MW01715950

STUDENT STUDY GUIDE

to accompany

Exceptional Lives
Special Education in Today's Schools

3rd Edition

Rud Turnbull
Ann Turnbull
Marilyn Shank
Sean Smith
Dorothy Leal

Prepared by
Margaret M. Cramer, Western Kentucky University

Previous Editions Prepared by
Dorothy Leal, Ohio University
Marilyn Shank, University of South Alabama

Merrill
Prentice Hall

Upper Saddle River, New Jersey
Columbus, Ohio

Vice President and Publisher: Jeffery W. Johnston
Acquisitions Editor: Ann Castel Davis
Editorial Assistant: Keli Gemrich
Production Editor: Sheryl Glicker Langner
Design Coordinator: Diane C. Lorenzo
Cover Designer: Alan Bumpus
Production Manager: Laura Messerly
Director of Marketing: Kevin Flanagan
Marketing Manager: Amy June
Marketing Services Manager: Barbara Koontz

Prentice-Hall International (UK) Limited, *London*
Prentice-Hall of Australia Pty. Limited, *Sydney*
Prentice-Hall Canada, Inc., *Toronto*
Prentice-Hall Hispanoamericana, S.A., *Mexico*
Prentice-Hall of India Private Limited, *New Delhi*
Prentice-Hall of Japan, Inc., *Tokyo*
Prentice-Hall Singapore Pte. Ltd.
Editora Prentice-Hall do Brazil, Ltda., *Rio de Janiero*

Copyright © 2002, 1999, 1995 by Pearson Education, Inc., Upper Saddle River, New Jersey 07458. All rights reserved. Printed in the United States of America. This publication is protected by Copyright and permission should be obtained from the publisher prior to any prohibited reproduction, storage in a retrieval system, or transmission in any form or by any means, electronic, mechanical, photocopying, recording, or likewise. For information regarding permission(s), write to: Rights and Permissions Department.

10 9 8 7 6 5 4 3 2

Merrill
Prentice Hall

ISBN: 0-13-094323-1

PREFACE

We have prepared these supplements to help you understand and memorize the information contained in the accompanying textbook *Exceptional Lives: Special Education in Today's Schools*, 3rd edition. However, we believe that the introductory special education class you are currently enrolled in is as much about attitude development as it is about memorizing information. In the text and throughout the supplementary materials, you will learn about how six core values—great expectations, positive contributions, inherent strengths, choices, relationships, and full citizenship—can make a remarkable difference in the lives of people with exceptionalities.

Student Study Guide: This Student Study Guide will help you understand, analyze, and evaluate the chapter concepts and prepare for in-class lectures and presentations. Each chapter in the Student Study Guide covers instructional objectives, key issues, and focus questions, and provides a guided review of the chapter content and vocabulary. Self-check quizzes (with answer key) will help you measure your level of comprehension and prepare for exams. Application exercises and ideas for completing individual or group projects are also included to encourage authentic, concrete learning experiences.

Companion Website: The Companion Website, located at ***http://www.prenhall.com/turnbull***, has been significantly upgraded for the third edition. The companion website will help you gauge your understanding of chapter content through the use of chapter-by-chapter *Overviews, Guided Reviews,* and interactive multiple choice *Chapter Quizzes*. The *Getting to Know People with...* module provides real artifacts (such as IEPs, evaluations, stories, and artwork) and photos from the individuals featured in the chapter vignettes. *My Voice Web Links* provide additional first-person accounts of living with a disability. *Web Links* to websites mentioned in the feature boxes and margin notes of the text will help you access additional information on chapter topics. The *CW Activities* offer 5 different types of web-based activities per chapter, including *Web Quests, Collaboration Activities, Media Challenges, Problem-Solving Activities,* and *Community Mapping Activities.* The *Resources* module houses blank IEP forms and collaboration charts, children's/young adult literature and video resource lists, lists of related organizations, books, journals and magazines, and a complete *Glossary*. The *Video* module will allow you to view on-line streaming videos that reinforce the themes of the text. Finally, you can collaborate and communicate with other students across the country using the *Message Board* and *Chat* features.

Our great expectation for *you* is that using the knowledge you gain from this class, you will make a difference in the lives of exceptional students by putting the six core values to work—in your professional activities and in your everyday life.

CONTENTS OF THE STUDENT STUDY GUIDE

The *Student Study Guide* is designed to provide you with a flexible, comprehensive review of the material presented in each chapter. The format for each chapter review is as follows:

Chapter Overview
Each chapter overview succinctly describes the chapter's highlights. It also provides a brief description of the exceptional life that is introduced in the chapter opening vignette and explains why the vignette subject was selected.

Chapter At-a-Glance
These charts provide you with an ordered preview of the chapter questions using the major four focus questions. After each focus question has asked, key parts of the chapter outline are presented in the first column. In the second column is a summary of instructional goals. The third column lists key concepts related to the focus question and objectives.

Project Options and Key Terms
Project options provide you with ideas for class projects, extra credit activities, and projects that will help extend your understanding of chapter concepts. Key terms will help you memorize important vocabulary and help you become familiar with professional terminology of the field.

Guided Review
This review follows the chapter outline and asks you to respond to questions that relate to the major concepts. The chapter section head and subsection for each guided review question are also provided to help you locate answers. Boxes that provide clarification or enrichment will help you understand the content. Human interest stories will help you to appreciate how the six values relate to people with different types of exceptionalities. The boxes contain minicase studies, book reviews, quotations, anecdotes, or additional information about the student featured in the chapter.

Application Exercises
Each chapter includes two to three application exercises that ask you to use key information presented in the chapter and apply it in meaningful contexts. This activity is designed to help you apply and extend your understanding to everyday situations.

Sample Quiz
A sample quiz is included to provide you with an opportunity to assess your ongoing knowledge. Questions in this quiz are similar to, but different from, those provided in the *Test Bank* and include true/false and multiple-choice questions only. The sample quiz also provides a balance of lower-level and higher-level multiple choice questions.

The answers to the Application Exercises, Sample Quiz Multiple-Choice Questions, and Sample Quiz Short Answer Questions are located in the back of this *Student Study Guide*.

At the end of the *Student Study Guide* you will also find a number of resources: a listing of literature for and about children and adolescents, as well as a listing of suggested videos by chapter, and a blank "Collaborating for Success" chart. These resources are also available on the *Companion Website* for this text (http://www.prenhall.com/turnbull). Also on the *Companion Website* are the sample quizzes contained in this *Student Study Guide,* with feedback covering the content of each chapter and links to special education resources on the Web.

TABLE OF CONTENTS

CHAPTER 1: OVERVIEW OF TODAY'S SPECIAL EDUCATION

CHAPTER OVERVIEW

Many factors influence students in today's world. This chapter examines the characteristics of today's students as well as important values that can influence their education for the better. It lays a foundation for understanding the characteristics, strengths, and concerns of students with exceptionalities. These issues are then examined in light of judicial decisions that have impacted students' lives and the lives of those involved in their education. Special attention is given to highlighting the six principles of the Individuals with Disabilities Education Act (IDEA).

The life of Danny Ramirez vividly illustrates how one student, his committed family, and his teachers and peers have made—through persistence and with the law on their side—a significant difference for both Danny and many other students, too. We chose Danny Ramirez in order to highlight a student whose family has strongly advocated for inclusion and who have secured—sometimes only after a lawsuit and sometimes after other great efforts—what they wanted. In addition, Danny's story raises issues related to cultural and linguistic diversity that are critically important to consider in providing an appropriate education for all students.

CHAPTER AT-A-GLANCE

Chapter Outline	Instructional Goals	Key Concepts
PROFILE OF SPECIAL EDUCATION STUDENTS AND PERSONNEL IN TODAY'S SCHOOLS		
Who Are the Students? • Total Number of Students Served • Age Groups of Students Served • Gender of Students • Provision of Gifted Education • Disability Categories • Labels and Language • Socioeconomic, Geographic, Racial, and Ethnic Profile • Disproportionate Education Who Are Special Education Personnel?	• Recognize how values guide teaching techniques • Identify the numbers, ages, categories of students identified with disabilities • Apply and understand the use of people-first language • Recognize the socioeconomic, geographic, racial, and ethnic profile • Note the disproportionate representation of students from culturally and linguistically diverse backgrounds • Explore the roles of different special education personnel	• Six values define the foundation for this book: envisioning great expectations, enhancing positive contributions, building on strengths, acting on choices, expanding relationships, and ensuring full citizenship. • Nearly 5.5 million students with disabilities were served in the 1997-1998 school year. • Special education includes thirteen categories of disabilities as well as students who are gifted and talented. • People-first language is preferred because labels can be demeaning. • Culturally and linguistically diverse students with disabilities are over-represented in special education. • Special education personnel include teachers, related service providers, administrators, paraprofessionals, and many others.
WHAT ARE THE RESULTS FOR STUDENTS WITH DISABILITIES?		
	• Examine actual results of special education • Describe goals for students with disabilities	• The actual outcomes of special education are not encouraging. • Goals include equal opportunity, independence, inclusion, and productivity.
THREE LEADERS WHO CHANGED SPECIAL EDUCATION: A HISTORY OF REFORM		
Lloyd Dunn Evelyn Deno James Gallagher	• Recognize how special education has changed as a result of the efforts and contributions of key people	• Lloyd Dunn questioned the efficacy of separate special education classes. • Evelyn Deno proposed a cascade of services. • James Gallagher proposed individualized contracts between educators and students. This contract was the precursor to IEPs.

JUDICIAL PRELUDES TO FEDERAL SPECIAL EDUCATION LAW: A HISTORY OF DISCRIMINATION		
Two Types of Discrimination Two Revolutionary Judicial Decisions	• Identify types of discrimination practiced in schools • Understand how the judicial system has worked to establish students' rights	• Schools practiced both exclusion and misclassification. • In the early 1970s, federal courts ruled those practices unconstitutional and gave students with disabilities a legal right to a free, appropriate public education. • The landmark cases were *Mills v. Washington, DC, Board of Education*, 1972 and *Pennsylvania Association for Retarded Citizens (PARC) v. Commonwealth of Pennsylvania*, 1972.
INDIVIDUALS WITH DISABILITIES EDUCATION ACT: INTRODUCTION AND ELIGIBILITY		
Introduction to IDEA: Progress but Problems Eligibility for Special Education: Need and Age Groups • Eligibility: Need • Eligibility for Special Education: Age-Specific Rights and Age Groups	• Identify the progress in special education over the last 25 years, and the problems that remain • Differentiate criteria for eligibility	• Despite progress, IDEA's implementation is still impeded by low expectations for students with disabilities and an insufficient focus on applying research-proven practices to the education of students with disabilities. • A student must have a disability and need special education and related services to be eligible for rights under IDEA, and age factors further determine those rights.
INDIVIDUALS WITH DISABILITIES EDUCATION ACT: SIX PRINCIPLES		
Zero Reject • Educability • Expulsion • Contagious Diseases	• List the six principles that govern IDEA • Identify the purpose • Explain when students may not be rejected • Understand the value, context, and application of the zero reject principle	• IDEA's six principles are zero reject, nondiscriminatory evaluation, appropriate education, least restrictive environment, procedural due process, and parent-student participation. • Zero Reject prohibits the exclusion from school of any student who has a disability. It means that students may not be excluded because they are regarded as "ineducable," have a behavior problem that is a manifestation of their disability, or have a contagious disease.
Nondiscriminatory Evaluation • Two Purposes • Evaluation to Eliminate Bias	• Identify the purposes • Understand the value, context, and application of a nondiscriminatory evaluation	• Nondiscriminatory evaluation determines whether a student has a disability and, if so, whether the student needs special education and what that education should be. • Non-biased evaluation is essential because of disproportionate representation of students from culturally and lingusitically diverse backgrounds in special education
Appropriate Education • Planning for Individual Needs • Interpreting "Appropriate"—the Benefit Rule and the Process Rule	• Identify the purpose • Understand the value, context, and application for an appropriate education	• Appropriate education includes an Individualized Education Plan (IEP) and occurs when the schools follow IDEA's processes, when the student benefits, and when related services are made available.

Least Restrictive Environment (LRE) • Reasons for the Rule • The Rule: A Presumption in Favor of Inclusion • Setting Aside the Presumption • The Continuum of Services • Nonacademic Inclusion • Courts and the LRE	• Identify the purpose • Understand the value, context, and application for the Least Restrictive Environment	• LRE requires students to be educated to the maximum extent appropriate with students who do not have disabilities. This means they must have access to the general education curriculum for academic and extracurricular activities.
Procedural Due Process • Due Process Hearing • Appeal to Court • Notice to Parents	• Identify the purpose • Understand the value, context, and application of procedural due process	• Procedural due process means parents and schools may use mediation or a due process hearing to resolve differences.
Parent-Student Participation	• Identify the purpose • Understand the value, context, and application of parent-student participation	• Parent and student participation encourages collaboration and shared decision making among parents, students, and educators.
FEDERAL FUNDING OF INDIVIDUALS WITH DISABILTIES EDUCATION ACT		
IDEA as Grant-in-Aid for States • Cost Pressures • Costs and Schools' Expanded Functions	• Describe reasons for cost pressures • Describe characteristics of funding issues and procedures	• Congress grants money to states to help states pay for services if they agree to comply with the six IDEA principles. • The number of students with disabilities in general education has increased, as have the per-pupil expenditures, so the overall costs of special education have risen. • Schools now perform many services formerly performed by agencies.
OTHER FEDERAL LAWS: ENTITLEMENTS AND ANTIDISCRIMINATION		
Entitlements and Other Services—the Rehabilitation Act and the Tech Act Prohibition of Discrimination—Section 504 and ADA	• Analyze how entitlements serve students • Identify how the law has worked to prohibit discrimination	• Entitlements include vocational rehabilitation services (job training and job location, and supported employment) and education about and access to assistive technology. • Federal law prohibits discrimination based solely on a person's disability. • Section 504 of the Rehabilitation Act prohibits discrimination in regard to federal funds while the ADA prohibits it in nearly every other sector of American life.

PROJECT OPTIONS

1. Prepare a class presentation on the different court cases that have affected the direction of special education throughout American history. Compare and contrast the differences and similarities among the different laws. As one resource, interview a special education director on legal issues surrounding special education. Another good resource is the following book: Turnbull, H. R. and Turnbull, A. P. (1998). *Free Appropriate Public Education.* (5th Ed.) Denver, CO: Love Publishing Company.

2. Create a survey for local special and general educators to assess their understanding of how the "least restrictive environment principles" are being carried out in your school district. Include at least ten questions and have a minimum of ten special and ten general educators fill out the survey. Then tally your answers and compare and contrast your findings. Chart your findings for the class.

3. Interview people from your local school board about how the procedural due process principle operates in your district. Present a written summary of how schools have been held accountable for complying with IDEA in your community.

4. Obtain permission to attend a committee meeting involving a student who may receive special education services, then write a report, without using any names of students or school systems, on how the six principles of IDEA were addressed.

KEY TERMS

Appropriate education

Benefit standard

Cross-categorical classes

Inclusion

Individualized Education Plan (IEP)

Individualized Family Services Plan (IFSP)

Integration

Job coach

Least restrictive environment

Mediation

National Council on Disability

Nondiscriminatory evaluation

Parent and Student Participation

Procedural due process

Process definition

Related services

Supported employment

Supplementary aids and support services

Zero reject

GUIDED REVIEW

Here Comes the SUN Team!
Collaborative Inclusion at Work

In the Boulder Valley School District, the SUN Team consultants worked with general and special educators and shared knowledge, skills and strategies for working with students with challenging needs. An inclusion model was developed to provide intensive support to ensure success to all students in their neighborhood schools. Beginning initially as a brainstorming session, staff was obtained solely by restructuring current personnel. The article highlights student, family, and educator outcomes during and after the intervention, collaborative program development and design, and benefits experienced by the district-level special education department. Read about "A Day in the Life of a SUN Team Consultant," in *Teaching Exceptional Children,* November/December 1999, *32*(2), p. 4.

Profile of Special Education Students and Personnel in Today's Schools

1. Identify the six values that guide special education practices as represented in your textbook. (*See* Profile of Special Education Students and Personnel in Today's Schools)
   a. ______________________________
   b. ______________________________
   c. ______________________________
   d. ______________________________
   e. ______________________________
   f. ______________________________

2. What percentage of all America's students were in special education during the school year 1997-1998? (*See* Who Are the Students?; Total Number of Students Served)

   ____

3. List the age groups of students served with special education and the percentage in each of the four categories. (*See* Who Are the Students?; Age Groups of Students Served)

Age Group	*Percentage of Total Students Served*

Early Inclusion Activities Form Lasting Friendships and Good Attitudes

Mall Elementary and North Liberty Schools in Burke County, North Carolina, set the goal of developing friendships and improving attitudes and interaction between peers with and without disabilities. The project, involving two schools with students ages five through thirteen, embarked upon an inclusion project that was supported by grant funding. Cathy Danford, who got the program funded, writes, "The regular education staff could see the successes of integration." Parents were involved as volunteers in the activity centers and in supervising trips. By the end of the year, children had new friends and were seen holding hands, singing, and laughing together. To learn more about this project, see "Early Inclusion Activities Form Lasting Friendships and Good Attitudes," in *Exceptional Parent,* September 1998, *28*(9). p. 31.

4. Which two categories of disabilities account for nearly three-fourths of all students with disabilities in the 1997-1998 school year? (*See* Who Are the Students?; Disability Categories)
   a. ______________________________
   b. ______________________________

5. List both advantages and disadvantages of labels for individuals with disabilities, noting which column is easiest to fill. (*See* Who Are the Students?; Labels and Language)

Advantages of Using Labels	***Disadvantages of Using Labels***

6. Identify where special education students from low-income families live (*See* Who Are the Students?; Socioeconomic, Geographical, Racial, and Ethnic Profile)

Residential Areas	***Percentages Who Live in These Areas***
Urban Areas	
Rural Areas	
Suburban Areas	

7. The fastest growing group of students in the country, taken without respect to race, is ______________________. This group of students primarily live in these three states:
   a. ____________________, b. ____________________, and c. ____________________.
   (*See* Who Are the Students?; Socioeconomic, Geographical, Racial, and Ethnic Profile)

8. What are the two largest groups of special educators? (*See* Who Are Special Education Personnel?)
   a. ______________________________
   b. ______________________________

What Are the Results for Students with Disabilities?

9. What is the graduation rate for students with disabilities? How does the dropout rate of students with disabilities compare to the dropout rate of students without disabilities? (*See* What Are the Results for Students with Disabilities?)
   a. ______________________________
   b. ______________________________

10. Match the term established by Congress to indicate the outcomes or results for individuals with disabilities with their definition. (*See* What Are the Results for Students with Disabilities?)

a. _____ Independence	1. Persons with disabilities will have income-producing work, or their work will contribute to a household or community.
b. _____ Productivity	2. Persons with disabilities will use the same community resources and participate in the same community activities as persons who do not have disabilities.
c. _____ Inclusion	3. Persons with disabilities will have the same chances people without disabilities have to an education and all aspects of American life.
d. _____ Equal Opportunity	4. Persons with disabilities will assert control and choice over their own lives.

Three Leaders Who Changed Special Education: A History of Reform

11. What characterized the three individuals who have changed special education practices? (*See* Three Leaders Who Changed Special Education: A History of Reform)

    ____

12. Match major accomplishments with the special education leaders who accomplished them. (*See* Three Leaders Who Changed Special Education: A History of Reform)

a. _____ Lloyd Dunn	1. Proposed the concept of a cascade of services, favoring individualized, student-centered education.
b. _____ Evelyn Deno	2. Advocated for a special education contract to safeguard against incorrect and permanent placements. This focus led the way for IEPs and a due process hearing.
c. _____ James Gallagher	3. Advocated for students with mild disabilities to have general class placements; recommended that labels describe the nature of the education the students would receive; focused the need for nondiscriminatory assessment.

Judicial Preludes to Federal Special Education Law: A History of Discrimination

13. Historically, name two ways schools discriminated against students with disabilities. (*See* Judicial Preludes to Federal Special Education Law: A History of Discrimination; Two Types of Discrimination)

    a. ____

    b. ____

14. What important outcome for special education sprang from the 1954 school race-desegregation case *Brown v. Board of Education*? (*See* Judicial Preludes to Federal Special Education Law: A History of Discrimination; Two Types of Discrimination)

    ____

    ____

15. What are the names of the two 1972 court cases that resulted in two jurisdictions: (a) creating free appropriate public education to all students with disabilities, (b) educating students with disabilities in the same schools as students without disabilities, and (c) putting into place certain procedural safeguards so that students with disabilities can challenge schools that do not live up to the courts' orders? (*See* Judicial Preludes to Federal Special Education Law: A History of Discrimination; Two Revolutionary Judicial Decisions)

    a. ____

    b. ____

Looking Back at *Brown v. Board of Education*

In 1994, the fortieth anniversary of *Brown v. Board of Education*, researchers reevaluated the issue of segregation (see *U.S. News and World Report*, May 23, 1994, pp. 33–36 and *Newsweek*, May 16, 1994, pp. 26–32; 53 for more information). They found that many African Americans still feel segregated in integrated public schools. Joanne Hayman, a grandmother, commented that she had "high hopes" when schools were integrated. But now she has changed her mind because she has seen her grandchildren struggle in integrated schools. "They all had such promise . . . . (In segregated schools) people pushed you because they believed in you. I can't say that is happening now" (Johnson, *U.S. News and World Report*, p. 35). Others, though, point to the value of integration. Edgar Epps, a professor, stated that people who want to go back to segregation "either have bad memories or weren't alive during segregation" (Johnson, *U.S. News and World Report*, p. 35).

The low self-esteem that many African-American students experience in public schools suggests that public policy can force schools to change their structure, but may have little effect on attitudes. The attitudes that you have as a teacher about the value of all your students, regardless of race, gender, religion, or exceptionality, can make a significant difference in their self-esteem.

Individuals with Disabilities Education Act: Introduction and Eligibility

16. What is the 1975 "Education of All Handicapped Students Act" now known as? (*See* Individuals with Disabilities Education Act: Introduction and Eligibility; Introduction to IDEA: Progress but Problems)

    ____

17. What does "IDEA" stand for? (*See* Individuals with Disabilities Education Act: Introduction and Eligibility; Introduction to IDEA: Progress but Problems)

    ____

18. According to Congress, IDEA's implementation has been impeded by (a)____________________ and (b) ____________________. (*See* Individuals with Disabilities Education Act: Introduction and Eligibility; Introduction to IDEA: Progress but Problems)

19. Match the components of IDEA's three parts: (*See* Individuals with Disabilities Education Act: Introduction and Eligibility; Introduction to IDEA: Progress but Problems)

a. _____ Part A	1. Benefits students who are between the ages of 3 and 21.
b. _____ Part B	2. Benefits infants and toddlers birth to two years.
c. _____ Part C	3. Sets out the findings of fact on which Congress justifies the rest of IDEA along with the purposes and policies that Congress intends to implement by enacting IDEA.

20. According to IDEA, what qualifies a student to be eligible for special education services? (*See* Individuals with Disabilities Education Act: Introduction and Eligibility; Eligibility for Special Education: Need, and Age-Specific Right and Age Groups)
    a. ____
    b. ____

21. According to the IDEA Part B, children age 3–9 exhibiting what characteristics may also be served at the discretion of each state? (See Individuals with Disabilities Education Act: Introduction and Eligibility; Eligibility for Special Education: Need, and Age-Specific Right and Age Groups)
    a. ____
    b. ____

IDEA: Six Principles

22. In the first column, list the names of each of the six principles governing the education of students with disabilities. In the second column, briefly identify the major characteristic of the principle. In the third column, write out questions you still want to know about IDEA. (*See* IDEA: Six Principles)

Name of Principle	*Major Characteristic*	*Questions About This Principle*
a.		
b.		
c.		
d.		
e.		
f.		

23. The written plan for serving students aged three through twenty-one is called a(n) __________ __________ __________.
(*See* IDEA: Six Principles; Appropriate Education)

24. The written plan for serving infants and toddler from birth through two (also called "zero to three") is called a(n) __________ __________ __________ __________.
(*See* IDEA: Six Principles; Appropriate Education)

25. Identify three other terms used to indicate the least restrictive environment principle. (*See* IDEA: Six Principles; Least Restrictive Environment)
    a. ____________________
    b. ____________________
    c. ____________________

Federal Funding of IDEA

26. What does the phrase "rights run with revenues" mean? (*See* Federal Funding of IDEA)
____
____

27. Congress grants federal money to state and local educational agencies (school districts) to assist them in educating students ages __________ to __________. (*See* Federal Funding of IDEA)

28. What is meant by referring to IDEA as a typical "grant-in-aid" law? (*See* Federal Funding of IDEA)
____
____

IDEA '97

Final Regulations Released

It is difficult to summarize all the changes in IDEA '97 and the final regulations, but this article does a good job of providing a sample of the issues that may be of particular interest to school personnel, teachers, and parents. Eligibility criteria, individualized education programs, statewide and districtwide assessments, discipline, and other important issues are covered. For more information see "IDEA '97: Final Regulations Released," in *Exceptional Parent*, September 1999, *29*(9), p. 56.

Other Federal Laws: Entitlements and Antidiscrimination

29. List two other federal laws (besides IDEA) that grant entitlements to students with special education needs. (*See* Other Federal Laws: Entitlements and Antidiscrimination)

____

____

30. Who is entitled to the assistance of a job coach? (*See* Other Federal Laws: Entitlements and Other Services)

____

31. How is "supported employment" defined in your textbook and how is this an entitlement? (*See* Other Federal Laws: Entitlements and Antidiscrimination; Entitlements and Other Services)

____

____

30. For legal purposes, Section 504 of the Rehabilitation Act and ADA defines a person with a disability as one who has the following three characteristics. (*See* Other Federal Laws: Entitlements and Antidiscrimination)

a. ____

b. ____

c. ____

31. How are Section 504 of the Rehabilitation Act and ADA different in scope?

____

____

Barrier Free Education

In this chapter, you learned about how the law demands appropriate accommodations to prohibit discrimination against people with disabilities. The law focuses on eliminating barriers.

The Internet is famous for leveling the playing field for people with disabilities. One website is expanding the field into education. *Barrier Free Education* (http://atlanta.arch.gatech.edu/BFE) promotes the philosophy that "Access to education is a universal right." The site, which is maintained by the College of Architecture at Georgia Tech, emphasizes that educators need to take a leadership role in providing appropriate accommodations. The site contains numerous links concerning generic disability, vision, mobility, speech, and cognitive issues to assist teachers, parents, and students.

As you read through your textbook, be sure to check out the other websites listed at the end of each chapter in Resources.

See Vanessa, Ira. (1998). "Barrier Free Education." *Exceptional Parent, 28*(2), 30.

APPLICATION EXERCISES FOR CHAPTER 1

Application Exercise 1a. Dignifying Labels

See how many alternate words with dignity you can generate for each word to avoid. Try thinking of other words to avoid to add to this list. Then generate a list of guidelines that helped you determine which words to use and which ones to eliminate.

Words to Avoid	*Words with Greater Dignity*
Cripple/ invalid	
Handicapped	
Birth defect	
Victim	
Normal (referring to persons without disabilities as "normal" infers that those with disabilities are abnormal)	
Deaf mute/deaf and dumb	
Crazy/ insane	
Slow	
Confined to a wheelchair	

<u>Application Exercise 1b. IDEA's Six Principles</u>

Reread the section on IDEA's six principles. Using what you have read, determine which principle is being described.

Principle	*Descriptors*
a. Zero reject	______ 1. Seeks to make the schools and parents accountable to each other for carrying out the student's IDEA rights
b. Nondiscriminatory evaluation	______ 2. Defines what kind of special education and related services the student will receive
c. Appropriate education	______ 3. Related services are not available to a student unless the student requires them in order to benefit from special education
d. Least restrictive environment	______ 4. A mechanism for shared decision making
e. Procedural due process	______ 5. The value of relationships is reflected in this principle
f. Parental and student participation	______ 6. Distinguishes between an appropriate education and the best education possible
	______ 7. Provides an opportunity for mediation and/or a due process hearing
	______ 8. Determines whether a student has a disability
	______ 9. Students may not be excluded based on educability, disability related behavior, or contagious diseases.
	______ 10. Plans for individual needs and follows the IDEA process
	______ 11. Requires notification concerning the school's decisions about their children
	______ 12. IDEA creates a presumption in favor of educating students with disabilities with those who do not have disabilities unless the student cannot benefit from being educated with students who do not have disabilities.
	______ 13. Includes another, less adversarial accountability technique: the parent-student participation principle
	______ 14. Evaluation to eliminate bias, including test bias
	______ 15. Schools must offer a continuum or range of services from more to less typical and inclusive.

Application Exercise 1c: Assessing What You've Learned

To summarize the major concepts in this chapter, identify how the six values* are important to the concepts for each major chapter section**.

* <u>Six Values</u>: envisioning great expectations, enhancing positive contributions, building on strengths, acting on choices, expanding relationships, and ensuring full citizenship.

** <u>Major Sections</u>: Profile of Special Education Students and Personnel in Today's Schools; What Are the Results for Students with Disabilities? Three Leaders Who Changed Special Education: A History of Reform; Judicial Preludes to Federal Special Education Law: A History of Discrimination; Individuals with Disabilities Education Act: Introduction and Eligibility; Individuals with Disabilities Education Act: Six Principles; Federal Funding of IDEA; Other Federal Laws: Entitlements and Antidiscrimination.

SAMPLE QUIZ FOR CHAPTER 1

MULTIPLE CHOICE

Circle the correct answer.

1. Which of the following is a leading court case for the "zero reject" principle of IDEA?
   a. Daniel R. R. v. State Board of Education (1989)
   b. PARC v. Commonwealth of Pennsylvania (1972)
   c. Timothy W. v. Rochester School District (1988)
   d. Larry P. v. Riles (1984)

2. For what is James Gallagher specifically known?
   a. Advocating for a special education contract safeguarding against incorrect and permanent placements
   b. Suggesting new roles for special educators
   c. Rejecting the term "mentally retarded"
   d. Urging system sorting to tailor treatment for each child

3. What had a major impact on some Congressional sponsors of antidiscrimination bills affecting persons with disabilities?
   a. PAC money from the NEA
   b. Family members with disabilities
   c. Testimony from AIDS patients who suffered discrimination
   d. Civil rights groups and progressive educators

4. In the Honig v. Doe (1988) court case what major principle of IDEA was addressed?
   a. Educability
   b. Appropriate education
   c. Expulsion
   d. Contagious diseases

5. What is the 1975 law known as (PL) 94-142 now called?
   a. FAPE
   b. ADA
   c. Section 504 of the Rehabilitation Act
   d. IDEA

6. Nathan's parents want him to have an assistant or paraeducator in the general education class because of his multiple disabilities. Must the school district provide such services?
   a. Yes, because he is in the category of multiple disabilities
   b. Only if his parents also volunteer their help in his class
   c. No, because it would cost too much money
   d. Only if he requires an aide in order to benefit from his special education

7. Hyung has active tuberculosis. Who will decide if he can attend public school?
   a. His parents
   b. The school
   c. A panel of medical experts
   d. The state disability determination board

8. What is the purpose of nondiscriminatory evaluation?
   a. To make sure minority students with disabilities can benefit from affirmative action in schools
   b. To determine whether a student has a disability and, if so, what special education and support services are needed
   c. To ensure that diversity is practiced in the public schools and its testing centers
   d. To make sure standardized tests are not biased against African Americans

9. You are a third grade teacher in a general education class. A new student has come into your class whom you feel does not belong there because of a disability, but her parents do not want her placed in an "MR" class and stigmatized. What is the IDEA rule?
   a. Your opinion as the lead teacher must be respected.
   b. The school district should avoid an expensive court case and thus adhere to the parents' wishes.
   c. The student must remain in a general education class unless, with the help of supplemental aids and support services, she cannot benefit from it.
   d. At the principal's discretion, the student can be moved to a special education class if she is taking up too much of your time.

10. What does IDEA provide when parents and state or local educational agencies disagree?
    a. A neutral judge to determine who should prevail
    b. Covered expenses for students' individual needs
    c. A mediator to meet weekly with parents to counsel them about the family's personal needs
    d. A court-appointed lawyer to present the family's case and usually a monetary settlement

11. What are the two leading IDEA categories for students with disabilities?
    a. Serious emotional disturbance and visual or hearing impairments
    b. Specific learning disabilities and speech or language impairments
    c. Mental retardation and serious emotional disturbance
    d. ADHD and mental retardation

12. Which of the following is true about gifted students in public schools?
    a. All states are complying with federal policies regarding screening to identify students who are gifted.
    b. Students who are gifted are covered by IDEA.
    c. Not all states require adapted instructional programs for students who are gifted.
    d. Hispanic Americans are overrepresented in national statistics regarding students who are gifted.

13. Why is it important to use "people-first" language?
    a. It emphasizes that the disability does not supersede all other characteristics of a person.
    b. It is politically correct.
    c. It is widely accepted by journalists and the public.
    d. It is expected by the U.S. Department of Education.

14. What are the two largest groups of special educators?
    a. Teachers of students who are mentally retarded or who have ADHD
    b. Teachers of students with specific learning disabilities and those who teach students in cross-categorical classes
    c. Teachers of students with physical disabilities and those with specific learning disabilities
    d. Teachers of students with ADHD or language impairments

15. Holly is a seven-year-old with disabilities. What is <u>not</u> true of how Deno's cascade system might affect her?
    a. It can promote relationships between Holly and students without disabilities.
    b. It can inhibit friendships from developing between Holly and students without disabilities.
    c. It promotes individualized, student-centered education.
    d. It will assure her placement in a general education classroom.

16. Which racial group is overrepresented among students with disabilities?
    a. Caucasian
    b. Hispanic
    c. Asian
    d. African American

17. In 1975, what did Congress find as it was considering passing the federal special education law?
    a. Most children with disabilities were receiving appropriate educational services, but states needed more funds to fully serve these students.
    b. One million students with disabilities were excluded from the public schools.
    c. All parents of children with disabilities demanded inclusion rather than separate special education classes.
    d. School buildings had become accessible to students with physical disabilities, but not enough assistive technology was available.

18. The Americans with Disabilities Act defines a person with a disability as one who has all of the following except:
    a. a record of such an impairment
    b. is regarded as having an impairment
    c. a learning disability that limits performance
    d. a physical or mental impairment that substantially limits one or more major life activities

19. In 1997–1998 school year, approximately how many students, ages six to twenty-one, received some form of special education services?
    a. About 500,000
    b. 1,750,000
    c. 3,500,000
    d. Approximately 5½ million

20. Under which category would a student with ADHD receive services?
    a. Traumatic brain injury
    b. Orthopedic impairments
    c. Other health impairment
    d. Emotional disturbance

SHORT ANSWER

21. How does IDEA define special education?

____

____

22. What is the two-part standard for eligibility for special education?

_______________________ and _______________________

23. Nearly three-fourths of all students with disabilities are classified into what two categories?

____

____

ESSAY

24. Discuss and rank the six values of this book from the point of view of (a) a special educator, (b) a general educator, (c) a parent, (d) a school administrator, and (e) a community member.

25. Compare and contrast and explain the purpose for each of the six principles of the Individuals with Disabilities Education Act.

CHAPTER 2: IMPLEMENTING IDEA'S PRINCIPLES

CHAPTER OVERVIEW

In this chapter you will learn how parents and schools jointly conduct nondiscriminatory evaluations and develop appropriate education with individualized approaches to teaching students with disabilities. A special focus in this chapter is on cooperative learning.

This chapter continues to look at the life of Danny Ramirez to provide a context for understanding how the six principles are implemented in one student's life. It also demonstrates how Danny can look forward to the future because school practices have changed.

CHAPTER AT-A-GLANCE

Chapter Outline	Instructional Goals	Key Concepts
FRAMEWORK FOR IMPLEMENTING IDEA		
	• Review the six values of the book and the six principles of IDEA	• The six values for this book are envisioning great expectations, enhancing positive contributions, building on strengths, acting on choices, expanding relationships, and ensuring full citizenship. • IDEA's six principles are zero reject, nondiscriminatory evaluation, appropriate education, least restrictive environment, procedural due process, and parent-student participation.
NONDISCRIMINATORY EVALUATION: SCREENING, PREREFERRAL, AND REFERRAL		
Screening	• Recognize the two purposes of nondiscriminatory evaluation • Become familiar with purposes and types of screening tests	• The purposes are (a) to determine whether a student has a disability and (b) to decide the nature of the special education and related services the student needs. • Screening involves routine tests of all students to help determine which students qualify for special education.
Prereferral	• Identify the purposes and context for prereferral	• Prereferral occurs to provide help to teachers experiencing challenges in teaching students and to guard against misidentifying students as having disabilities. • Prereferral occurs when a student's general education teacher (a) determines that a child is having learning difficulties, and (b) seeks help from others to identify instructional strategies to address these difficulties.
Referral	• Explain the deciding factors for a referral	• A referral occurs when an educator or a parent submits a formal request for the student to be considered for a full and formal nondiscriminatory evaluation.

NONDISCRIMINATORY EVALUATION		
Nondiscriminatory Evaluation Procedures and Standards	• Identify why a nondiscriminatory evaluation is given • Explore the characteristics of a nondiscriminatory evaluation	• A nondiscriminatory evaluation is given to determine whether the student has a disability and, if so, what the student's special education and related services needs are. • IDEA contains detailed procedural safeguards to ensure that evaluation is free of cultural and linguistic bias. • Procedural safeguards relate to the breadth of the assessment, assessment procedures, timing of the assessment, parental notice and consent, and interpretation of assessment information.
Assessment Instruments • Norm-Referenced Tests • Criterion-Referenced Tests • Summary of Tests	• Recognize the difference between norm-referenced and criterion-referenced tests	• Norm-referenced tests are standardized and compare a student with his or her age- or grade-level peers. • Criterion-referenced tests determine whether a student has mastered a particular skill and compares the student to a standard of mastery.
Administration of Nondiscriminatory Assessments • Guarding Against Cultural and Linguistic Bias • Parent and Student Input on the Evaluation Team • Compiling Assessment Data and Making Evaluation Decisions	• Describe which aspects of a nondiscriminatory evaluation can highly influence the resulting treatment and outcome	• Cultural and linguistic bias can result in differential treatment. • Broader, more comprehensive assessment procedures are less likely to be biased against students from culturally and linguistically diverse backgrounds than are traditional assessments. • Parents and students provide invaluable information. • The 1997 reauthorization of IDEA added the requirement that parents be part of the evaluation team. • The nondiscriminatory evaluation is the foundation of the student's appropriate education.

APPROPRIATE EDUCATION		
Developing the IFSP/IEP • IDEA Requirements • Contents of the IFSP/IEP • Age-Specific Provisions • Participants Who Develop the IFSP/IEP • Timelines • IFSP/IEP Conferences	• Become familiar with IDEA requirements • Describe characteristics of IFSP/IEP conferences	• IDEA authorizes services for individuals from birth through age twenty-one. • The IFSP serves infants and toddlers (age birth through 3). The federal government gives states money to operate programs for individuals ages 3–21. • All states must serve students 6–21, and students in this age group receive an IEP. States decide whether to serve students ages 3–5. • Participants on the IFSP/IEP team must include the same people from the evaluation team. • The IFSP must include the present levels of development; family's resources, priorities, and concerns; major outcomes; early intervention services; natural environments; dates and duration of services; name of family service coordinator; the transition plan. • The IFSP must be developed within 45 days of the child's referral and reviewed at six-month intervals. • The IEP must contain the student's present levels of educational performance; annual goals and short-term objectives; related services; extent of non-participation; assessment modifications; dates and duration of services; transition plans; and measurement of progress toward annual goals. • Transition plans have special provisions for students beginning at age 14, at age 16, and one year before the students reaches the age of majority (usually 18). • The IEP must be in effect at the beginning of each school year and be reviewed at least once a year. • IDEA requires that parents be members of the educational team; it expects school and family collaboration.

PROJECT OPTIONS

1. With several other students, write a script for a multidisciplinary team conference that demonstrates the value of collaboration. This may be either a referral conference or an IEP conference. Present this as a skit to the class, having each person take a different team member role. Be sure to include a parent and the student and to consider all aspects discussed in this chapter.
2. In a local school, get permission to examine IEPs for three different students. Discuss, compare, and contrast the stated objectives on the basis of clarity and practicality. Evaluate the related services as they relate to the objectives. Then, take what you have learned and prepare overhead transparencies to demonstrate your findings about the practical usefulness of IEPs.
3. Conduct further research and prepare a class presentation on assessment instruments. Create compare/contrast diagrams to illustrate substantial differences and similarities among the different tests. Prepare a lesson plan and test for your peers. Make the test based on the best characteristics that you've learned about assessment instruments.

KEY TERMS

Adaptive behavior

Assessment

Bell-shaped curve

Criterion-referenced tests

Evaluation

Evaluation team

Nondiscriminatory evaluation

Norm-referenced tests

Portfolio Assessment

Prereferral

Referral

Reliability

Screening

Validity

GUIDED REVIEW

Your Baby's First Tests

Doctors now examine newborns during their first 48 hours of life to immediately assess a newborn's health (Apgar Test), test for common conditions, test for various diseases or genetic disorders, and prevent delays. For details on why the tests are performed and what is involved, read "Your Baby's First Tests," in *Parenting*, March 2000, p. 35.

Framework for Implementing IDEA

1. In your own words, summarize the six IDEA principles and their purpose and the key components for each one. (See Framework for Implementing IDEA)

IDEA Principle	*Purpose*	*Key Components*
1.		
2.		
3.		
4.		
5.		
6.		

Nondiscriminatory Evaluation: Screening, Prereferral, and Referral

2. What are the two purposes of nondiscriminatory evaluation? (*See* Nondiscriminatory Evaluation; Screening, Prereferral, and Referral)
   a. ______________________________
   b. ______________________________

3. List the four steps of a nondiscriminatory evaluation. Circle the ones that are NOT required by IDEA but are a matter of good practice. (*See* Nondiscriminatory Evaluation; Screening, Prereferral, and Referral)
   a. ______________________________
   b. ______________________________
   c. ______________________________
   d. ______________________________

4. Match the definitions for a nondiscriminatory evaluation. (*See* Nondiscriminatory Evaluation; Screening, Prereferral, and Referral)

1. Prereferral	(a) _____ A routine test that helps school staff identify which students might need further testing to determine whether they qualify for special education.
2. Screening	(b) _____ Occurs when an educator or a parent submits a formal request for the student to be considered for a full and formal nondiscriminatory evaluation.
3. Referral	(c) _____Occurs when a student's general education teacher asks others (educators and families) to help problem-solve in order to identify instructional strategies to adequately address learning and behavioral challenges.

5. List some examples of screening tests. (*See* Nondiscriminatory Evaluation; Screening, Prereferral, and Referral; Screening)
   a. ____________________
   b. ____________________
   c. ____________________

6. What students do not undergo the screening process in order to have disabilities identified? (*See* Nondiscriminatory Evaluation; Screening, Prereferral, and Referral; Screening)
____

7. What are the two purposes for prereferral? (*See* Nondiscriminatory Evaluation; Screening, Prereferral, and Referral; Prereferral)
   a. ____________________
   b. ____________________

8. Identify some of the consequences and dangers of classification and explain the danger. (*See* Nondiscriminatory Evaluation; Screening, Prereferral, and Referral; Prereferral)
   a. ____________________
   b. ____________________
   c. ____________________

9. IDEA prohibits schools from classifying into special education any students who have
   a. ____________________ or
   b. ____________________.
   (*See* Nondiscriminatory Evaluation; Screening, Prereferral, and Referral; Prereferral)

10. What types of information is a typical part of the referral form? (*See* Nondiscriminatory Evaluation; Screening, Prereferral, and Referral; Referral)
   a. ____________________
   b. ____________________
   c. ____________________
   d. ____________________

Nondiscriminatory Evaluation

When you review test instruments, we encourage you to pay attention to the sample of students or families for whom the standardization was done. Pay particular attention to the racial, ethnic, and exceptionality characteristics of the people represented in the standardization sample. Do these characteristics reflect a cross-section of students? What is the likelihood of the test being used to assess only those students who were represented in the standardization sample? What difference do you think it makes if some racial, ethnic, and exceptionality groups are left out of standardization?

11. What two questions does a nondiscriminatory evaluation answer? (*See* Nondiscriminatory Evaluation Procedures and Standards)
    a. ______________________________
    b. ______________________________

The Assessment/Instruction Relationship
Does your local news media discuss the results of your district's yearly standardized assessment? One of the major concerns about classwide standardized assessment is that teachers feel pressured to teach to the test: they find out the content of the test and develop their instruction around it. Instead, appropriate instruction starts with goals and objectives from the curriculum's scope and sequence charts and individual IEPs. Assessment measures are constructed to measure the student's progress toward those goals and objectives. If a student fairs poorly on a test, the teacher uses this information to improve instruction for that student. Assessment becomes meaningless without the goal/instruction/assessment link.

12. Under the 1997 amendments to IDEA, who must be included on the evaluation team? (*See* Nondiscriminatory Evaluation Procedures and Standards)
    a. ______________________________
    b. ______________________________
    c. ______________________________
    d. ______________________________
    e. ______________________________
    f. ______________________________

13. Explain the difference between assessment and evaluation: (*See* Nondiscriminatory Evaluation Procedures and Standards; Assessment Instruments)

	Refers to	***Examples of***
Assessment		
Evaluation		

14. Norm-referenced tests compare a student with ______________________________, while criterion-referenced tests compare a student to ______________________________. (*See* Nondiscriminatory Evaluation Procedures and Standards; Assessment Instruments)

15. A test is said to be ________________________ if it yields similar results across time and among raters. It is said to be _________________ if it measures what it says it measures. (*See* Nondiscriminatory Evaluation Procedures and Standards; Assessment Instruments)

Integrating Standards: Including All Students

The 1997 Amendments to the Individuals with Disabilities Education Act (IDEA, Public Law 105-17) align special education policies with standards-based reforms. If you are concerned about new requirements for individualized education programs, collaboration, and assessment, then this article can help. Several new provisions in four major areas are covered.

See "Integrating Standards: Including All Students," in *Teaching Exceptional Children*, January/February, 1999, *31*(3), p. 66.

16. A nineteen-year-old student took an IQ test and found he had a mental age of 17. Based on the IQ formula given in your textbook, what would be his IQ?______________________

(*See* Nondiscriminatory Evaluation Procedures and Standards; Assessment Instruments)

17. Identify at least five problems that may arise when administering norm-referenced intelligence tests to students with exceptionalities. (*See* Assessment Instruments; Norm-referenced tests)
    a. ________________________________
    b. ________________________________
    c. ________________________________
    d. ________________________________
    e. ________________________________

18. Explain why criterion-referenced tests tend to be more helpful than norm-referenced tests for determining placement and educational needs of students with exceptionalities. (*See* Assessment Instruments; Criterion-referenced Tests)

____
____
____
____

19. Identify the three aspects of a nondiscriminatory evaluation that are involved in the administration of tests, typical expectations, and alternatives that meet the need. (*See* Nondiscriminatory Evaluation Procedures and Standards; Administration of Nondiscriminatory Assessments)

Aspect of Nondiscriminatory Assessment	*Typical Expectations*	*Alternative Possibilities*
a.		
b.		
c.		

20. Explain why portfolio assessment is so effective in assessing student learning. (*See* Administration of Nondiscriminatory Assessments; Guarding Against Cultural and Linguistic Bias)

____

____

21. One of the most challenging times for many families is the ______________________ ______________________________. (*See* Administration of Nondiscriminatory Assessments; Compiling Assessment Data and Making Evaluation Decisions)

A Transition Portfolio for Jeff, a Student with Multiple Disabilities

In an effort to make the transition from middle to high school smooth for Jeff, a fourteen-year-old student, one of his teachers developed a transition portfolio with assistance from team members. The transition portfolio documented critical information about Jeff that new teachers might need. Information gathering usually extends over one year as members of the team jot down important details and strategies, and then document these items in a more formal way at the end of the year. For example, the team felt it was important to document the types of medications Jeff was taking and the effect of these medications.

To learn more about what a transition portfolio is and what individual components should be included see "A Transition Portfolio for Jeff, A Student with Multiple Disabilities," in *Teaching Exceptional Children,* July/August 2000, *32*(6), p. 44.

Appropriate Education

22. How are the rules for students ages 14 to 21 different than for students age three to twenty-one? (*See* Contents of the IFSP/IEP; Age-Specific Provisions)

____

____

23. What individuals must be part of the IFSP/IEP team? (*See* Contents of the IFSP/IEP; Participants Who Develop the IFSP/IEP)

____

24. Examine Figures 2-7 and 2-8 and identify unique characteristics of the contents of the IFSP and the IEP. (*See* Contents of the IFSP/IEP)

Unique to IFSP	*Unique to IEP*

25. If a parent does not want to participate in the IEP meeting, what happens next? (*See* Contents of the IFSP/IEP; Participants Who Develop the IFSP/IEP)

____

____

26. By what point in the school year must the IEP be developed? (*See* Contents of the IFSP/IEP, Time Lines)

____

27. What is the one principal reason for a mandatory review conference? (*See* Developing the IFSP/IEP; IFSP/IEP Conferences)

____

28. List the five separate matters that must be addressed when reviewing an IFSP/IEP. (*See* Contents of IFSP/IEP; IFSP/IEP Conferences)

____

____

____

____

____

APPLICATION EXERCISES FOR CHAPTER 2

Application Exercise 2a. Identifying Stages of a Nondiscriminatory Evaluation

After reading the "Nondiscriminatory Evaluation: Screening, Prereferral, and Referral" section of the text, select which of the three stages of evaluation (screening, prereferral, referral) is taking place in each of the following situations:

1. Jami has been bringing home poor work for months now. Jami's parents have asked for a full and formal nondiscriminatory evaluation.

   Stage: ________________________________

2. Jill has not been paying attention in class and not completing her work. Jill's teachers have been examining her records to see how she performed on both intelligence and achievement tests. They also asked the school nurse to administer a vision and hearing test.

   Stage: ________________________________

3. George has been having learning difficulties. He can't seem to grasp the math concepts presented in class and has been steadily falling behind with his classwork. Mr. McCutcheon, his teacher, has asked the guidance counselor and school nurse to help assist him. Ms. Safran, the guidance counselor, sat in one day when Mr. McCutcheon was teaching and later gave him some suggestions for how to deliver the instruction more effectively for that student. Together they brainstormed ways to help George.

   Stage: ________________________________

4. Chanpen has only been in the U.S. a few months. Her English is limited and she doesn't seem to be making any effort to communicate. Ms. McMath, her third grade teacher, has expressed concern that she may have a serious disability. Several other school personnel have been asked to assist to determine if Chanpen's difficulties arise from a disability or from the cultural and linguistic differences she is experiencing.

   Stage: ________________________________

5. Mr. Martin has tried everything he knows to help Sam learn science. Sam appears not only disinterested, but hostile. He becomes angry when Mr. Martin tries to help him. Ms. Sexton has observed Mr. Martin teaching and trying to help Sam. Together they brainstormed some new ideas and Mr. Martin tried them, but without success.

   Stage: ________________________________

Application Exercise 2b. IQ Scores in the Classroom

Reread Box 2-5, "Into Practice: Collaborating with Parents in IFSP/IEP Conferences." Then match the practice with the place in the process where this practice belongs. You will use some of the items in the left-hand column more than once.

a. Preparing in Advance	_____ 1. Introduce each participant, briefly describing his or her role in the conference
b. Connecting and Getting Started	_____ 2. Give family members a written copy of all evaluation results.
c. Sharing Visions, Great Expectations, and Strengths	_____ 3. Clarify who—student, family, professionals—is responsible for reaching the goals and objectives and ensuring their generalization or mastery.
d. Reviewing Formal Evaluation and Present Level of Performance	_____ 4. Ask the family about their preferences and needs regarding the conference.
e. Sharing Resources, Priorities and Concerns	_____ 5. Consider the five special factors identified in IDEA (for example, positive behavioral support, limited English proficiency, use of Braille, language and communication modes for people who are deaf and hard of hearing, and assistive technology), and make plans as needed for the student.
f. Developing Goals and Objectives (or Outcomes)	_____ 6. Determine evaluation criteria, procedures, and schedules for goals and objectives and how parents will be regularly informed.
g. Determining Placement, Supplementary Aids/Services, and Related Services	_____ 7. Avoid educational jargon as much as possible, and clarify any terms that seem to puzzle the family, student, or their advocates.
h. Addressing Assessment Modifications and Special Factors	_____ 8. Assign the follow-up responsibility for any task requiring attention.
i. Concluding the Conference	_____ 9. Share the results of Making Action Plans (MAPs) process, or incorporate it into the conference.
	_____10. Explain the extent to which the child will not participate in the regular education program.
	_____11. Encourage all participants to express their concerns about their own roles in supporting the student, especially in areas where they believe they will need support or assistance.
	_____12. Prepare an agenda to cover the remaining components of the IEP conference.
	_____13. Affirm the value of a reliable alliance, and cite specific examples of how having an alliance enhanced the quality of decision-making.

Application Exercise 2c: Assessing What You've Learned

Based upon the major sections* in this chapter, construct a twenty-question criterion-referenced test to summarize the major concepts covered in this chapter.

*Major Sections: Framework for Implementing IDEA; Nondiscriminatory Evaluation: Screening, Prereferral, and Referral; Nondiscrimination Evaluation; and Appropriate Education.

SAMPLE QUIZ FOR CHAPTER 2

MULTIPLE CHOICE

Circle the correct answer.

1. The content of the student's IEP is the foundation for all of the following <u>except</u>?
   a. Appropriate education
   b. Insurance of benefit from special education
   c. Total inclusion into a general education classroom
   d. Opportunities for the outcomes of independence

2. What are the purposes of prereferral?
   a. Safeguarding against misidentification and providing immediate help to teachers with challenging students
   b. Screening for learning difficulties and exploring cultural differences that might exist
   c. Assessing strategies for evaluation and interpreting test results
   d. Determining classification and accommodating students in the general education classroom

3. Norm-referenced tests compare a student's performance to what other students?
   a. Students randomly chosen to represent the entire population
   b. The normal distribution of a characteristic of students in the general population
   c. The students with IQs in the normal range of 90–110
   d. The students in a general education class who do not require special education

4. Nine-year-old Lupe is undergoing an assessment of her adaptive behavior. What will be considered during this process?
   a. Her adaptive behavior skills as compared to those of peers her age
   b. How she performs on a norm-referenced test
   c. Whether she is ready for the transition process
   d. Whether her outcome-oriented rights have been considered

5. Shawnine's nondiscriminatory evaluation team has determined that she has a disability. What is the next step for the team?
   a. Place her in the least restrictive educational environment
   b. Develop an IEP
   c. Identify the closest Parent to Parent program for her family
   d. Determine the special instruction that she needs

6. A student with average performance would score within which IQ range?
   a. 70–85
   b. 90–109
   c. 80–89
   d. 110–119

7. For what ages does IDEA provide federal money to guarantee students with disabilities a free appropriate public education?
   a. Birth to eighteen
   b. Birth to twenty-one
   c. Three to eighteen
   d. Preschool through high school

8. What is the formula for calculating IQ?
   a. Chronological age divided by mental age
   b. Mental age × 100 × chronological age
   c. Mental age ÷ chronological age × 100
   d. Chronological age × mental age ÷ Wechsler score

9. In implementing the IFSP/IEP, what are two issues that need to be addressed?
   a. Conducting annual assessments and selecting an appropriate placement
   b. Assuring parent participation and fostering cooperative learning
   c. Training the parents in supplementing instruction and emphasizing great expectations
   d. Selecting appropriate instructional methods and determining evaluation strategies

10. Which of the following is <u>not</u> considered a basic component of cooperative learning?
   a. Interpersonal skills
   b. Face-to-face interaction
   c. Positive interdependence
   d. Individual compctition

11. Which of the following is <u>not</u> one of the six IDEA principles?
   a. Procedural due process
   b. Nondiscriminatory evaluation
   c. Parent and student participation
   d. Full inclusion

12. Andreas's general education teacher has asked the school psychologist and Andreas's parents to assist in problem solving and identifying strategies to improve this student's behavioral challenges. Which term best refers to this process?
   a. Screening
   b. Prereferral
   c. Referral
   d. Nondiscriminatory evaluation

13. Which of the following does <u>not</u> apply to the reevaluation of a student?
   a. Occurs every three years
   b. Occurs as often as is warranted
   c. Occurs if a parent or teacher requests it
   d. Occurs every year

14. When should nondiscriminatory evaluation occur?
   a. After initial placement
   b. Before initial placement
   c. After writing the IEP
   d. During the prereferral process

15. Mohan is receiving a nondiscriminatory evaluation. What test will <u>most</u> likely be used to measure his intelligence?
   a. A norm-referenced test
   b. A criterion-referenced test
   c. A portfolio of his class work, since he has motor difficulties
   d. A functional assessment

16. Christopher's nondiscriminatory evaluation shows that he is in the second percentile on his IQ score. What does this result indicate?
    a. He is intellectually challenged.
    b. His IQ is low average.
    c. He is almost in the top category for giftedness.
    d. He is scoring in the average range of intelligence.

17. Which of the following people must administer the assessments required for evaluation?
    a. School psychologists
    b. Trained personnel
    c. School administrators
    d. Special education teachers

18. To what does the testing term "validity" refer?
    a. How well a test yields similar results in different situations
    b. How well the raters agree on the scores of test-takers
    c. How well the test measures what it says it measures
    d. How consistent the test questions are

19. How often must an IFSP be reviewed with the family?
    a. Every six months
    b. At least once a year
    c. Every three years or more often if warranted
    d. Whenever the family requests a review

20. What is the essential purpose of a nondiscriminatory evaluation?
    a. To eliminate students who do not have disabilities
    b. To find out if the student has a disability and, if so, what the student's needs are
    c. To help teachers work together on behalf of students facing learning challenges
    d. To identify student weaknesses and strengths

SHORT ANSWER

21. What are the four steps typically followed in accomplishing the purposes of nondiscriminatory evaluation?

a. ______________________________
b. ______________________________
c. ______________________________
d. ______________________________

22. What are the two types of frequently used tests?

a. ______________________________
b. ______________________________

23. Define reliability and validity in tests.

____
____
____

ESSAY

24. Describe the nondiscriminatory evaluation procedures and standards.

25. Explain how the IFSP and IEP serve as tools to help students succeed in their education. Integrate important points about the contents, time lines, and implementation for the IFSP and IEP.

CHAPTER 3: SPECIAL EDUCATION TODAY: INCLUSION AND COLLABORATION

CHAPTER OVERVIEW

Students with exceptionalities can benefit greatly from inclusion and collaboration. A background of the various reforms in general and special education provides the framework for understanding how inclusion builds on and draws together the strengths offered by each reform. Each stage of the evolution of inclusion is closely examined, including the new 1997 amendments to IDEA. Collaboration is explored through an explanation of the roles of various potential collaborators.

This chapter examines the role of inclusion and collaboration in the life of eighteen-year-old Danny Ramirez. Danny's experience of being part of other students' lives and being part of the school has meant being in the same programs as the students who do not have disabilities. His experiences mirror some of the major issues surrounding both inclusion and collaboration today.

CHAPTER AT-A-GLANCE

Chapter Outline	Instructional Goals	Key Concepts
GENERAL AND SPECIAL EDUCATION SCHOOL REFORM		
School Reform via Standards-Based Reform	• Describe how the Goals 2000 law serves as a vehicle for making the promise of IDEA a reality for all students • Describe the controversy over standards-based reform	• Goals 2000 seeks to have all students, including students with disabilities, meet 8 national education goals. • More and more states are implementing standards for learning, although this standard-setting is not necessarily a product of collaboration between special and general educators.
School Reform via the Individuals with Disabilities Education Act	• Describe how the 1997 changes in IDEA have sought to improve services to students • Identify the two themes of school reform in special education	• IDEA now uses an outcome-based approach to special education and also connects state and local educational agencies to school reform. • The two themes of school reform in special education are inclusion and collaboration.
FORERUNNERS TO INCLUSION: MAINSTREAMING AND THE REGULAR EDUCATION INITIATIVE		
Mainstreaming	• Recognize characteristics of mainstreaming	• Mainstreaming integrates students with disabilities only in nonacademic portions of the general education program.
The Regular Education Initiative • Madeleine Will and Special Education Reform • Controversy over the Regular Education Initiative	• Explain Will's role in the Regular Education Initiative • Analyze the issues involved in the controversy	• Madeleine Will criticized the shortcomings of special education services. • The REI focused on the way students are taught as well as the structure and organization of special education.

FIRST-GENERATION INCLUSION		
The Evolution Toward Inclusion	• Understand influences on the evolution of inclusion	• Opposition to the REI was both financial and logistical in nature.
Extent of Implementation	• Recognize that first-generation inclusion has been successful to an extent	• The placement of students with disabilities in general education classrooms jumped 16% in nine years.
Three Key Components • Home-School Placement • Age- and Grade-Appropriate Placements • Special Education Supports Exist Within General Education Classes	• Identify options for achieving the home-school principle • Explain key issues at the heart of the inclusion debate • Define how supports for inclusion differ	• Three components of first-generation inclusion are (a) all students receive education in their neighborhood school, (b) placements are age- and grade-appropriate, (c) special education supports exist in the general classroom. • Three options to achieve the home-school principle include the neighborhood school, a transportation school, and a school of choice. • Issues include eliminating the continuum of services, increasing the amount of time students spend in the general education classroom, and defining "all students." • First-generation models <u>add</u> teaching procedures and resources while second-generation models are characterized by <u>systemic</u> change.
Challenges Encountered in Inclusion • Teachers' perspectives • Parents' perspectives • Students' perspectives • Research perspectives	• List specific obstacles to inclusion • Note perspectives on inclusion from each group	• Obstacles include time, training, personnel resources, materials resources, class size, consideration of severity of disabilities.
SECOND-GENERATION INCLUSION		
Crossroads: From First- to Second-Generation Inclusion	• Summarize the major difference between first- and second-generation inclusion	• Second generation requires that change must be systemic and the education enterprise needs to be redesigned at the systems level.
Overview of Second-Generation Inclusion • Universal Design	• Explain the expectations for second-generation inclusion • Define universal design, and explain why it is a strategy for all students.	• Second-generation inclusion expects schoolwide reform, teacher renewal, intensive support for students, and a retreat from education based on labels. • Universal design is a strategy for modifying curricular goals and instructional strategies to ensure full access by all students, including those with exceptionalities, linguistic differences, and varied learning styles. • Universal design provides flexible means of representation, expression, and engagement.

COLLABORATION AS A PREREQUISITE FOR INCLUSION		
Definition of Collaboration	• Define the key components of collaboration	• Collaboration is an interactive process that builds on the expertise, interests, and strengths of everyone involved in the educational process to solve problems.
Rationale for Collaboration	• Explain how collaboration can be justified	• Historically, general and special education teachers worked in isolation from one another, preventing them from capitalizing on each others' potentially valuable contributions.
Roles of Potential Collaborators • Students • Parents • Teachers • Related-Service Providers • Paraprofessionals • Language Translators and Interpreters • Administrators	• Identify the roles of potential collaborators	• For students, self-determination is an important part of their curriculum and leads to them being effective collaborators in their own education. • For parents, collaboration is best done through power-sharing; teachers' power over parents' discourages collaboration. • For teachers, collaboration requires them to make time and reconceptualize their roles. • For related-service providers, paraprofessionals, language translators and interpreters, and administrators, it includes being essential parts of a collaboration team.
State-of-the-Art Collaborative Approaches	• Explain the characteristics and benefits of cooperative teaching	• Cooperative teaching involves two or more educators sharing the responsibility for planning, delivering, and evaluating instruction for students. • Benefits of cooperative teaching include reduced need for pullout programs, and more effective individualized instruction in the general education environment.
Process of Creating Collaborative Teams	• Explain the necessary elements in creating a collaborative process.	• Five important elements are: (a) frequent face-to-face interaction, (b) a feeling of positive interdependence, (c) well-developed small-group interpersonal skills, (d) regular assessment's of the team's functioning, and (e) methods for holding team members accountable.

PROJECT OPTIONS

1. Create a survey for local special and general educators to assess their understanding of how the "least restrictive environment principle" is being carried out in your school districts. Include at least ten questions and have a minimum of ten special and ten general educators fill out the survey. Then tally your answers and compare and contrast differences. Chart your findings for the class.
2. Obtain a copy of IDEA. Make a time line, comparing and contrasting beliefs about inclusion during the last five decades in educational history.
3. Compose a poem or short story illustrating both the positive and negative stances on inclusion. Then illustrate the beliefs with either original pictures or pictures from magazines.
4. Based on a thorough search of websites on inclusion, construct a chart demonstrating the most recent implementations of inclusion for the four different age levels discussed in this text: early childhood, elementary, middle and secondary, and transitional postsecondary. Then create a presentation to the class that requires group discussion and collaboration to solve specific problems uncovered.

KEY TERMS

Continuum of services

Facilitative role

Information-giving role

Paraprofessional

Prescriptive role

Self-determination

Supportive role

Transportation school

GUIDED REVIEW

Perspectives on Inclusion

A parent of a young child with autism expressed the following perspective on the value of inclusion:

"Young people with disabilities only aspire to what is expected of them. You put them in special education, they learn to wash dishes. You mainstream, they can learn to live in a normal society. We will not allow Jason to use his handicap as an excuse to achieve less than his full potential."

However, another parent expressed her concern about the social isolation that can occur for students with exceptionalities who are placed in but do not participate in general classrooms:

"My son sits at the same table as general education kids, but there is no interaction . . . .Some of his classes contain joint activities, but 'togetherness' is not being facilitated."

In this chapter, you read about the second-generation inclusion movement, which emphasizes making sure that justification is written in IEPs for not including students. Furthermore, when students are included, they are expected to be active participants in general education.

School Reform Via Standards-Based Reform

1. Explain the arguments for and against holding students with disabilities accountable to state-mandated standards.(*See* School Reform via Standards-Based Reform)

____

____

____

2. The provisions of the 1997 IDEA reauthorization seek to improve services to students in five important ways. Identify the goals or outcomes and then define what is involved in these improved services. (*See* School Reform via IDEA)

Goal/Outcome	*Explanation of Goal*
a.	
b.	
c.	
d.	
e.	

You can read about a principal who personally reformed her school in inner-city Philadelphia in the book *For the Children* (Madeline Cartwright, 1993, Doubleday Books). She considered the filthy, vermin-ridden school, which housed a discouraged staff and troubled children "a challenge made to order."

3. What are the four consecutive phases of special education reform for inclusion? (*See* School Reform via IDEA)
   a. ____
   b. ____
   c. ____
   d. ____

Alternative Schools
Can you imagine attending a school that was run by the Walt Disney Co.? Disney has built the Celebration School and Teaching Academy outside of Orlando, Florida. The school houses 1,400 students in prekindergarten through twelfth grade. This is only one example of private enterprise taking over schools in hopes of improving education and making a profit at the same time. Impatient with school reforms, many parents are demanding change and welcoming businesses into their schools. Jane Carroll, a parent in Hartford, Connecticut, explained her reasons for doing so: "Nothing has changed over the years, nothing has happened. Now, I want something to happen." (Gibbs, *Time*, p. 48.) That something was Education Alternatives, Inc., a company that agrees to pay the bills, train the teachers, and develop the curriculum in exchange for one-half of every dollar it saves the school system.

Forerunners to Inclusion: Mainstreaming and the Regular Education Initiative

4. In the early days of mainstreaming, students normally participated in what portions of the program? (*See* Forerunners to Inclusion; Mainstreaming)

____

Inclusion Resources
Do you want to learn more about inclusion? *Toward Inclusive Classrooms* (National Education Association) has many practical, helpful ideas on promoting inclusion by curricular activities. It emphasizes inclusion at all levels from elementary to secondary schools and includes a helpful resource list. The book moves beyond philosophy to answer some of the difficult "how-to" questions. *Exceptional Children* (1994, Vol. 60, No. 6) contains articles that address the relationship of inclusion to the development of positive self-identity, a policy study on implementing the IDEA least restrictive environment principles, and the current status of inclusion for students with learning disabilities. In addition, Expectations Unlimited, Inc. (P.O. Box 655, Niwot, CO 80544, 303-652-2727) has a free catalog that lists videotapes, audiotapes, and books on inclusion and related issues.

First-Generation Inclusion

5. What were some of the key influencing factors in the evolution toward inclusion? (*See* First-Generation Inclusion; The Evolution Toward Inclusion)

____

____

6. Match the stage of inclusion with its characteristics. (*See* First-Generation Inclusion)

Mainstreaming The Regular Education Initiative	a. ______ Madeleine Will criticized special education services for its lack in several key areas. b. ______Special educators called on general educators to assume more responsibility and general educators viewed this as outsiders' attempt to direct them into undesired roles. c. ______Placed students with disabilities in general education classes with their peers who do not have disabilities to the maximum extent appropriate. d. ______ Most of the students with disabilities participated in the nonacademic portions of the program only.

7. What was the basic goal of the inclusive school movement? (*See* First-Generation Inclusion; The Evolution Toward Inclusion)

____

8. Identify strengths and weaknesses for each of the following stages of inclusion. (*See* First-Generation Inclusion; The Evolution Toward Inclusion)
   a. Mainstreaming:

   ____

   ____

   b. The Regular Education Initiative:

   ____

   ____

   c. First-Generation Inclusion:

   ____

   ____

9. Match the latest percentages for educational placements of students with disabilities. (*See* First-Generation Inclusion; Extent of Implementation)

Placement Location	***Percentage***
1. _______ Separate facility	a. 46%
2. _______ Separate class	b. 27%
3. _______ Residential facility	c. 22%
4. _______ General education classroom	d. 3 %
5. _______ Home/ hospital	e. 0.7%
6. _______ Resource room	f. 0.7%

10. Identify the three components of first-generation inclusion. (*See* First-Generation Inclusion; Three Key Components)
    a. ____
    b. ____
    c. ____

Inclusion Can Work

Judith Heumann, Assistant Secretary for Special Education and Rehabilitative Services, U.S. Department of Education, states her perspective on the current inclusion debate: "Historically, we have had two educational systems: one for students with disabilities and one for everyone else. We are working to create an educational system that values all students." Heumann goes on to say that the general education classroom in the neighborhood school ought to be the first option for students with disabilities. She also emphasizes that teachers and administrators will need special training for that option to work.

See *Exceptional Parent,* September 1994, p. 37.

11. Home-school placement means that students should attend their ______________________.
    This means that they should attend the same school that they would attend if ______________
    ____. (*See* Three Key Components; Home-School Placement)

12. What are three options to achieve the home-school principle? (*See* Three Key Components; Home-School Placement)
    a. ____
    b. ____
    c. ____

13. Describe the pros and cons for each of the major issues at the heart of the inclusion debate. (*See* Three Key Components; Age- and Grade-Appropriate Placements)
    a. Eliminating the continuum of services:

    ____

    ____

    b. Increasing the amount of time students spend in general education classrooms:

    ____

    ____

    c. Defining "all students":

    ____

    ____

14. Explain the difference between being "based-in" and "confined to" general education classrooms. (*See* Three Key Components; Age- and Grade-Appropriate Placements)

    ____

    ____

15. The core issue of the debate over inclusion is whether the dominant theme in education·decision making for students with exceptionalities is and should be ______________________ or should be ______________________________________
    (*See* Three Key Components; The Meaning of "All")

16. Which factor most distinguishes first- and second-generation inclusion? (*See* Three Key Components; Special Education Supports Exist Within General Education Classes)

    ____

Inclusion and Racism

Students of color are often overrepresented in special education. However, in their article "The Color of Inclusion," Terry Meier and Cheryl Render Brown emphasize that students of color can be "labeled, marginalized, even rendered invisible, without ever leaving the general classroom." The authors contend that even if these students are taken out of special education classes, a dual educational system will continue to exist, unless we are "willing to examine honestly the role that racism plays in meting out educational opportunities in our schools."

See *The Journal of Emotional and Behavioral Problems* (1994), *3*(3), pp. 15–18.

17. The focus of general education practice is on the ________________ ,while the special educator's focus has always been on the __________________. (*See* First-Generation Inclusion; Challenges Encountered in Inclusion)

18. List the six major themes research has shown to be critical to inclusion. (*See* First-Generation Inclusion; Challenges Encountered in Inclusion)
    a. ______________________________
    b. ______________________________
    c. ______________________________
    d. ______________________________
    e. ______________________________
    f. ______________________________

Second-Generation Inclusion

19. First-generation inclusion focuses on how to make ______________________ and ______________________; in contrast, second-generation inclusion focuses on ______________________ change. (*See* Second-Generation Inclusion; Crossroads: From First- to Second-Generation Inclusion)

20. Identify expectations for second-generation inclusion along with the required change. (*See* Second-Generation Inclusion; Overview of Second-Generation Inclusion)

	Expectation	***Change Needed***
Expectation 1		
Expectation 2		
Expectation 3		
Expectation 4		

Collaboration as a Prerequisite for Inclusion

21. Define *collaboration.* (*See* Collaboration as a Prerequisite for Inclusion; Definition of Collaboration)
    ____

22. Name the four roles you will play as a professional educator. (*See* Collaboration as a Prerequisite for Inclusion; Definition of Collaboration)
    a. ______________________________
    b. ______________________________
    c. ______________________________
    d. ______________________________

Community Education

Community members are not the only ones who can experience awkwardness when they encounter a child with a disability. Sometimes parents experience awkwardness with knowing how to speak to others about their child. Lisa Abelow Hedley describes this dilemma. Her daughter, who has dwarfism, contrasts dramatically with her mother's six-foot stature.

At first, Lisa found herself accosting strangers who were little people, trying to make a connection This was an overreaction, she says, especially when she found herself providing one of these strangers with a ride in her car. She discovered that stature is "a relatively superficial bond." Lisa had to contend with the insensitivity of a friend who suggested that she have her daughter put up for adoption, for the good of the community. And then she also experienced the openness of a child who asked if her daughter was really a dwarf. When she answered yes, the child said, "That's okay. It doesn't matter how tall you are if your heart's in the right place." Lisa believes that people's reaction often reveals more about themselves than they want others to know. Her suggestions for other parents? "Speak out of respect [about your child] and from the heart."

See Hedley, L. A. "A Child of Difference." *The New York Times Magazine* (October 12, 1997), pp. 94–98.

23. Identify the roles of future potential collaborators by listing the benefits and outcomes of collaboration for each collaborator. Use the IEP form provided in this Student Study Guide to be sure you cover the breadth of collaboration required for the success of students with exceptionalities. (*See* Collaboration as a Prerequisite for Inclusion; Roles of Potential Collaborators, as well as the "Collaborating for Success" chart in the Student Study Guide)

Collaborator	*Role of Collaborator*	*Outcomes for Student*
a. Student		
b. Parents		
c. Teachers		
d. Related-Service Providers		
e. Paraprofessionals		
f. Language Translators and Interpreters		
g. Administrators		

24. Define "power-relationships" and describe some of the benefits of "power-sharing." (*See* Collaboration as a Prerequisite for Inclusion; Roles of Potential Collaborators)

25. Define cooperative teaching and explain some of its benefits. (*See* Collaboration as a Prerequisite for Inclusion; State-of-the-Art Collaborative Approaches)

____

____

____

____

26. List the five critical steps for creating collaborative teams. Circle the one that is most important. (*See* Collaboration as a Prerequisite for Inclusion; Process of Creating Collaborative Teams)
    1. ________________________________
    2. ________________________________
    3. ________________________________
    4. ________________________________
    5. ________________________________

Cooperative Learning

Cooperative learning is one technique that allows students to help each other to learn curricular content. There are several different types of cooperative learning formats, and we suggest that you read more about this valuable instructional tool. Two good sources are the *Cooperative Learning Center* (202 Pattee Hall, University of Minnesota, Minneapolis, MN 55455, 612-624-7031) and the *Team Learning Project* (Center for Research on Elementary and Middle Schools, The Johns Hopkins University, 3505 N. Charles Street, Baltimore, MD 21218, 301-338-8248). Norma Dyke (1990) suggests that when you are using cooperative learning in your classes, you will want to teach your students the following guidelines:

1. Make sure everyone knows the material.
2. No one is finished until everyone knows the answers.
3. Ask all teammates for help before asking the teacher.
4. Talk with a soft voice.
5. Tell your teammates HOW to get the answer.
6. Be sure everyone agrees on the answer before checking the answer sheet.

APPLICATION EXERCISES FOR CHAPTER 3

Application Exercise 3a. Identifying Placements for Students with Disabilities

Identify which educational placement is most typical as represented in the following scenarios. Also tell what percentage of students have placements in this setting.

1. Josephina has multiple physical disabilities and requires many paraprofessionals helping her everyday. She enjoys other children, but requires full time on-site supervision.
   Setting: ________________
   Percentage: ________________

2. Rolando benefits from daily interactions with peers, even though his hearing loss is moderate. He enjoys the many hours he spends in the general education class, but also receives additional help from the speech-language pathologist four afternoons a week.
   Setting: ________________
   Percentage: ________________

3. Abdul's learning disabilities have not prevented him from being one of the most popular kids in the class. His sense of humor and ability to make his teachers smile make the school day more pleasant for all of his peers. He has several peer buddies who help him with difficult assignments. A special tutor for reading comes to his class and works with him there.
   Setting: ________________
   Percentage: ________________

4. Jenny's swimming accident resulted in a traumatic brain injury. She has required extensive rehabilitation following hospitalization and has received special education services during this time. With continued collaboration on the part of her teachers and rehabilitation personnel, her parents expect her to one day be back in a regular class.
   Setting: ________________
   Percentage: ________________

5. Gopal was born blind, but his parents soon recognized how bright he was. Since he was a preschooler he has benefited from excellent instruction from teachers who were visually impaired as well as enjoyed interactions with peers who were blind. His school participates in collaborative sports and extracurricular activities with the local elementary school.
   Setting: ________________
   Percentage: ________________

6. Erin's speech difficulties require extensive teaching from the speech language pathologist. However, for math, art, and physical education, she often participates with other children at her own grade level.
   Setting: ________________
   Percentage: ________________

Application Exercise 3b. Matching Collaborators with Professional Roles

Collaboration is been defined as "an interactive process that enables people with diverse expertise to generate creative solutions to mutually defined problems." First, define the professional role. Then, match the collaborator with the most typical professional roles.

Collaborator	*Professional Role and Definition*
1. ____________Students	a. Supportive role:
2. ____________Parents	
3. ____________Special educators	b. Facilitative role:
4. ____________General educators	
5. ____________Related-service providers	c. Information-giving role:
6. ____________Paraprofessionals	
7. ____________Language translators and interpreters	d. Prescriptive role:
8. ____________Administrators	

Application Exercise 3c. Collaborating for Success

Working collaboratively with two partners, construct a written summary of the major concepts in this chapter. In addition to the written summary, submit a list of activities that you did collaboratively. Then evaluate which aspects of collaboration worked most effectively for an assignment like this.

Major Sections: General and Special Education School Reform, Forerunners to Inclusion, First-Generation Inclusion, Second-Generation Inclusion, Collaboration as a Prerequisite for Inclusion

SAMPLE QUIZ FOR CHAPTER 3

MULTIPLE CHOICE

Circle the correct answer.

1. Which of the following is not a key component of first-generation inclusionary practices?
   a. Placements that are age-appropriate and grade-appropriate
   b. Education in the school students would attend if they had no disability
   c. Special education supports within general education classes
   d. Provision of an individual assistant or paraprofessional

2. Which of the following is a criticism of special education that was raised by supporters of the Regular Education Initiative?
   a. Excluding many students who need special education support
   b. Stigmatizing students placed in special education
   c. Withholding special programs until the student fails
   d. All of the above

3. Second generation inclusion encourages which of the following?
   a. Schoolwide reform
   b. Teacher renewal
   c. Intensive support for students
   d. All of the above

4. What is a difference between charter schools and magnet schools?
   a. Magnet schools are free; charter schools charge tuition.
   b. Charter schools cannot discriminate, while magnet schools can have competitive admission.
   c. Charter schools are created by parents and teachers to reflect their educational philosophy and values.
   d. Magnet schools focus on math, science, and technology and often use a lottery system for admission.

5. Which of the following is not true about the services provided by paraprofessionals or paraeducators who work with special educators and general educators to assist with the provision of services to students with special needs in inclusive classrooms?
   a. Teachers have more time to respond to students' needs when paraprofessionals or paraeducators are available.
   b. Students make more academic gains because of the help from paraprofessionals or paraeducators.
   c. Paraprofessionals or paraeducators are paid well for their assistance in inclusive classrooms.
   d. Administrators are usually pleased with the use of paraprofessionals or paraeducators.

6. Who are the primary advocates for inclusive education?
   a. Leaders in the field of severe and multiple disabilities
   b. Parents of children with mild to moderate disabilities
   c. Researchers, political appointees in Washington, D.C., and university professors
   d. Special education teachers and The American Association of Paraprofessionals

7. What is necessary for successful second-generation inclusion?
   a. Increase the number of special education teachers and paraprofessionals to meet the individual needs of students with disabilities
   b. Curriculum adaptations
   c. Increased federal funding to fulfill IDEA mandates
   d. A redesign of the educational system

8. Under the inclusion requirements of IDEA, services to students with disabilities begin in which of the following settings?
   a. Self-contained classrooms
   b. General education classroom
   c. Resource rooms
   d. Special schools

9. Mike is a student with special needs in your class. He has an apparently poor attitude toward other students. What is the most appropriate way to include him?
   a. Collaborate with the school counselor to set up a reward system for completing class assignments.
   b. Assign an assistant to distract him when he exhibits poor behavior.
   c. Ask Mike which peers he would like to work with and form a small group to practice verbal responses with him.
   d. Carefully choose activities that allow him to work alone.

10. Madeleine Will is usually associated with which of the following?
   a. REI
   b. LRE
   c. FAPE
   d. IDEA

11. What is a major change that is expected to occur for students with disabilities as a result of Goals 2000?
   a. A greater emphasis on the extent to which they meet challenging standards associated with their school's curriculum
   b. All fourth-, eighth-, and twelfth-grade students with learning disabilities having to pass their state's proficiency test
   c. Promotion of vocational skills so all students with disabilities can be part of the workforce
   d. Strong push to develop literacy, math, science, and social skills so the United States will be first in the world

12. What did Madeleine Will believe should be the outcomes of special education for students with disabilities?
   a. The development of vocational skills, adaptive behavior, and satisfaction in personal preferences
   b. Supported partnerships with parents and great expectations
   c. Human relationships, literacy, responsibility, and happiness
   d. Adult independence and a network of friends

13. How did advocates for inclusion challenge the very nature of schools?
   a. They wanted to eliminate the continuum of services.
   b. They tried to persuade school authorities to create special classes for students within general education schools.
   c. They supported REI's emphasis on improving the academic achievement of students with mild and moderate disabilities.
   d. They supported full inclusion with no pull-out programs, resource rooms, or special services.

14. What is an advantage of the "critical mass" approach to special education?
    a. It is less costly, more efficient, and more effective than using home schools.
    b. It develops a sense of community and responsibility.
    c. It offers greater opportunities for neighborhood activities.
    d. It enhances racial and ethnic balances among students with disabilities so they have better peer relationships.

15. Which of the following is <u>not</u> one of the three major issues mentioned as being at the heart of the inclusion debate?
    a. Defining <u>all students</u>
    b. Eliminating the continuum of services
    c. Students with special needs becoming a member of a real class
    d. Providing students with transportation services to and from schools

16. According to the authors, what characterizes second-generation inclusion?
    a. Curriculum modification and individualization of instructional techniques
    b. Systemic change in delivering educational services to all students
    c. Increased collaboration between parents, paraprofessionals, teachers, and administrators
    d. Intense instruction, great expectations, skills for independent living, and social relationships

17. What is seen by many general educators as a reason for endorsing resource or pull-out programs?
    a. Lack of individualization in general education
    b. The increased severity of disability in current students
    c. The constant disruptive entrance and exit of paraprofessionals in the classroom
    d. Disruption of normal peer relationships because of the stigma attached to special education students

18. What is cited as a major barrier to collaboration?
    a. Finances and in service training
    b. Arranging schedules
    c. Resentment by general education teachers of the new roles into which they are being forced
    d. Lack of respect for special education teachers and paraprofessionals

19. Chloe's work is acceptable but she needs constant supervision as a student with special needs. What would be an appropriate action to take as her teacher?
    a. Assign an assistant to work with her.
    b. Allow her to complete her unfinished work at home.
    c. Ask peers to work with her to construct a tracking system for class assignments.
    d. Collaborate with the school counselor to teach her specific social skills.

20. In general education, school reform is guided by which of the following?
    a. ADA
    b. IDEA
    c. Goals 2000
    d. Local school systems

SHORT ANSWER

21. Identify four of the eight goals for Goals 2000.

    a. ______________________________
    b. ______________________________
    c. ______________________________
    d. ______________________________

22. What are the two related themes of school reform in special education?

 a. ______________________ b. ______________________

23. Identify the four roles you as a professional will be able to play in school-wide collaboration.

 a. ____
 b. ____
 c. ____
 d. ____

ESSAY

24. Describe obstacles to inclusion reported by teachers and possible appropriate solutions.
25. Describe the major themes of successful inclusion.

CHAPTER 4: LEARNING DISABILITIES

CHAPTER OVERVIEW

A specific learning disability is the most commonly identified disability in today's schools. This chapter examines the changes and controversies occurring in the field and how these impact students, families, and communities today. In chapter 4, you will learn to (a) recognize students who have learning disabilities, (b) become sensitive to their needs, and (c) provide appropriate learning opportunities for them, whether they are in general education or special education settings. You will study the difficult concept of *discrepancy* as it relates to specific examples. You will learn how individual states identify students with learning disabilities because the criteria vary so much across states. Curriculum-based assessment measures as well as the importance of standardized intelligence and achievement tests for establishing discrepancy will be discussed. You will discover how to use learning strategies, graphic organizers, computers, anchored instruction, and other approaches to improve instruction for students with learning disabilities.

The life of sixth grader Julia Goldberg provides an illustration of a typical student with learning disabilities. Julia has a significant discrepancy between her ability and achievement in several academic areas. Her evaluation presented special challenges, however, because she has a hearing impairment. The team needed to determine whether her reading and written expression discrepancies were actually due to specific learning disabilities or her hearing loss. Julia has made tremendous strides in her academic development as a result of the use of strategies that emphasize her learning how to learn independently and generalizing these skills and behaviors to new situations in and outside of the school environment.

CHAPTER AT-A-GLANCE

Chapter Outline	Instructional Goals	Key Concepts
WHO ARE STUDENTS WITH LEARNING DISABILITIES?		
Defining Learning Disabilities • Classification Criteria	• Grasp the complexity in defining learning disabilities	• The definition of learning disabilities has been much debated, but the IDEA and NJCLD definitions are commonly used.
Describing the Characteristics • Learning Characteristics • Reading • Written Language • Mathematics • Memory • Metacognition • Behavioral, Social, and Emotional • Interpersonal Skills • Motivation and Self-Concept • Subtyping Learning Disabilities	• Describe key characteristics of learning disabilities • Recognize the diversity of characteristics experienced by students with learning disabilities	• Each state has criteria for identifying students with learning disabilities which typically include three parts: a severe discrepancy between demonstrated ability and actual achievement, exclusion of other factors, and substantiated need for special services. • Students with learning disabilities are a heterogeneous population with varied learning, behavioral, and social characteristics.
Identifying the Causes of Learning Disabilities • Neurological Causes • HereditaryGenetic Causes • Teratogenic/Pollutant Factors	• Identify potential causes of learning disabilities	• Research suggests that learning disabilities may be caused by central nervous system dysfunction that results in deficits in visual-spatial processing and phonological awareness.
Identifying the Prevalence of Learning Disabilities	• Recognize prevalence rates and recent trends	• Approximately 50% of all students with disabilities have learning disabilities. In 1998-1999, 2.7 million public-school students had learning disabilities.

HOW ARE STUDENTS WITH LEARNING DISABILITIES EVALUATED?		
Determining the Presence of a Learning Disability	• Explain the characteristics of different types of assessments used to determine the presence of learning disabilities	• Nondiscriminatory evaluation includes the use of standardized intelligence and achievement tests to determine discrepancy. • Curriculum-based assessment can be norm-referenced or criterion-referenced.
Determining the Nature and Extent of Special Education and Related Services • Curriculum-Based Assessment • Developing the IEP	• Recognize the importance of careful planning and explanations in developing the IEP plan for students with learning disabilities	• The IEP process should include careful explanation of the term *learning disabilities* to the student and family.
HOW CAN YOU ESTABLISH EFFECTIVE TEACHING PRACTICES?		
Set Curricular Goals	• Differentiate among curriculum options available for use with students with learning disabilities	• Specific curricular approaches in reading (phonological awareness), written expression (process approach), and mathematics (creating active learners) benefit students with learning disabilities. • Learning strategies can encourage independent learning, generalization, and age-appropriate content skills in general education classrooms.
Implement Instruction • Learning Strategies • Anchored Instruction	• Evaluate different methods that are effective for varied student needs	• Effective methods such as specific learning strategies, graphic organizers, overcoming learned helplessness, and computer technology help students to compensate for learning disabilities.
Early Childhood Years	• Describe characteristics of effective preschool programs	• Strategies like the Embedded Learning Opportunities help build a child's interest and increase their motivation.
Elementary Years	• Describe characteristics of effective elementary programs for students with learning disabilities	• The goal of an effective program is for the student to develop tools that will assist the child in learning how to learn.
Middle and Secondary Years	• Describe characteristics of effective programs for middle and secondary students	• Anchoring instruction to previous student experience allows a student to tackle a familiar problem, develop problem-solving techniques, and transfer this skill to another learning environment.
Transitional and Postsecondary Years	• Describe characteristics of effective program options for adults with learning disabilities	• Today's universities and colleges have created support systems that assist students in developing appropriate learning strategies, organizational skills, and self-advocacy skills to succeed in the postsecondary learning environment.

HOW CAN YOU ENCOURAGE PARTICIPATION?		
Practice Inclusion	• Examine how students are best served in an enabling environment	• The Least Restrictive Environment must focus on the student, rather than the place, in order to be the most enabling environment.
Foster Collaboration • Professional-to-Professional Collaboration • Collaboration with Students	• Explore ways to collaborate on behalf of students with learning disabilities	• Effective collaboration methods include CLASP for general and special educators and peer tutoring for students. • Making collaboration successful involves the development of specific skills through an effective training model.

PROJECT OPTIONS

1. Investigate recent research about one type of academic learning disability (reading, math, written language). Include a web search through the web challenge activity. Summarize the newest and best of what you find by presenting the new information according to the section headings of this chapter. Discuss how the new research changes expectations for students with learning disabilities. Include a list of your sources.
2. Get permission to work with the learning disabilities specialists in two local schools. Find out about a particular student's program. With parental permission, ask the specialists to identify (1) the specific learning problem, (2) the diagnostic assessment used, and (3) the interventions used. Observe at least three different students receiving intervention and evaluate the strengths and weaknesses of the interventions.
3. Write a dramatic presentation demonstrating best/worst practices when working with students with learning disabilities. For example, you might choose a parent/student, teacher/student, or administrator/student interaction. Include demonstrations of effective methods, interventions, or programs contrasted with ineffective ones.
4. Write a narrative poem about a student with learning disabilities who has been helped by some type of cooperative learning, peer tutoring, or other collaborative intervention.

KEY TERMS

Anchored instruction

Basic psychological processes

Central nervous system dysfunction

Concomitance

Curriculum-based assessment

Dysgraphia

Dyslexia

Embedded learning opportunities

Generalization

Learning strategies

Metacognition

Mnemonic

Phonological awareness

Severe discrepancy

Subtyping

Teratogens

GUIDED REVIEW

"I'm going to do what I promised. I'm going to save your life."

Dr. Fred Epstein whispered these lines to a young patient immediately before surgery. Dr. Epstein, who is coauthor with Elaine Shimberg of *Gifts of Time* (1993, William Morrow & Co.), is a pediatric neurosurgeon. Many of his colleagues refer to him as a miracle worker. He has been willing to perform surgeries that others considered impossible and, as a result, has saved many young lives.

Dr. Epstein also has learning disabilities. His grades in college were only average, and his chemistry grades were "abysmal." He applied to four medical schools and was rejected by all of them. His father, a psychiatrist, intervened and Dr. Epstein was finally accepted by New York Medical College.

Perhaps his struggles with learning disabilities have helped him to develop the patience and tenacity that resulted in his success. He emphasizes, "I don't accept children dying."

See *Reader's Digest,* February 1993, pp. 192–228.

Who Are Students with Learning Disabilities?

1. When students reach the point of ______________________________ ________________________, they refuse to risk failure in order to safeguard their fragile self-esteem. (*See* Who Are Students with Learning Disabilities?)
2. The definition adopted by the National Joint Committee on Learning Disabilities (NJCLD) differs from IDEA's definition. Fill in the blanks in the chart to compare and contrast the IDEA and NJCLD definitions. (*See* Who Are Students with Learning Disabilities?; Defining Learning Disabilities)

Definition	*IDEA*	*NJCLD*
Perceived cause		
Areas affected		
Inclusionary criterion		
Exclusionary criterion		
Need criterion		

3. Some states and local school districts require that students with learning disabilities be identified by a severe discrepancy between ______________________________ and ______________________________. (*See* Who Are Students with Learning Disabilities?; Defining Learning Disabilities; Classification Criteria)
4. Name and describe the three criteria required to receive the learning disabilities classification. (*See* Who Are Students with Learning Disabilities?; Defining Learning Disabilities; Classification Criteria)
   a. Criterion: ______________________________
      Description: ______________________________
   b. Criterion: ______________________________
      Description: ______________________________
   c. Criterion: ______________________________
      Description: ______________________________

5. No matter what characteristics manifest, students with learning disabilities often face challenges related to ____________________, ____________________, and ____________________ ____________________. (*See* Who Are Students with Learning Disabilities? Describing the Characteristics)

Collective Perspectives on Issues Affecting Learning Disabilities (Pro-Ed, 8700 Shoal Creek Boulevard, Austin, TX 78757, 512-451-3246) contains brief position statements on a variety of topics by the National Joint Committee on Learning Disabilities (NJCLD). This relatively inexpensive book would be an excellent addition to your library.

6. Describe identifying characteristics for each of the five categories of learning disabilities. (*See* Who Are Students with Learning Disabilities?; Describing the Characteristics)

Category of Learning Disability	***Identifying Characteristics***
Reading	
Written language	
Mathematics	
Memory	
Metacognition	

7. Dyslexic characteristics are a subgroup of reading disability characteristics that represent a developmental ____________________ ____________________.
   Recent research suggests that dyslexia may stem from difficulty in ____________________ ____________________. (*See* Who Are Students with Learning Disabilities?; Describing the Characteristics; Reading)
8. Students with learning disabilities in mathematics may also have difficulties with ____. (*See* Who Are Students with Learning Disabilities?; Describing the Characteristics; Mathematics)

9. List three different subtypes of learning disabilities classified by the underlying cognitive processing disorder. (*See* Who Are Students with Learning Disabilities?; Identifying the Causes of Learning Disabilities; Neurological Causes)
   a. ____
   b. ____
   c. ____

You may have heard of controversial treatments or methods for assisting students with learning disabilities, such as vision training, megavitamin therapy, the Feingold diet, Irlen (colored) lenses (also referred to as scotopic lenses), or chiropractic manipulation. The research on these approaches is inconclusive, at best. It is important to note that megavitamin therapy can actually be dangerous to a student's health.

10. As a result of research involving brain-mapping, three types of problems in how language is processed have been identified. List these three types of problems. (*See* Who Are Students with Learning Disabilities?; Identifying the Causes of Learning Disabilities; Neurological Causes)
    a. ______________________________
    b. ______________________________
    c. ______________________________
11. Research studies, especially those involving twins, indicates that almost ____________% of reading disabilities are caused by genetic factors. (*See* Who Are Students with Learning Disabilities?; Identifying the Causes of Learning Disabilities; Hereditary/Genetic Causes)
12. Students with learning disabilities represent close to ____________% of all students served in special education. Between 1977 and 1998–1999, the percentage of students identified as having learning disabilities increased from 1.8% to ______________ of total public K–12 enrollment. Based on those figures, it is probable that at least __________students in every class of 30 students will be identified as having a learning disability. (*See* What Are Learning Disabilities?; Identifying the Prevalence of Learning Disabilities)

How Are Students With Learning Disabilities Evaluated?

13. In the field of learning disabilities, what is the most common intelligence test used to identify learning disabilities? ______________________________. This test is often used concurrently with the ______________________________ Test, that measures student ____________________. (*See* How Are Students with Learning Disabilities Evaluated?; Determining the Presence of a Learning Disability)
14. What are three types of discrepancies that are used in various states to identify learning disabilities? Name and describe each one. (*See* How Are Students with Learning Disabilities Evaluated?; Determining the Presence of a Learning Disability)
    a. ______________________________
    b. ______________________________
    c. ______________________________
15. What three things must be taken into account when developing curriculum-based assessment? (*See* How Are Students with Learning Disabilities Evaluated?; Determining the Nature and Extent of Special Education and Related Services; Curriculum-Based Assessment)
    a. ______________________________
    b. ______________________________
    c. ______________________________
16. What is one of the most important components of the IEP process for students with learning disabilities? (*See* How Are Students with Learning Disabilities Evaluated?; Determining the Nature and Extent of Special Education and Related Services; Developing the IEP)

    ____

Making Sense of What's in Print

You can find many articles about learning disabilities in the popular press and on the Internet. How do you decide whether these articles accurately portray learning disabilities? Joan Rankin and Susan Phillips, in their article "Learning Disabilities in the Popular Press: Suggestions for Educators," emphasize that there are several questions you should ask while you read: What is the major focus or intent of the article? What is the author's perspective (e.g., medical/neurological, educational/instructional, telling a story about a real or fictitious person with learning disabilities, trying to get you to buy a product)? What are the author's qualifications? Is the information supported by research or expert opinion? How are *learning disability* and other terms defined by the author? Are parental rights addressed? Does the article provide advice? If so, what are the recommendations? You can ask these questions as you read about other exceptionalities besides learning disabilities.

See *Teaching Exceptional Children,* Spring 1995, pp. 35-39.

How Can You Establish Effective Teaching Practices?

17. Describe methods for teaching students with learning disabilities more effectively in reading, written language, and mathematics. (*See* How Can You Establish Effective Teaching Practices?; Implement Instruction)

Curricular Area	***Effective Teaching Approaches***
Reading	
Written Language	
Mathematics	

18. Name and describe examples of three academic tasks for instruction in learning strategies. (*See* How Can You Establish Effective Teaching Practices?; Implement Instruction)
Strategy: ____________________
Examples: ____________________
Strategy: ____________________
Examples: ____________________
Strategy: ____________________
Examples: ____________________

19. Describe some classroom adaptations useful in an inclusionary setting for students with learning disabilities. (*See* How Can You Establish Effective Teaching Practices?; Implement Instruction)
____
____
____

20. What are ways to determine effective best practice techniques to be used in developing academic programs for students with learning disabilities? (*See* How Can You Establish Effective Teaching Practices?; Implement Instruction; Into Practice)
____
____
____

Freebies

The HEALTH Resource Center, a national clearinghouse on postsecondary education for individuals with disabilities, offers free booklets on numerous topics. A few of their many titles include "Focus on College Admissions Tests," "Young Adults with Learning Disabilities and Other Special Needs: Guide for Selecting Postsecondary Transition Programs," "Technology and Learning Disabilities," and "National Resources for Adults with Learning Disabilities." The address is One Dupont Circle, Suite 800, Washington, DC 20036. The phone number is 800-544-3284.

21. Identify support services being created by universities and colleges to accommodate learning needs of individuals with learning disabilities in the postsecondary learning environment (*See* Observe Programs in Practice; Transitional and Postsecondary Years)

22. List key features for each of the following programs for students with learning disabilities. (*See* Observe Programs in Practice)

Program	***Key Features***
Embedded Learning Opportunities	
Learning strategies	
Anchored Instruction	
Western Colorado College	

How Can You Encourage Participation?

23. What is the most common placement for students with learning disabilities? (*See* How Can You Encourage Participation?; Practice Inclusion)

____

24. Describe the major components of the successful collaboration Project CLASP. (*See* How Can You Encourage Participation?; Foster Collaboration; Professional-to-Professional Collaboration)
   a. ________________
   b. ________________
   c. ________________
   d. ________________
   e. ________________

25. Two factors that ensure continuous improvement in general/special educator teams are ________________ and ________________.
   (*See* How Can You Encourage Participation?; Foster Collaboration; Professional-to-Professional Collaboration)

26. Describe components and benefits of peer tutoring. (*See* How Can You Encourage Participation?; Foster Collaboration; Collaboration with Students)
   a. Components: ________________
   ____
   b. Benefits: ________________
   ____

27. Developing the necessary skills for effective collaboration involves skill development for teachers, both general and special educators. Visit the Power of 2 learning modules and list four lessons focused on developing partnership skills (*See* How Can You Encourage Participation?; Foster Collaboration; Into Practice)
    a. ______________________________
    b. ______________________________
    c. ______________________________
    d. ______________________________

<u>Don't Waste Your Time</u>

When Janice Anderson Connolly entered her Period 7 class on her first day of teaching, she knew she was in for a challenge. One of the students commented, "Lady, don't waste your time. We're the retards."

She later learned that most of the students were children of migrant workers. Their attendance and motivation were poor, and no one expected them to graduate from high school. Janice decided that she wouldn't give up on them as others had. She went to the board the next day and wrote "ECINAJ" and told them that was her first name. After a few comments about her weird name, she wrote "JANICE" on the board. She explained to them that she had a learning disability and couldn't write her own name when she began school. Janice also told them that she couldn't spell words or do math. "That's right. I was a 'retard'. I can still hear those awful voices and feel the shame."

Her understanding of their dilemma reached the kids. She maintained high expectations for them and helped them to discover that they could learn and learn well. Two years later all fourteen of her Period 7 students graduated and six received college scholarships.

See "The First Year of Teaching: Real World Stories from America's Teachers," 1992, *Mentor*, pp. 26–31.

APPLICATION EXERCISES FOR CHAPTER 4

Application Exercise 4a. Identifying Characteristics of Learning Disabilities

See if you can tell by the description provided which characteristic of learning disabilities each of the following students demonstrates.

1. Shayla thinks that when Andrew says "Yeah, right" in a sarcastic manner, he means that he agrees with what she is saying.

   ____

2. Nigel refuses to try whenever his teacher tries to show him how to add with regrouping.

   ____

3. Mina often forgets her homework.

   ____

4. Miguel doesn't know how to study for a test.

   ____

5. Ingrid doesn't seem to be able to concentrate on her work.

   ____

6. Tobias interrupts when others are talking.

   ____

7. Pei-lin is good in math but performs below grade level in reading.

   ____

Application Exercise 4b. Determining Eligibility Based on Severe Discrepancy

You have read that when schools determine a severe discrepancy, they typically compare the discrepancy between a student's IQ and achievement scores. A particular state uses a one-and-one-half standard deviation discrepancy between full-scale IQ and achievement to determine learning disabilities (23 points). In which subject areas does each student qualify for services in that state?

	Full-Scale IQ	Reading	Mathematics	Written Language
Jose	116	92	99	101
Chanpen	103	100	86	81
Julie	123	100	96	89

Application Exercise 4c. Metacognitive Learning Strategies

Based upon the major questions addressed in this chapter, use a different metacognitive strategy to summarize the major concepts concerning learning difficulties. For each major chapter question, describe the strategy you used to learn the concepts of this section.

Major Questions: Who Are Students with Learning Disabilities? How Are Students with Learning Disabilities Evaluated? How Can You Establish Effective Teaching Practices? How Can You Encourage Participation?

SAMPLE QUIZ FOR CHAPTER 4

MULTIPLE CHOICE

Circle the correct answer.

1. What should be the focus of a program that provides the most enabling environment for a student with a learning disability?
   a. The student rather than the "place"
   b. The special education teacher rather than the general education teacher
   c. The resource room
   d. The general education classroom

2. Jaime has dyslexia. In school, what difficulties will he <u>most</u> likely face?
   a. Poor concentration during story time
   b. Difficulties in word recognition, reading comprehension, and spelling
   c. Difficulties in motor skills and metacognition
   d. Poor handwriting and memory

3. Among the students served in special education, what is the percentage of those with learning disabilities?
   a. 15%
   b. 30%
   c. 50%
   d. 65%

4. Whose work with central nervous system dysfunction laid the foundation for the field of learning disabilities?
   a. Samuel Kirk
   b. Evelyn Deno
   c. Lloyd Dunn
   d. James Hinshelwood

5. What is a benefit of concurrently using the Wechsler tests for intelligence and achievement?
   a. Both tests had the same original norm group, thus simplifying the comparison of a student's IQ and achievement scores.
   b. When ordered together, a purchase discount is available.
   c. All states use these basic tests, thus facilitating student transfers to other districts.
   d. Severe discrepancies tend to be lessened in scores, which clarifies the criteria for standard deviations.

6. Which of the following is <u>not</u> typically reviewed by the evaluation team during a reevaluation of a student with learning disabilities?
   a. Portfolio assessment
   b. Ecological assessment
   c. Behavior rating scale
   d. Neurological causes

7. Meg is developing a criterion-referenced, curriculum-based assessment instrument. Which of the following will <u>not</u> be necessary for her to consider?
   a. The time limit and level of mastery are reasonable.
   b. The test items directly reflect the objectives emphasized in the curriculum.
   c. The norm group is composed of a representative group of students from the district.
   d. The items are clearly stated.

8. What does the "P" in the POSSE strategy stand for?
   a. Predict ideas.
   b. Prepare the student for new ideas.
   c. Plan for the student's different ideas.
   d. Propose new ideas to the student.

9. What causes the downward spiral once students experience learned helplessness?
   a. Lack of instruction or misidentification of disabilities
   b. Peer ostracism
   c. Lowered self-esteem and achievement
   d. Parental neglect and/or scolding

10. Which of the following is <u>not</u> mentioned as a benefit of peer tutoring?
    a. Mastering skills
    b. Gaining confidence
    c. Lessening teacher workload
    d. Increasing socialization

11. Karen meets the inclusionary criterion. What does this mean?
    a. A rejection by the school to provide inclusion
    b. A significant difference between academic performance and IQ
    c. A demonstrated lack of opportunity
    d. A discrepancy between potential and scores on an individually administered intelligence test

12. What are the five categories of learning characteristics in students with disabilities, according to the CLD?
    a. Reading, mathematics, memory, metacognition, and written language
    b. Motor skills, mathematics, reading, writing, and fine arts
    c. Cooperation, creativity, task commitment, self-control, and humor
    d. Intrapersonal, interpersonal, athletic, musical, and academic

13. Most students with learning disabilities are educated in which classroom setting?
    a. Combination of resource room and general education classroom
    b. Combination of resource room and self-contained classroom
    c. Classroom in a special school
    d. General education classroom only

14. To assist the transfer of knowledge to generalizable tasks, students with learning disabilities <u>must</u> be exposed to which of the following?
    a. Excellent textbooks
    b. Experienced teachers
    c. Meaningful learning experiences
    d. Repetitive assignments

15. What is the purpose of an ecological assessment in a nondiscriminatory evaluation?
    a. To determine that the student's environment does not cause the learning disability
    b. To assess the student's knowledge of ecology
    c. To eliminate ineffective instruction as the reason for academic difficulty
    d. To reveal the student's abilities according to anecdotal records

16. What popular strategy helps students become more actively engaged in learning by situating or anchoring instruction around a topic that is interesting to them?
    a. Direct instruction
    b. Strategy instruction
    c. Anchored instruction
    d. Self-esteem instruction

17. What is the most lacking and desired component of self-esteem in students with learning disabilities?
    a. Power
    b. Love
    c. Significance
    d. Competence

18. Which of the following is not suggested in using computers with students who have learning disabilities?
    a. Computers can be used to make individualized drill and practice more enjoyable.
    b. Computers can be used to read orally what students write.
    c. Computers should be used primarily as a reward for good behavior.
    d. Computers are able to teach social skills through the use of simulation experiences.

19. An important aspect of nondiscriminatory evaluation for students with learning disabilities is establishing which of the following?
    a. A discrepancy between ability and achievement
    b. A discrepancy between social skills and achievement
    c. The existence of a neurological problem
    d. The existence of a learning problem

20. To accommodate students with learning disabilities, many colleges and universities have done which of the following?
    a. Provided individual tutors for all students with learning disabilities
    b. Equipped "Offices of Disability Services" to ensure equal learning opportunities
    c. Established special evaluation services for students with disabilities
    d. Provided special training to instructors to assist students with learning disabilities

SHORT ANSWER

21. How does a learning disability differ from mental retardation?

____

____

22. What are the three criteria most states use to identify students as having learning disabilities?
    a. ____
    b. ____
    c. ____

23. List some of the areas of difficulty a student with dyscalculia might have.

____

____

ESSAY

24. What are four types of reading difficulties mentioned in the chapter, and state appropriate interventions for each one?
25. Give suggestions for encouraging a discouraged student in mathematics.

CHAPTER 5: EMOTIONAL OR BEHAVIORAL DISORDERS

CHAPTER OVERVIEW

This chapter examines two of the many and varied definitions associated with emotional and behavioral disorders. It also examines both emotional and behavioral characteristics of students, with a discussion of how to distinguish between externalizing and internalizing behavior patterns. Both biological and environmental causes are examined and explored. Evaluation procedures focus on direct observations with applied behavior analysis and contingency contracts. Concentration in this chapter is on restoring hope, setting limits, and encouraging a productive self-concept and personal wellness. Productive ways to include and collaborate on behalf of students with emotional or behavioral disorders are discussed, with a particular focus on peer mediation. Program options that successfully help students with emotional or behavioral disorders to overcome difficulties and lead productive lives are presented.

The life of ten-year-old Tijuane demonstrates the challenges and joys of working with students with emotional or behavioral disorders. Tijuane, a bright, vibrant girl, experienced some challenges that characterize students with emotional or behavioral disorders. One day, like many youngsters with emotional or behavioral disorders, she was upset by a change in the routine at school. Now, after positive support from her teachers and strategy instruction, Tijuane is happier and more socially well-adjusted. She is now an honor student and won a sportsmanship trophy at school.

CHAPTER AT-A-GLANCE

Chapter Outline	Instructional Goals	Key Concepts
WH0 ARE STUDENTS WITH EMOTIONAL OR BEHAVIORAL DISORDERS?		
Defining Emotional or Behavioral Disorders	• Identify key components among models for defining emotional or behavioral disorders	• Students with emotional or behavior disorders are those whose behavior and adjustment problems are chronic, severe, and adversely affect their lives. • Numerous definitions of emotional or behavioral disorders have been proposed over the years, but no single definition is universally embraced.
Describing the Characteristics • Nature of Emotional and Behavioral Disorders and Associated Characteristics • Behavioral Characteristics • Social Characteristics • Cognitive and Academic Characteristics	• Describe key characteristics of emotional or behavioral disorders	• Students may exhibit emotional disorders, including, but not limited to, anxiety disorder, major depression, bipolar disorder, oppositional defiant disorder, conduct disorder, eating disorders, or schizophrenia. • There are two broad categories of behavioral disorders: externalizing (aggressive, acting-out, antisocial behaviors) and internalizing (withdrawn, fearful, anxious, depressed, or lacking in social competence). • Most students with emotional or behavioral disorders have academic problems.

Identifying the Causes of Emotional or Behavioral Disorders • Biological Causes • Genetics • Environmental Factors • Living Conditions • Lack of System Support • Child Abuse	• Explain differences between biological and environmental causes of emotional or behavioral disorders	• Biological causes include genetics and biological influences. • Environmental causes include living conditions and child abuse. • There is rarely one determining factor.
Identifying the Prevalence of Emotional or Behavioral Disorders	• Examine prevalence rates overall as well as within special education	• Prevalence estimates vary considerably from 3% to 5%. However, only about 1% are identified. • Emotional or behavioral disorders is the fourth largest category in special education.
HOW ARE STUDENTS WITH EMOTIONAL OR BEHAVIORAL DISRODERS EVALUATED?		
Determining the Presence of Emotional or Behavioral Disorders	• Identify specific tools useful for determining emotional and behavioral disorders	• A checklist of internalizing and externalizing behaviors can be useful for teachers.
Determining the Nature and Extent of Special Education and Related Services	• Understand how to use direct observations and applied behavior analysis to help educate students with emotional or behavioral disorders	• Direct observations of student behavior along with applied behavior analysis and contingency contracts allow professionals to monitor student performance toward achieving specific objectives.
HOW CAN YOU ESTABLISH EFFECTIVE TEACHING PRACTICES?		
Set Curricular Goals	• Ensure that goals relate directly to the characteristics of students with emotional or behavioral disorders	• Curriculum should address emotional and behavioral, social, and academic and career goals.
Implement Instruction	• Utilize techniques such as applied behavioral analysis to eliminate problem behaviors	• Follow the six principles of any applied behavioral analysis program as an effective behavioral intervention. • Use peer mediation to help students develop good social skill, solve problems, and address conflicts.
Early Childhood Years	• Describe characteristics of effective preschool programs	• Regional Intervention Program (RIP) uses applied behavioral analysis and provides parent training and support.
Elementary Years	• Describe characteristics of effective elementary school programs	• LaGrange Department of Special Education (LADSE) uses a wrap-around approach to providing services.
Middle and Secondary Years	• Describe characteristics of effective programs for middle and secondary students	• M. L. King, Jr., Law and Public Service Magnet High School WAVES Program uses peer mediation to develop students' skills.
Transitional and Postsecondary Years	• Describe characteristics of effective program options for adults	• Project STRIVE addresses work-inhibiting attitudes of adults in the inner city.

HOW CAN YOU ENCOURAGE PARTICIPATION?		
Practice Inclusion	• Summarize issues affecting the inclusion of students with emotional or behavioral disorders	• There are differing perspectives on the most appropriate place to educate these students. • Once identified as having emotional or behavioral disorders, most students are educated in self-contained classes.
Foster Collaboration • Professional-to-Professional Collaboration • Family and Professional Collaboration • School, Student, Family, and Community Collaboration	• Examine ways to collaborate on behalf of students with emotional or behavioral disorders	• Many students with emotional or behavioral disorders require multiple services that involve several disciplines, including education, mental health, public welfare, and the juvenile justice system. • Peer mediation involves the voluntary resolution of differences between peers in the presence of trained peer mediators.

PROJECT OPTIONS

1. Find a cooperating teacher who will allow you to observe that class and do direct observations on a student. Then develop a contingency contract for the student and teacher to use.
2. Interview a school counselor to ascertain (a) how many students with emotional or behavioral problems have a record of juvenile delinquency, (b) how delinquency has been handled in the school, and (c) what the philosophy of the school counselor is for these students. Based on observation, after permission is obtained from the school and parents, select two students and classify the type of behavior problems they have experienced. Then, based on what you have learned in this chapter, plan additional ways to help these students.
3. Research discipline methods that have been proven effective in all classrooms. Evaluate these methods and prioritize them for students with emotional and behavioral disorders.

KEY TERMS

Active listening

Anxiety disorder

Applied behavior analysis

Bipolar disorder

Conduct disorder

Contingency contract

Direct observation

Eating disorders

Emotional or behavioral disorder

Frequency

Generalized anxiety disorder

Heterogeneous

Externalizing behavior

Internalizing behavior

Latency

Magnitude

Major depression

Obsessive-compulsive disorder

Panic disorder

Phobia

Post-traumatic stress disorder

Schizophrenia

Social maladjustment

Topography

GUIDED REVIEW

The Emotional Roller Coaster

By the age of two, a child has a whole range of emotions. Because feelings come and go so quickly, their power can sometimes be underestimated. Dr. Susanne Denham, a psychologist at George Mason University in Fairfax, Virginia, has discovered through research that children whose parents talk with them about feelings learn how to control their emotions more readily. "When we talk about feelings, even with toddlers, we're giving our children a set of important tools they'll use for the rest of their lives," she says. The article discusses emotional education, talking about feelings, the frustration factor, the roots of empathy, and the emotional power of play. To learn more, see *Parents*, March, 2000, pp. 185–188.

Who Are Students with Emotional or Behavioral Disorders?

1. IDEA defines "emotionally disturbed" in two ways. Fill in the missing information that helps clarify the many facets of this disorder. (*See* Defining Emotional or Behavioral Disorders)
   a. The term means a condition exhibiting one or more of the following characteristics over a long time and to a marked degree that adversely affects a student's educational performance:

      ____

      ____

      ____

      ____

      ____

   b. The term includes schizophrenia. The term does not apply to students who are ______________ ______________________, unless it is determined that they have an emotional disturbance.

2. IDEA limits what schools may do by way of disciplining students with disabilities. Summarize the two major rules concerning discipline procedures. (*See* Defining Emotional or Behavioral Disorders)
   a. ______________________________

      ____

   b. ______________________________

      ____

Teaching Good Behavior in the Whole School

Disruptive behavior has become one of the most pressing issues facing educators today. The foundation for one schoolwide discipline plan is a lively, engaging curriculum and effective teaching practices. The plan has three interrelated components: (a) the ecological arrangements of the common areas of the school; (b) establishing clear and consistent behavioral guidelines or expectations for common area routines; and (c) the supervision of the common area routines to prevent disruptive behavior from occurring and to respond effectively when it does occur. To learn more, read the complete article written by Nelson, Crabtree, Marchand-Martella, and Martella in *Teaching Exceptional Children,* March/April 1998, *30*(4), pp. 4–9.

3. Identify the main points of the definition for emotional or behavioral disorders that is preferred by the Mental Health and Special Education Coalition (MHSEC). (*See* Defining Emotional or Behavioral Disorders)
   a. ____
      ____
   b. ____
      ____
   c. ____
      ____

4. The primary difference between IDEA's and MHSEC's definitions is that IDEA's definition does not include students with ________________ ____________________, while the MHSEC definition does include them. (*See* Defining Emotional or Behavioral Disorders)

5. Describe emotional characteristics that lead to students being identified as having emotional or behavioral disorders. (*See* Describing the Characteristics; Nature of Emotional and Behavioral Disorders and Associated Characteristics)

	Key Word Descriptors	***Indicators/ Symptoms***
Anxiety disorder		
Major depression		
Bipolar disorder		
Oppositional defiant disorder		
Conduct disorder		
Eating disorders		
Schizophrenia		

6. What percentage of young people are affected by anxiety disorders, the most common childhood disorder? (*See* Describing the Characteristics; Emotional and Behavioral Disorders and Associated Characteristics)
   ______________% to ________________%

The Discipline Expert's Toughest Cases
Although none of your student's may display behavioral challenges that are as extreme as the ones mentioned in this article, some of the same techniques can be utilized. Such issues as the aggressive child, the withdrawn child, and the stubborn child are covered. To learn how child therapists handle their most challenging patients and how to make the same techniques work for you, read the article by Sherry Suib Cohen in the February 2000 edition of *Parents* magazine (V. 75, No. 2).

7. Externalizing and internalizing behaviors are two broad categories of behavioral disorders.
   Externalizing behaviors are characterized by

   ____

   Internalizing behaviors are characterized by

   ____

   (*See* Describing the Characteristics; Behavioral Characteristics)

8. Would you describe each of these students as demonstrating internalizing or externalizing behaviors? If they are externalizing, are they overt or covert? (*See* Describing the Characteristics; Behavioral Characteristics)

Behavior	*Internalizing/Externalizing*	*Overt/Covert*
a. Sondra pouts when she is asked to do her work.		
b. Janika shoves students as she changes classes.		
c. Matilda daydreams a lot and seems to be lost in another world.		
d. Habib isolates himself in the back of the room during group activities.		
e. Eric tells you to "shove it" whenever you give him an assignment.		

9. Fire setting, sleep disturbances, self-abuse, and depression are examples of behavioral ______________________. (*See* Describing the Characteristics; Behavioral Characteristics)

10. What type of academic performance would you expect from a student identified as having emotional or behavioral disorders? Why?

    ____

    ____

    (*See* Describing the Characteristics; Cognitive and Academic Characteristics)

11. The graduation rate for students with emotional or behavioral disorders is __________%, while the rate for students without disabilities is ______________% and students with disabilities is ______________% (*See* Describing the Characteristics; Cognitive and Academic Characteristics)

12. Some examples of biological causes include

    ____.

    (*See* Identifying the Causes of Emotional or Behavioral Disorders; Biological Causes)

13. As an educator, you will want to be familiar with medications that students with emotional or behavioral disorders take. List five things you should find out from parents about students' medication. (*See* Identifying the Causes of Emotional or Behavioral Disorders; Biological Causes)
    a. ______________________________
    b. ______________________________
    c. ______________________________
    d. ______________________________
    e. ______________________________

> ***A Child Called "It"***
>
> David Peltzer has written powerful books about the horrible physical and emotional abuse he suffered as a child. A caring substitute teacher recognized his pain and initiated procedures to have Dave removed from his home. Although he developed emotional and behavioral disorders from the abuse, he eventually overcame them. Dave has received commendations from Presidents Reagan, Bush, and Clinton. He was also the only American who received the prestigious Outstanding Young Person of the World award in 1994. If you have not read his books, we recommend that you do so. The titles are *A Child Called "It": An Abused Child's Journey from Victim to Victor* (Health Communications, 1995) and *The Lost Boy: A Foster Child's Search for the Love of a Family* (Health Communications, 1997). The third book in the series is *A Man Called Dave*.

14. Name and describe three factors that can trigger emotional or behavioral disorders. (*See* Identifying the Causes of Emotional or Behavioral Disorders; Environmental Factors)
    a. ______________________________
    b. ______________________________
    c. ______________________________

15. Prevalence estimates vary considerably for this population, varying from __________% to __________% of all children. However, only ___________ % of all school-age students receive services, even though this is the ________________-largest category of students receiving special education services. (*See* Identifying the Prevalence of Emotional or Behavioral Disorders)

How Are Students with Emotional or Behavioral Disorders Evaluated?

16. What are some tools used to determine the presence of emotional or behavioral disorders? (*See* Determining the Presence of Emotional or Behavioral Disorders and Figure 5.5)
    a. During prereferral or referral:______________________________
    b. During the nondiscriminatory evaluation process:
    ____

17. Direct observation requires you to ____________________ and ____________________, the specific behaviors of a student for a specified time while students are engaged in a specific activity. Name and describe the five observable and measurable dimensions of behavior recorded during direct observations. (*See* How Are Students with Emotional or Behavioral Disorders Evaluated ; Determining the Presence of Emotional or Behavioral Disorders)
    a. ______________________________
    b. ______________________________
    c. ______________________________
    d. ______________________________
    e. ______________________________

How Can You Establish Effective Teaching Practices?

18. Explain how applied behavior analysis works, including the role of a contingency contract. (*See* Implement Instruction; Applied Behavior Analysis)

____

____

____

____

19. List the three main goals for students with emotional or behavioral disorders. (*See* How Can You Establish Effective Teaching Practices?; Set Curricular Goals)
    a. ____
    b. ____
    c. ____

20. Describe the main characteristics of the frequently used instructional techniques for students with emotional or behavioral disorders. (*See* How Can You Establish Effective Teaching Practices; Implement Instruction)

Techniques	***Main Characteristics***
ABA	
Peer Mediation	

21. Define the following: (*See* Implement Instruction; Applied Behavior Analysis)
    a. Applied Behavioral Analysis

    ____

    ____

    b. Baseline Data

    ____

    ____

    c. Contingency Contract

    ____

    ____

    d. Positive Behavioral Supports

    ____

    ____

22. List the steps that mediators and students must follow to solve problems by constructive, proactive means. (*See* How Can You Establish Effective Teaching Practices?; Peer Mediation)
    1. ____
    2. ____
    3. ____
    4. ____
    5. ____
    6. ____
    7. ____

23. Describe important characteristics of how the wraparound process works in schools. (*See* Observe Programs in Practice; Elementary Years)

____

____

24. One of the characteristics of some students with emotional or behavioral disorders is their ________________ ________________ behavior. (*See* Observe Programs in Practice; Transitional and Postsecondary Years)

25. Summarize key features for each of the following programs. (*See* Observe Programs In Practice)

Program	***Key Features***
Regional Intervention Program (RIP)	
LADSE's Emotional and Behavioral Dis-order Network	
WAVES Program	
Project STRIVE	

Therapeutic Teachers

What makes a therapeutic teacher? According to Brian Abrams and Amiel Segal (1998), such a teacher has several identifiable characteristics. The first is good mental health. Therapeutic teachers also communicate caring, respect, and confidence in themselves and others. They exhibit and model self-control and stress-coping skills, with an ability to de-escalate tension in a classroom. By establishing trust and rapport with students, therapeutic teachers can tell when students are frustrated or experiencing anxiety. They also identify and respect student's needs, values, interests, and talents. Therapeutic teachers protect their students' dignity and do not resort to threats or confrontations. Instead, they create a positive classroom climate and display enthusiasm and positive expectations. How do you measure up?

See "How to Prevent Aggressive Behavior" in *Teaching Exceptional Children, 30*(4), pp. 10–15.

How Can You Encourage Participation?

26. CCBD supports a full continuum of ________________ ________________ and special education services for children and youth with emotional or behavioral disorders. (*See* How Can You Encourage Participation?; Practice Inclusion)

27. Rank order the educational placements of students with serious emotional disturbances, from (a) largest to (e) smallest percentages: Resource room, separate school, residential facility, homebound/hospital, regular class. (*See* How Can You Encourage Participation?; Practice Inclusion)

a. ____________________ d. ____________________

b. ____________________ e. ____________________

c. ____________________

28. Using the chapter's text, figures, and boxes, identify ways different people are collaborating on behalf of students with emotional or behavioral disorders. (*See* How Can You Encourage Participation?; Foster Collaboration)

Collaborator	***Strategies, Guidelines, and Approaches***
Professional	
Family	
Community	
Peer	

The Compassionate School

How can schools work with students and families when abuse is involved? In her book *The Compassionate School: A Practical Guide to Educating Abused and Traumatized Children*, Gertrude Morrow offers some effective practices. She includes tested procedures for detecting and reporting child abuse, along with suggestions for helping students in the classroom. The book also discusses how to help depressed or suicidal students.

29. Professional _________________ is believed to have a serious impact on the success of inclusive schools. (*See* How Can You Encourage Participation?; Professional Collaboration)

30. Name the five steps of problem-solving. (*See* How Can You Encourage Participation?; School, Student, and Family Collaboration)
    a. ____
    b. ____
    c. ____
    d. ____
    e. ____

APPLICATION EXERCISES FOR CHAPTER 5

Application Exercise 5a. Identifying Emotional Characteristics

Match the name of the disorder with the student's symptoms.

1. Anxiety disorder	a. _______ Jonee seems like a content child on some days, always talking with anyone who will listen. On others she withdraws and appears unhappy and morose.
2. Major depression	b. _______ Sita can't go to sleep at night unless she says the alphabet forward and backward. She also holds her breath for ten seconds between each bite of food she eats.
3. Bipolar disorder	c. ________ Jaime can never admit someone else is right. His insistence on being right often leads to violent outbursts of swearing and angry accusations.
4. Oppositional defiant disorder	d. ________ Rochelle binges on large amounts of chocolate and sweets and then later vomits the food. She denies taking or eating the food and tries to cover for her cravings.
5. Conduct disorder	e. ________ Tomas experiences a rapid heartbeat and dizziness associated with unpleasant situations.
6. Eating disorders	f. ________ Jonathan sleeps whenever he has a chance. When he's awake, he's convinced he's ugly and worthless. He often cries for long periods.
7. Schizophrenia	g. ________ Anita feels as though she does not receive the attention she needs. Recently, when others weren't looking, she started small fires in trash cans. She also steals food from other lunches.
	h. ________ Lois feels hopeless no matter what she does. She has once attempted suicide, but was unsuccessful.
	i. _________ Ragy is unable to experience pleasure and spends large amounts of time daydreaming. During this time, hallucinations are common.

Application Exercise 5b. Identifying Types of Observations

Identify which of the five types of observations is being demonstrated in the following examples. Types include: frequency, magnitude, duration, latency, and topography.

1. Mr. Singh measures how long it takes Diane to begin her work after he asks her to do so.

   Type of Observation: ____

2. Ms. Mitias measures how many times Maria talks during a class period.

   Type of Observation: ____

3. Mrs. Norris uses a rating scale to determine the severity of Garland's acting out behaviors.

   Type of Observation: ____

4. Mr. Martin measures how long Jill is out of her seat.

   Type of Observation: ____

5. Miss Eaglesfly records specific responses that Amelia gives when students greet her and then decides whether they were appropriate or inappropriate.

   Type of Observation: ____

Application Exercise 5c. A Collaborator's View of Emotional or Behavioral Disorders

Explain how a specific collaborator might answer each of the major questions addressed in this chapter. Summarize each of the major concepts through the eyes of your selected collaborator.

Major Questions: Who Are Students with Emotional or Behavioral Disorders? How Are Students with Emotional or Behavioral Disorders Evaluated? How Can You Establish Effective Teaching Practices? How Can You Encourage Participation?

SAMPLE QUIZ FOR CHAPTER 5

MULTIPLE CHOICE

Circle the correct answer.

1. To what does DSM-IV refer?
   a. Diagnostic and Statistical Manual of Mental Disorders
   b. Direct Supervisory Measures for Mental Health, Major Behavior Disorders, and Maladjustment
   c. Disorders related to Schizophrenia and Mental Health (four major categories)
   d. Handbook on Defiance, Suicide and Major Depression

2. Which of the following is not considered an anxiety disorder?
   a. Phobia
   b. Obsessive-compulsive disorder
   c. Post-traumatic stress disorder
   d. Schizophrenia

3. Which of the following is not a curricular goal that applies to almost all students, including those with emotional and behavioral disorders?
   a. Learning socially valued ways to express emotions
   b. Learning how to aggressively demand attention from a group of peers
   c. Developing reciprocal friendships
   d. Learning how to increase school and career options

4. Professionals often use which of the following techniques to evaluate students with emotional or behavioral disorders?
   a. Indirect observation
   b. Self-observation
   c. Peer observation
   d. Direct observation

5. One-third of all students with emotional or behavioral disorders receives services in which type of classroom?
   a. General education classroom
   b. Self-contained classroom
   c. Resource room
   d. Special school

6. Which of the following children is most likely to be overlooked in prereferral for services?
   a. Paige, a girl who has a history of substance abuse
   b. Caitlin, who is anorectic
   c. Masud, an African American boy
   d. Ramiro, who causes no problems but is withdrawn

7. What does research indicate will improve the conduct and engagement of students with emotional or behavioral disorders?
   a. Incorporating personal interests into curriculum assignments
   b. Substituting communitywide activities on campus instead of school dances and other dating events
   c. Bringing sports heroes to school assemblies for motivational talks
   d. Mandating community work assignments for students who have been suspended

8. Danielle, one of your students who has an emotional disorder, is trying to hurt you by spreading a false rumor about you. What is the best way to handle the situation?
   a. Tell Danielle that you care about her no matter what she says or does, but you will enforce consequences for her actions.
   b. Ignore the rumor and concentrate on making your class such an enjoyable place that the students will defend you.
   c. Discuss the situation with Danielle's IEP team and request her reassignment to another class.
   d. Advise the principal that the rumor is false and avoid the subject with Danielle so she can see that you cannot be hurt by her.

9. Which of the following has been shown to reduce drop-out rates, suspensions, and student assaults?
   a. Intensive counseling
   b. Community support
   c. Peer mediation
   d. Hospitalization followed by controlled medication

10. STRIVE, a transition program in East Harlem, New York, addresses what special issue faced by some students with emotional or behavioral challenges?
   a. Panic attacks
   b. Oppositional defiant behavior
   c. Obsessive compulsive behavior
   d. Depression

11. How does the behavior of an emotionally disturbed child differ from behavior in normal conflicts that can occur with other students?
   a. The problems are chronic and interfere with learning.
   b. The problems result in physical violence.
   c. The problem is diagnosed by a psychiatrist as maladjustment or schizophrenia.
   d. The problem can be controlled by medication.

12. To what does manifestation determination refer?
   a. The student's ability in self-determination
   b. The relationship between the student's disability and the student's behavior
   c. The appropriateness of the student's IEP in determining what services are needed
   d. A decision by the student to control his or her own destiny and behave appropriately

13. Yasmine suffers frightening flashbacks of a bombing she witnessed. What kind of anxiety disorder does she have?
   a. Generalized anxiety disorder
   b. Phobia
   c. Post-traumatic stress disorder
   d. Panic disorder

14. What is one of the most frequently used instructional techniques for students with emotional or behavioral disorders?
   a. Direct instruction
   b. Peer mediation
   c. Self-evaluation
   d. Applied behavior analysis

15. What has recent research found to be an effective tool for increasing homework productivity of students with emotional or behavioral disorders?
   a. Have parents sign a homework journal.
   b. Ground the student until homework is done.
   c. Use peer buddies to study together at the home of the student experiencing trouble.
   d. Turn off the television until homework is completed.

16. J. B. is undergoing a nondiscriminatory evaluation for a possible emotional or behavioral disorder. Which of the following will most likely not be included?
    a. WISC-III
    b. Projective test
    c. Achievement test
    d. Torrance Test of Creativity

17. What is the document that helps students by specifying in writing the relationship between behavior and its consequences?
    a. Interaction skills management agreement
    b. Self-monitoring strategy plan
    c. Numerical baseline form
    d. Contingency contract

18. Which of the following is the most effective method for dealing with and preventing children's emotional and behavioral challenges?
    a. Intervention in elementary school years
    b. Early intervention
    c. Middle school intervention
    d. Intervention during transition years

19. Which of the following is an example of Dreikurs's mistaken goal of "inadequacy".
    a. John blurts out in class to get the other students to listen to him.
    b. Sue screams back at the teacher to get her attention.
    c. Because he is mad, Jim tells the other students that Joe stole the toy.
    d. Bill finds his homework too hard to do and gives up.

20. Due to his inappropriate social behavior, Donnell has been placed in a residential school. How can this placement affect him negatively?
    a. He can obtain drugs more easily from the other delinquent boys there.
    b. He will pick up jargon that may interfere with the development of effective communication.
    c. His opportunities to learn and practice appropriate interpersonal skills may be further restricted.
    d. He will be more at risk for abuse from his caregivers.

SHORT ANSWER

21. Name the two major eating disorders and their characteristics.

____

____

22. Define *child abuse* and state what you should do if you suspect one of your students is being abused.

____

____

23. Identify three academic characteristics you may frequently see in students with emotional or behavioral disorders
    a. ______________________________
    b. ______________________________
    c. ______________________________

ESSAY

24. Discuss the difficulties associated with externalizing and internalizing behavior patterns and identify ways to handle these patterns in a classroom.
25. Explain the relationship between causes and characteristics of emotional and behavioral disorders.

CHAPTER 6: ATTENTION-DEFICIT/HYPERACTIVITY DISORDER

CHAPTER OVERVIEW

Attention-deficit/Hyperactivity disorder (AD/HD) has become a prominent disability in American education. This chapter examines the controversy over AD/HD and clarifies the different types and characteristics. An in-depth look at the causes is reported, with recent research findings that shed light on ways to best serve students with AD/HD. Several relevant evaluation procedures are presented and discussed. The importance of effective curriculum and methods is highlighted with successful examples. The role of inclusion and collaboration are explained with more examples of ways to seek the success of students with AD/HD. Key components of successful programs at four levels are presented as a means to further understand and apply ways to build on students' inherent strengths and abilities.

The life of Taylor Wiggand, who has the combined type of AD/HD, which manifests characteristics of inattention and hyperactivity-impulsivity, helps demonstrate and clarify issues revolving around students who daily experience the challenges associated with AD/HD. Taylor comes from a large, supportive family, including foster children. As with many other students with AD/HD, he receives accommodations for his AD/HD in the general classroom and does not need special education or related services.

CHAPTER AT-A-GLANCE

Chapter Outline	Instructional Goals	Key Concepts
WHO ARE STUDENTS WITH ATTENTION-DEFICIT/ HYPERACTIVITY DISORDER?		
Defining Attention-Deficit/ Hyperactivity Disorder	• Examine different ways to define and identify students with AD/HD	• Students with AD/HD are served under the other health impairments category. • There are three types of AD/HD: inattentive type, hyperactive-impulsive type, and combined type
Describing the Characteristics of AD/HD • Predominantly Inattentive Type • Predominantly Hyperactive-Impulsive Type • Combined Type • A Conceptual Model of Self-Regulation Characteristics • Positive Traits Associated with AD/HD	• Describe key characteristics of students with AD/HD • Identify positive characteristics of students with AD/HD	• Students with AD/HD appear to experience a developmental delay of inhibition, which affects their ability to separate facts from feeling, use self-directed speech, and break apart and recombine information. • Students with AD/HD often demonstrate creativity and a sense of humor.
Identifying the Causes of AD/HD • Environmental Explanations • Biological Explanations	• Compare and contrast environmental and biological causes of AD/HD	• Probable causes are more likely biological than environmental, and it is likely that more than one cause is responsible.
Identifying the Prevalence of AD/HD	• Provide prevalence figures for AD/HD today	• Prevalence estimates of AD/HD are 3% to 5% of the general population.
HOW ARE STUDENTS WITH ATTENTION-DEFICIT/ HYPERACTIVITY DISORDER EVALUATED?		
Determining the Presence of AD/HD • Assessment Instruments for AD/HD • New Developments in Diagnosis • Cultural Issues in Diagnosis	• Compare different ways to determine the presence of AD/HD	• Diagnosis of AD/HD is often by a psychologist, psychiatrist, or physician. • Behavior rating scales designed for AD/HD and continuous performance tests are often used. • People may falsely appear to have AD/HD to evaluators outside their culture.

Determining the Nature and Extent of Special Education and Related Services	• Recognize the ways students with AD/HD may receive appropriate services	• Students may receive an IEP, if needed, or they may receive a 504/ADA plan. • Appropriate accommodations for skill deficits are included in each plan.
HOW CAN YOU ESTABLISH EFFECTIVE TEACHING PRACTICES?		
Set Curricular Goals	• Identify instructional goals that benefit students with AD/HD	• A multimodal approach to intervention, which may include medication, behavior management, coaching, education, counseling, and/or organization training, is essential for students with AD/HD.
Implement Instruction	• Ensure that instruction addresses attention to learning and student involvement • Address academic, behavioral, physical, and self-efficacy issues	• Students benefit from instruction that incorporates relevance, novelty, variety, choices, and activity. • Utilize a professional organizer or coach to provide organizational training.
Early Childhood Years	• Describe characteristics of effective preschool programs	• Multidisciplinary Diagnostic and Training Program increases academic progress and social success through the use of multimodal treatments.
Elementary Years	• Describe characteristics of effective elementary school programs	• Multisensory motivational program such as KanDoo utilizes a unique curriculum program to teach management skills.
Middle and Secondary Years	• Describe characteristics of effective programs for middle and secondary students	• LeHigh University-Consulting Center program includes in-service programs, on-site consultation, and follow-up.
Transitional and Postsecondary Years	• Describe characteristics of effective program options for adults with AD/HD	• Vassar College Campus Support Services Program provides accommodations and emphasizes self-efficacy skills.
HOW CAN YOU ENCOURAGE PARTICIPATION?		
Practice Inclusion	• Examine placement options where students with AD/HD are best served	• The general classroom is the appropriate placement for most students with AD/HD.
Foster Collaboration • Professional-to-Professional Collaboration • Family and Professional Collaboration • School, Student, Family and Professional Collaboration	• Explore ways to collaborate on behalf of students with AD/HD	• Professional collaboration provides students with consistency to monitor the effects of medication. • Families need to learn positive and negative strategies to use to survive the Big Struggle. • Sometimes simply having one close friend can make a positive difference for a student with AD/HD.

PROJECT OPTIONS

1. Volunteer at least three hours of your time to tutor a student with AD/HD. Write a report of what you learned from your experience. (You may need to have this approved through the Department of Special Education at least two weeks in advance.)
2. Read a book written for children or adolescents about an individual with AD/HD. Choose one of the following options:
   a. Write a report or do an art project that demonstrates how the six values were or were not met in the life of the individual with AD/HD.
   b. Write a skit for one of the critical scenes in the book that could be reenacted by students.
   c. Describe how you would use this book in a classroom to develop sensitivity and respect toward individuals with AD/HD.
3. Develop a friendship with an individual with AD/HD. Write a report near the end of the quarter telling what that friendship has meant to you.

KEY TERMS

Attention-deficit/hyperactivity disorder (AD/HD)

Behavioral inhibition

Combined type of AD/HD

Continuous performance tests

Executive functions

Hyperactive

Hypoactive

Multimodal treatment

Polygenetics

Predominantly hyperactive-impulsive type of AD/HD

Predominantly inattentive type of AD/HD

Pseudo-ADD

Psychotropic medication

Selective attention

Self-efficacy

Stress-induced agitation syndrome

Teratogens

GUIDED REVIEW

> "If a man does not keep pace with his companions, perhaps it is because he hears a different drummer. Let him step to the music which he hears, however measured or far away."—Henry David Thoreau

Who Are Students with Attention-Deficit/Hyperactivity Disorder?

1. In the controversy over AD/HD, what are two identified concerns? (*See* Who Are Students with Attention-Deficit/Hyperactivity Disorder?)
   a.____
   b.____
2. Who is often considered the father of AD/HD? (*See* Who Are Students with Attention-Deficit/Hyperactivity Disorder?)
   ____
3. Under what category does IDEA offer services for students with AD/HD? Why is it considered under this category? (*See* Defining Attention-Deficit/Hyperactivity Disorder)
   Category: ____
   Explanation: ____
4. Between _________% and ___________% of children with AD/HD also have a learning disability. (*See* Defining Attention-Deficit/Hyperactivity Disorder)
5. To be eligible to receive a diagnosis of AD/HD as an additional diagnosis, students must have symptoms that are excessive for his or her ____________________age rather than ______________________age. (*See* Defining Attention-Deficit/Hyperactivity Disorder)
6. List the four criteria that the American Psychiatric Association uses to define AD/HD. (*See* Defining Attention-Deficit/Hyperactivity Disorder)

	Criterion Characteristics
Criterion A	
Criterion B	
Criterion C	
Criterion D	

Calvin and Hobbes

Calvin, from the "Calvin and Hobbes" comic strip by Bill Watterson, exemplifies the combined type of AD/HD. One minute Calvin is staring into space, oblivious to everything around him and daydreaming that he is fleeing awful bug beings from Zartron-9. The next, he has to face the principal for a comment he impulsively blurted out in class. He explains to the principal that the comment was "not an attitude, it's a fact!" You can learn a great deal about AD/HD from reading "Calvin and Hobbes."

7. What is "pseudo-ADD" and how do you distinguish it from AD/HD? (*See* Defining Attention-Deficit/Hyperactivity Disorder)
   ____
   ____

8. Match the type of AD/HD with the identifying descriptions. (*See* Defining Attention-Deficit/Hyperactivity Disorder)

1. Inattentive Type	a. _____ Usually an underachiever
2. Hyperactive-Impulsive Type	b. _____ Students who are inattentive and hyperactive
3. Combined Type	c. _____ Students who can't sit still and talk excessively
	d. _____ Students who are forgetful and easily distracted
	e. _____ Students who may be accident-prone
	f. _____ Students who daydream, lose things, and do not follow through
	g. _____ Students with hyperactive thinking but bodies in slow motion
	h. _____ Students who may become workaholics

How to Manage Your Students with ADD/ADHD

Odds are that you will be teaching at least one student with ADD/ADHD. Teachers have to make accommodations in the physical setup of the classroom, try some new instructional approaches, and implement a variety of classroom management techniques. This article provides an extensive checklist to help teachers get started or to improve upon strategies already in place. References are included.

See " How to Manage Your Students with ADD/ADHD," in *Primary Educator,* 1997, *3*(3), p. 63.

9. Name and briefly describe the four characteristics of a developmental delay of inhibition. (*See* Describing the Characteristics of AD/HD)

a. ______________________________

____

b. ______________________________

____

c. ______________________________

____

d. ______________________________

____

10. Explain the process of reconstitution that students with AD/HD find so difficult. (*See* Describing the Characteristics; Breaking Apart and Recombining Information)

____

____

11. List some positive traits associated with AD/HD. (*See* Describing the Characteristics of AD/HD; Positive Traits Associated with AD/HD)

a. ____________________ c. ____________________

b. ____________________ d. ____________________

A Triumph Over Human Suffering

Ned Hallowell, a psychiatrist who also has AD/HD, says that the diagnosis and treatment of AD/HD represent a triumph of "science over human suffering." AD/HD is only one of the many brain syndromes society is learning to address, he says, "without scorn or hidden moral judgment. As we begin to bring mental suffering out of the stigmatized darkness it has inhabited . . . we all have reason to rejoice."

See "What I Learned from ADD." (1997, June/July) *Psychology Today, 30*(3), pp. 40–45.

12. Describe the three biological explanations for AD/HD that have moved to the forefront. (*See* Identifying the Causes of AD/HD; Biological Explanations)

Biological Explanation	***What It Means***	***What It Suggests***
Genetics		
Pre-, peri-, and postnatal trauma		
Brain differences		

13. Name some teratogens that may increase the likelihood that a child will develop AD/HD. (*See* Identifying the Causes of AD/HD; Biological Explanations; Pre-, Peri-, and Postnatal Trauma)

_______________ _______________

_______________ _______________

_______________ _______________

14. What have position emission therapy scans on adults and children with and without AD/HD shown about causes of AD/HD? (*See* Identifying the Causes of AD/HD; Biological Explanations; Brain Differences)

____

____

15. What is the effect of neurochemical imbalances in AD/HD? (*See* Identifying the Causes of AD/HD; Biological Explanations; Brain Differences) _______________

____

____

16. How many students in a typical general education classroom would you expect to find with AD/HD?____________ to ______________ children. What is the current reported ratio of boys to girls? _____________ boys to _____________ girls. (*See* Identifying the Prevalence of AD/HD)

17. What are some possible reasons why AD/HD seems to occur more often in the United States than other countries? _______________

_______________ (*See* Identifying the Prevalence of AD/HD)

How Are Students with Attention-Deficit/Hyperactivity Disorder Evaluated?

I Write from Experience

After I helped write the first edition of this textbook, I was diagnosed with the inattentive type of AD/HD by a psychologist. The diagnosis was later confirmed by a neuropsychologist. Why did I ask to be tested? *DSM IV* had just been published, and as I researched the inattentive type for the first edition, I started thinking about my own history. Years of disorganization, daydreaming, missed deadlines, and forgotten important events and tasks rushed into my awareness. I thought about the time I was called down to the nurse in high school for a hearing test, probably because a teacher was concerned about my inattentiveness. I received the nickname "Lightning" from one person, a sarcastic response to my tendency to move in slow motion.

Despite having the typical AD/HD abilities to hyperfocus and be creative, which allowed me to complete a doctorate and write chapters for *Exceptional Lives*, the condition had severely impacted my adulthood. No matter how much I accomplished, I always had a sense that I would be able to do so much more if I could just get myself together.

Receiving the diagnosis gave me permission to stop beating myself up for my symptoms and ask for support. I take medication for the condition; the result has been that I feel like part of a cloud has lifted from my brain. I still face challenges in managing my everyday life. I am a client of Lee Donald, the professional organizer who shared suggestions for you in the textbook. Her assistance has been invaluable.

I share this with you to help you realize that people who seem successful can struggle with AD/HD. Many adults have never been diagnosed, and the result can be a life of frustration and low self-esteem.

—Marilyn Shank

18. What should you do if you suspect a child may have AD/HD? (*See* Determining the Presence of Attention-Deficit/Hyperactivity Disorder)

____

____

19. Name, give the purpose for, and describe three assessment instruments for determining the presence of attention-deficit/hyperactivity disorder. (*See* Determining the Presence of Attention-Deficit/ Hyperactivity Disorder)

Name	*Purpose*	*Description*

20. Explain how stress-induced agitation syndrome is both similar to and different from AD/HD. (*See* Determining the Presence of Attention-Deficit/Hyperactivity Disorder; Cultural Issues in Diagnosis)

Similarities:

____

____

Differences:

____

____

21. In addition to IDEA, two other laws provide protection against discrimination for students with disabilities such as AD/HD. Explain how each of these laws function in determining the nature and extent of special education and related services. (*See* Determining the Nature and Extent of Special Education and Related Services)

Law	*Function*
Section 504 of the Rehabilitation Act	
Americans with Disabilities Act (ADA)	

22. Typical factors that contribute to the inappropriate behavior of students with AD/HD stem from what four deficits? (*See* Determining the Nature and Extent of Special Education and Related Services)
    a. ______________________________
    b. ______________________________
    c. ______________________________
    d. ______________________________

How Can You Establish Effective Teaching Practices?

23. A common academic challenge for students with AD/HD is ____________________ ____________________. (*See* How Can You Establish Effective Teaching Practices?; Set Curricular Goals)

24. Seven key words that are important to successful curriculum presentation for students with AD/HD are ____________________, ____________________, ____________________, ____________________, ____________________, ____________________, and ____________________. (*See* How Can You Establish Effective Teaching Practices?; Implement Instruction)

Now or Not Now?

When you are given an assignment at the beginning of the semester, how do you plan for completing it? According to Dave deBronkart, the tendency for people with AD/HD is to think of tasks in only two ways: now or not now. With an extraordinary ability to finish things "all at once," they can unexpectedly and creatively complete tasks in "a mad flurry of activity." Others, seeing these remarkable results, chide the person with comments such as, "See what you can do when you apply yourself?" It's not a matter of willpower or laziness, deBronkart contends. Instead, the problem is a lack of depth perception for the passage of time, resulting in an inability to perceive that task deadlines are getting closer. Your students with AD/HD will need to understand their misperception of time and how to work around it.

See "The ADD Sense of Time" at http://www.ruralnet.net/~bobseay/debr.htm

25. The use of concurrent treatment approaches is called ____________________ treatment. (*See* How Can You Establish Effective Teaching Practices; Set Curricular Goals)

26. Match the type of intervention method with its characteristics. (*See* Implement Instruction; Physical Issues)

1. Medical Management	a. _____ Lack of relevance becomes an issue
2. Education	b. _____ Helps students to structure developmental tasks
3. Coaching	c. _____ As many as 60% to 80% of students with hyperactivity/impulsivity respond favorably to use of stimulants.
4. Self-Efficacy	d. _____ Rewards a student for completion of each task and subtask
5. Organizational Training	e. _____ Includes instruction on regulating motivation and enlisting help
6. Behavior Management	f. _____ Encourages and provides help to students

27. Use of medication may increase ______________________________, _________________________, and ______________________________. It also may decrease ___________________________, ______________________________, and ______________________________.(*See* Implement Instruction; Physical Issues)

28. Identify the needs of students with AD/HD and name some proven ways to meet those needs at each of the following age levels. Use ideas discussed in each of the program options discussed in this chapter. (*See* How Can You Establish Effective Teaching Practices; Observe Programs in Practice)

Age Level	***Student Needs***	***Effective Ways to Meet Student Needs***
Early Childhood Years		
Elementary Years		
Middle and Secondary Years		
Transitional and Postsecondary Years		

AD/HD-Friendly Jobs

Making the transition from school to work is often challenging for people with AD/HD. In school, they had clear assignments and deadlines. Many times in the workplace workers must set their own deadlines and perform with minimal direction. According to Kathleen Nadeau, an editor of *ADDvance*, AD/HD-friendly jobs minimize paperwork, allow immediate response to short-term tasks, provide support and structure, emphasize the worker's interest, allow variety and stimulation, have a comfortable stress level, and are supervised by an organized, supportive individual.

See www.addvance.com/article2.html

How Can You Encourage Participation?

29. Willingness to incorporate different ________________________ ________________________ in teaching is essential for students with ADHD. (*See* How Can You Encourage Participation?; Practice Inclusion)

30. Identify the benefits for all involved in a student's success when different collaborators participate. (*See* How Can You Encourage Participation?; Foster Collaboration)

Collaborator	*Benefits*
Professional-to-Professional Collaboration	
Family and Professional Collaboration	
School, Student, Family, and Professional Collaboration	

31. What is the "Big Struggle" and how can it be lessened? (*See* How Can You Encourage Participation?; Family and Professional Collaboration)

____

____

APPLICATION EXERCISES FOR CHAPTER 6

Application Exercise 6a. Identifying Types of AD/HD

Match the type of AD/HD experienced with the characteristics. Choose from inattentive, hyperactive-impulsive, and the combined types.

1. Jaime can't seem to sit still. He has trouble controlling his body as well as what he says.

   Type: ______________________________

2. Gopal always forgets his homework, even when his teacher calls the night before. He often appears to be daydreaming when the teacher is giving whole group instruction.

   Type: ______________________________

3. Hannah talks all the time. She loves to explain everything to everyone. Her peers call her "motor-mouth," while others make fun of her. She often blurts out answers before the teacher has finished the question. Her talking tends to annoy her neighbors.

   Type: ______________________________

4. When the teacher needs help organizing things in the classroom, he knows not to enlist the aid of Matilda. Matilda can't keep track of papers and loses things every day. On field trips she has been known to get lost.

   Type: ______________________________

5. Nadia spends a lot of time doodling. Even when she's supposed to be taking notes, her pages are cluttered with pictures. She never seems to be paying attention and can't seem to sit still in class. She leaves her seat to show her pictures to peers and has a hard time connecting to the teacher's lessons.

   Type: ______________________________

6. Otis tries hard to do well on tests, but he makes careless mistakes. He doesn't seem to listen to directions and then invents his own.

   Type: ______________________________

Application Exercise 6b. Accommodations for Students with AD/HD

Match the teaching accommodation for the specific AD/HD need.

1. Inattention	a. ____ Set up and practice appropriate ways for Linda to relate to her peers.
2. Impulsiveness	b. ____ Develop a self-monitoring system for Jose for his talking during class.
3. Motor Activity	c. ____ Make sure Kissan writes down his homework assignments and then ask him to tape-record his homework.
4. Academic Skills	d. ____ Help Marcy set short-term goals for the term project due in one month.
5. Organization and Planning	e. ____ Give Samena specific times when she can get up and take notes to peers during class.
6. Compliance	f. ____ Set up a contract with Benjamin to reward him for each five times he raises his hand before speaking out.
7. Socialization	g.____ Encourage Maeghan to use a word processor and/or tape recorder for written assignments in order to compensate for her difficulty in writing ability.

Application Exercise 6c. Coaching the Concepts

Based upon the major questions addressed in this chapter, write or tape-record a short play detailing the interactions between a student with AD/HD and his/her coach summarizing the major concepts dealing with AD/HD. Include cueing behavior by the coach.

Major Questions: Who Are Students with Attention-Deficit/Hyperactivity Disorder? How Are Students with AD/HD Evaluated? How Can You Establish Effective Teaching Practices? How Can You Encourage Participation?

SAMPLE QUIZ FOR CHAPTER 6

MULTIPLE CHOICE

Circle the correct answer.

1. Which of the following is not a positive trait of the inattentive type of AD/HD?
   a. Imaginative
   b. Intuitive
   c. Excellent attending skills
   d. Ability to hyperfocus

2. Which of the following commonly used acronyms refers to the inattentive type of AD/HD?
   a. ADD
   b. AD/HD-HI
   c. AD/HD-C
   d. ADD-H

3. Blaine has been diagnosed with AD/HD. He has trouble paying attention in class, is easily distracted, and cannot seem to sit still. What type of AD/HD does he most likely have?
   a. Predominantly inattentive
   b. Predominantly hyperactive-impulsive
   c. Predominantly neurologically kinesthetic
   d. Combined type

4. Kara is 13 and has lost interest in all classes except art since entering junior high school. She cannot seem to concentrate, her grades have plummeted, and she appears bored. She stares out the window much of the time and seems to have no friends. Can she be diagnosed with AD/HD?
   a. No, because she did not exhibit these symptoms early enough.
   b. No, because most adolescents go through this stage.
   c. Yes, because she is obviously inattentive, at risk, and needs special help.
   d. Yes, because otherwise she is not eligible for the help she needs to get the most appropriate education.

5. What are current estimates of the ratio of boys to girls who have AD/HD?
   a. 9:1
   b. 6:1
   c. 4:1
   d. 3:1

6. For most students with AD/HD, which of the classroom settings below is the most appropriate?
   a. General education classroom
   b. Resource room
   c. Self-contained classroom
   d. Special instruction

7. Diagnosis of AD/HD by a psychologist, psychiatrist, or physician often occurs in which of the following settings?
   a. In the student's home
   b. Outside the school system
   c. In the doctor's office
   d. In the special education classroom

8. Victoria suspects that a child in her first grade class has AD/HD. What should be her first step?
   a. Talk to the child's physician.
   b. Keep a record of characteristics that she notices in the classroom.
   c. Ask the child's parents to request a screening.
   d. Request a referral.

9. To improve peer relationships, CHADD recommends all of the following steps except?
   a. Praise and reward appropriate behaviors
   b. Directly coach and model behaviors
   c. Role play desired behaviors
   d. Focus on multiple behaviors

10. Which of the following is <u>not</u> a common side effect of stimulants?
    a. Insomnia
    b. Increased heart rate
    c. Dizziness
    d. Decreased appetite

11. Which of the following is <u>not</u> true about the identification of AD/HD, according to the APA?
    a. The symptoms occur exclusively during the course of a Pervasive Developmental Disorder.
    b. Some of the symptoms that caused impairment were present before the age of seven.
    c. Some impairment from the symptoms is present in two or more settings.
    d. There is clear evidence of significant impairment in social, academic, or occupational functioning.

12. Natalie, who has AD/HD, fidgets, talks excessively, and has difficulty engaging in quiet activities. What type of AD/HD does she have?
    a. Predominantly inattentive
    b. Predominantly disruptive
    c. Predominantly hyperactive-impulsive
    d. Combined type

13. Which of the following is <u>not</u> included in a multimodal approach to remediation for students with AD/HD?
    a. Medication
    b. Behavior management
    c. Counseling
    d. Visual imaging

14. Which of the following is true about middle and secondary school years for students with AD/HD?
    a. Very few students with AD/HD drop out or are expelled from high school.
    b. Larger schools at the secondary level are more personal.
    c. Social skills improve significantly in middle school.
    d. Eighty percent of these students continue to experience AD/HD into adolescence.

15. Blood flow and activity in what part of the brain differ in those with AD/HD?
    a. Posterior areas
    b. Limbic system
    c. Frontal areas
    d. Hippocampus

16. Jackson, age 5, has just received an initial diagnosis of AD/HD from the evaluation team at his school. What should happen next?
    a. He should be seen by a pediatrician or a psychiatrist.
    b. His parents should hire a professional to counsel him weekly.
    c. He should be given Ritalin on a daily basis.
    d. He should be given an individualized intelligence test.

17. The Freedom from Distractibility Scale is part of what larger assessment?
    a. Wechsler Intelligence Scale for Children
    b. Intermediate Visual and Auditory Continuous Performance Test
    c. Child Behavior Checklist
    d. Attention Deficit Disorder Assessment Scale

18. Harlan suffers from stress-induced agitation syndrome. What is likely true about him?
    a. He comes from a home where his parents put great pressure on him to excel.
    b. He lives in poverty amid violence.
    c. He is an overachiever.
    d. He is lethargic but can concentrate.

19. Students with AD/HD benefit from a curriculum that incorporates all of the following except?
    a. Novelty
    b. Choice
    c. Variety
    d. Continuous repetition

20. What percentage of children with AD/HD continue to experience the disorder into adolescence?
    a. 25%
    b. 40%
    c. 65%
    d. 80%

SHORT ANSWER

21. What four specific skill deficits are mentioned which relate to behavioral issues for students with AD/HD?
    a. ______________________________
    b. ______________________________
    c. ______________________________
    d. ______________________________

22. What can you as a teacher do to help a student with AD/HD who needs help in improving peer relationships?

    ____

    ____

    ____

23. List at least five suggestions for an effective preschool program for children with AD/HD.
    a. ______________________________
    b. ______________________________
    c. ______________________________
    d. ______________________________
    e. ______________________________

ESSAY

24. Compare and contrast the three types of AD/HD in relation to characteristics and accommodations for the classroom.
25. Discuss the causes of AD/HD as are presently understood. Describe the influence of both environmental and biological explanations. Include a discussion of the relationship of medical management to the causes of AD/HD.

CHAPTER 7: GIFTEDNESS

CHAPTER 7 OVERVIEW

The nature of giftedness is a subject that has intrigued educators and philosophers in every generation. Although IDEA does not cover students who are gifted and talented, they too need special services not ordinarily provided by the school. This chapter explores the nature of giftedness by examining changes in definition, the controversy over characteristics, and a discussion of the causes and prevalence rates. It also examines assessment tools unique to giftedness, such as Torrances' tests for creativity and Maker's DISCOVER assessment for determining multiple areas of giftedness. Product and process measures, including instructional rubrics, are examined as a means to involve students who are gifted in the evaluation of the nature and extent of special education services needed. The many facets of setting curricular goals and implementing instruction are examined along with a description of some excellent program options being utilized in today's schools and communities. The chapter concludes by probing benefits and concerns with inclusion and collaboration.

The life of twelve-year-old Breá Thornton helps demonstrate and clarify issues revolving around students who daily experience both the benefits and the challenges of being gifted. Breá was selected because she exemplifies the typical student who is gifted as well as the need to find ways to help her reach her full potential. She is typical because of her high test scores, love of reading, and her deep academic interest in learning. While she has a photographic memory and learns things easily, she also is socially mature. Her life and daily circumstances form a platform for evaluating the many and varied dimensions of what it means to be gifted today.

CHAPTER-AT-A-GLANCE

Chapter Outline	Instructional Goals	Key Concepts
WHO ARE STUDENTS WITH GIFTEDNESS?		
Defining Giftedness • Historical Definitions • Recent Perspectives • Sociocultural Perspectives	• Differentiate among models for defining giftedness in today's classrooms	• Definitions of giftedness vary according to whether they are based on a conceptual model or a domain specific model. Definitions also vary by culture.
Describing the Characteristics Commonly Recognized Characteristics • General Intellect • Specific Academic Aptitude • Creative Productive Thinking • Leadership Ability • Visual and Performing Arts Behavioral, Social and Emotional Characteristics of Giftedness	• Describe key characteristics of both expected aspects of giftedness • Identify behavioral, social, and emotional characteristics of giftedness	• The Federal definition lists five expected characteristics associated with giftedness. • Giftedness is not always easily recognized. Some behavior associated with AD/HD is also typical of giftedness. In addition, gender bias also hides girls' giftedness.
Identifying the Causes of Giftedness	• Discuss differences between the nature vs. nurture explanation of causes of giftedness	• Most researchers attribute giftedness to a combination of genetic and psychosocial factors.
Identifying the Prevalence of Giftedness	• Apply prevalence figures to an average classroom	• If an IQ of 125–130 is the standard, then 2 to 3% of the population are gifted. If a "talent pool" is the standard, then 15 to 20% of students may be considered gifted.

HOW ARE STUDENTS WHO ARE GIFTED EVALUATED?		
Determining the Presence of Giftedness • Multiple Intelligences DISCOVER Assessment • Creativity Assessment	• Compare the characteristics of different assessment tools used to determine the presence of giftedness	• A balance of IQ and creativity tests along with rating scales and documentation helps determine the presence of giftedness.
Determining the Nature and Extent of Special Education and Related Services • Product Evaluation • Process Evaluation	• Recognize the need for culture fair tests for students from different backgrounds • Analyze the nature and extent of special education needed	• Standardized tests are biased against students from culturally and linguistically diverse populations. New assessment tools such as DISCOVER help to alleviate this bias. • Student responsibility for the nature and extent of special education can be built into IEP goals using instructional rubrics.
HOW CAN YOU ESTABLISH EFFECTIVE TEACHING PRACTICES?		
Set Curricular Goals	• Explain ways to differentiate instruction for students who are gifted.	• Curriculum modifications may include tailoring the pace of instruction, ensuring a depth of content coverage, and relating instruction to students' interests.
Implement Instruction • Accelerated Instruction • Content Enriched Instruction • Magnet School Instruction	• Evaluate how different methods are most effective for varied student needs.	• Proven instructional methods focus on acceleration, content enrichment, and magnet school programs.
Early Childhood Years	• Decide on key features of effective programs.	• Montgomery Knolls Elementary School serves underserved gifted pre-schoolers.
Elementary and Middle Years	• Decide on key features of effective programs.	• The WINGS program tailors the pace of instruction for up to 1,000 students.
Secondary Years	• Decide on key features of effective programs.	• Secondary options include early college programs, such as at Mary Baldwin College, for girls who are gifted.
Transitional and Postsecondary Years	• Decide on key features of effective programs.	• Mensa is a social organization for people of all ages who are gifted.
HOW CAN YOU ENCOURAGE PARTICIPATION?		
Practice Inclusion	• Summarize benefits and problems associated with inclusion for students who are gifted.	• Inclusion means more work for the general educator, but collaboration with mentorship and in-services can strengthen the programs offered for all children.
Foster Collaboration • Professional-to-Professional Collaboration • Family and Professional Collaboration • School, Student, Family and Community Collaboration	• Explore ways to collaborate on behalf of students who are gifted	• All types of collaboration contribute toward successful student learning

KEY TERMS

Acceleration

Collaboration

Creativity

Documentation

Domain-specific giftedness

Emotional intelligence

Evaluation

Expertise

Genius

Gifted

Inclusion

Instructional rubric

Magnet schools

Multiple intelligences

Prodigy

Talent pool

PROJECT OPTIONS

1. Obtain a checklist of characteristics to assess giftedness from a local school. Complete this checklist on three students. Ask the cooperating teacher to fill them out on the same students. Then, based on your evaluations, discuss the areas of giftedness in terms of one of the models discussed in this chapter along with students' potential for positive contributions to society.
2. Along with several other students in the class, read works by Bruer, Doman, Elkind, and others on causes of giftedness, and structure a debate based on the best arguments of each side. Present your debate to the class and ask the class to assess your arguments.
3. Find and learn about as many types of creativity tests as you can, including Torrance's two main tests. Take each test yourself, and then create a chart to compare the strengths and weaknesses of each one. You may also choose to do this with different IQ tests.
4. From the existing programs discussed, create a new program model for gifted students that would amplify on the best of each program model as well as build on involvement and collaboration across age levels and the community.

GUIDED REVIEW

Teaching Prodigies

"Prestige had nothing to do with anything," Itzhak Perlman's violin teacher Dorothy DeLay comments. Children realize that their parents are happiest when they are the best. Therefore, they fear losing love if they do not perform well. Outstanding performance may bring admiration, power, or influence, but not love. "I'm always hunting around for whatever is tying children up so that they are not free," she says.

DeLay emphasizes that highly gifted children need to learn three things: no matter what happens, you can always build; curiosity should always be the motivating force to learn and grow; and give something to people that they can value, rather than focusing on pleasing them.

See *U.S. News and World Report,* 103, p. 59.

Who Are Students with Giftedness?

1. Although IDEA (does, does not) cover gifted and talented, many states have shown their priority for students who are gifted by providing quality programs. (*See* Defining Giftedness; Historical Definitions)
2. Write out the federal definition that provides the foundation for guiding programs for students who are gifted. (*See* Defining Giftedness; Historical Definitions)

   ____
   ____
   ____

3. What two misconceptions arose from Terman's important studies of individuals who are gifted? (*See* Defining Giftedness; Historical Definitions)
   a. ____
   b. ____
4. Compare the traditional understanding of giftedness with today's emerging paradigm by filling in the characteristic differences. (*See* Companion Website 7-01)

	Traditional Paradigm	Emerging Paradigm
Basis for giftedness		
Potential for trait changes		
Identification basis		
Social orientation		
Influences on expression		
Model for instruction		
Location orientation		
Cultural diversity		

5. What are the five categories of giftedness specified in the federal definition? (*See* Defining Giftedness; Recent Perspectives)
   a. ______________________________ d. ______________________________
   b. ______________________________ e. ______________________________
   c. ______________________________

6. Match the classification system for identifying students who are gifted with the researcher: (*See* Defining Giftedness; Recent Perspectives)

a. _____ Gardner	1. Above-average ability + creativity + task commitment
b. _____ Renzulli	2. Five areas of giftedness: general intellect, specific academic, performing/visual arts, leadership, creative
c. _____ Sternberg and Zhang	3. Giftedness expressed in 8 different domains: Linguistic, musical, bodily-kinesthetic, spatial, logical-mathematical, intrapersonal, interpersonal, and naturalist.
d. _____ Federal definition	4. Pentagonal theory: excellence + rarity + productivity + demonstrability + value

7. According to Howard Gardner (*See* Defining Giftedness; Recent Perspectives)
   a. The difference between giftedness and prodigiousness is _______________.
   b. _______________ is the technical mastery of skills and lore.
   c. _______________ is a unique expression within a domain of giftedness.
   d. _______________ is when a person's works assume a universal significance.

8. List and describe five commonly recognized characteristics of giftedness. (*See* Describing the Characteristics)

Characteristics	Description
General intellect	
Specific academic aptitude	
Creative productive thinking	
Leadership ability	
Visual and performing arts	

Whiz Kid with Dyslexia

Identifying students who are gifted can be a complex process. Many unexpected characteristics can hide giftedness. The giftedness of Benjamin Bolger could easily have been over looked and undeveloped, if not for a mother who recognized his unique abilities.

Benjamin graduated from the University of Michigan at age 17 and at 19 was the youngest student at Yale Law School. However, Benjamin has dyslexia and cannot read. Although he is a member of Mensa, he can't read a menu at a restaurant. Benjamin has a hard time reading a number from a phone book or keeping track of time. Sometimes he must ask strangers for help.

As a child, his teachers did not understand his problem and labeled him as lazy or stupid. In fourth grade, his mother, a former teacher, began teaching Benjamin herself because she couldn't find a school that could help her son. He flourished under her tutelage, and at age 13 Benjamin entered the University of Michigan.

How does Benjamin keep up with the reading required in his demanding program? His mother reads his assignments to him. Frequently they are in the library until 3 a.m. due to this laborious task. His friends know about his problem and also help—with encouragement as well as academic support.

Despite the challenges he experiences, Benjamin says, "I've learned not to look at dyslexia as a liability."

See Jill Johnson, "Not Your Typical Whiz Kid," *React*, January 15–21, 1996, p. 10.
See also www.react.com for information about Benjamin.

9. Identify three differences between giftedness and AD/HD. (*See* Describing the Characteristics; Behavioral, Social, and Emotional Characteristics of Giftedness)

10. Most researchers agree that giftedness is the result of a combination of _____________ (or _____________) and _______________ (or __________________). (*See* Identifying the Causes of Giftedness)

11. The prevalence of giftedness is identified by using either IQ cut-off scores of ___________ to _________ or by using a talent pool that includes the top _____________% to _______________% of all students. (*See* Identifying the Prevalence of Giftedness)

How Are Students Who Are Gifted Evaluated?

12. Serving gifted students from ethnically diverse backgrounds is essential. They will soon represent more than _______________ of public school children. (*See* Determining the Presence of Giftedness)

13. What forms of documentation can be used to ensure that assessments do not discriminate against students from culturally diverse backgrounds? (*See* Determining the Presence of Giftedness)
    a. ____________________________ c. ____________________________
    b. ____________________________ d. ____________________________

14. The DISCOVER performance-based assessment evaluates students in which six of Gardner's eight domains of intelligence? (*See* Determining the Presence of Giftedness; Multiple Intelligences DISCOVER Assessment)
    a. ____________________________ d. ____________________________
    b. ____________________________ e. ____________________________
    c. ____________________________ f. ____________________________

<u>Ayinde Jean-Baptiste</u>

When he was four years old, Ayinde Jean-Baptiste memorized Martin Luther King's "I Have A Dream" speech and was delivering original speeches to school assemblies at Marva Collin's West Side Preparatory School. At age six, Ayinde appeared on the Oprah Winfrey show. At age twelve, he spoke to more than a million Black men. This highly sought-after high school sophomore, who at the age of six was testing at eleventh and twelfth grade levels in some subjects, enjoys friends, sports, and collecting comic books. He hopes to be a lawyer or a scientist, but whatever career he chooses, he will continue to use his oratorical abilities to better the lives of others. "It's not a performance," he comments. "It comes from the heart. . . . I have an ability to get a message out and have people act on it. That's what's important."

See J.B. Kinnon. (1997). "Ayinde Jean-Baptiste: Superstudent." *Ebony 52*(4), pp. 148–152.

15. What criteria does Maker use for evaluating giftedness? ___________________ (*See* Determining the Presence of Giftedness; Multiple Intelligences DISCOVER Assessment)
    ____
    ____

16. Identify the two Torrance's creativity tests. Tell what domain of giftedness is assessed for each of these tests. (*See* Determining the Presence of Giftedness; Creativity Assessment)
    a. ____________________________________; ____________________________
    b. ____________________________________; ____________________________

17. Instructional rubrics have two basic components: ______________ and _________________. (*See* Determining the Nature and Extent of Special Education and Related Services: Process Evaluation)

How Can You Establish Effective Teaching Practices?

18. Identify three ways to set curricular goals. (*See* Set Curricular Goals)
    a. ____
    b. ____
    c. ____

19. Match the type of instruction used with students who are gifted with its description: (*See* Implement Instruction)

a.___	A school with an instructional emphasis on a specific domain of talent, such as math	1. Acceleration
b.___	Compacting or telescoping the curriculum	2. Content enrichment
c. ___	Pull-out programs	3. Magnet school
d. ___	Moving faster through the grades or a particular subject area	
e. ___	Revolving Door Model	

20. What three types of underserved children are offered opportunities to develop their gifts at the Montgomery Knolls preschool program? (*See* Observe Programs in Practice; Early Childhood Years)
a. ______________________________
b. ______________________________
c. ______________________________

21. In the WINGS (Working with the Individual Needs of Gifted Students) program, what three instructional areas assure content coverage related to elementary and middle school students' aptitudes and diverse interests? (*See* Observe Programs in Practice; Elementary and Middle Years)
a. ______________________________
b. ______________________________
c. ______________________________

22. Name at least four types of programs available for middle- or secondary-level students. (*See* Observe Programs in Practice; Secondary Years)
a. ____________________ c. ____________________
b. ____________________ d. ____________________

23. Name the one requirement for membership in Mensa, the international organization primarily for adults who are gifted. ______________________ (*See* Observe Programs in Practice; Transitional and Postsecondary Years)

Putting It All Together

Breá Thornton's mother Elvia likes to tell about Breá's creative ability to put things together, converting abstract things into concrete ones. One Christmas, when Breá was in second grade, there were many gifts that came unassembled and "it seemed there were never enough parts, too few screws, or too many washers, and not enough instructions. But I gladly passed the baton onto Breá and she took the challenge like a sponge to water. At the ripe old age of eight, Breá became the family member responsible for 'putting it all together.'" Building on Gardner's model of multiple intelligences, what does Breá's behavior in this situation indicate about her giftedness?

How Can You Encourage Participation?

24. List at least two benefits and two concerns of inclusion for students who are gifted (*See* Practice Inclusion)

Benefits:______________________________
____

Concerns:______________________________
____

25. Explain how Winebrenner's differentiated assignments help general education teachers serve the needs of students who are gifted. (*See* Practice Inclusion)

____

____

26. Identify at least four key collaborators who may be involved in adapting the classroom environment for helping an unproductive student who is gifted: (*See* Foster Collaboration)

a. ____________________ c. ____________________
b. ____________________ d. ____________________

27. Resource consultation shares responsibility among personnel at what three levels? (*See* Foster Collaboration; Professional-to-Professional Collaboration)

a. ____
b. ____
c. ____

28. Mentorships are a good example of collaboration because ____________________
____.
(*See* Foster Collaboration; School, Student, Family, and Community Collaboration)

An Update on Michael Kearney and Family

Michael Kearney and his family continue to live in Murfreesboro, Tennessee. Maeghan, now fourteen, is completing her undergraduate work in veterinary medicine. She is getting good grades and realizing that she has what it takes to make a difference. Following the completion of his bachelor's at the age of ten, Michael, now sixteen, is hard at work on his second master's degree in computer science. His first masters degree was in biochemistry. He is fascinated with artificial intelligence as well as fencing, and he enjoys making others laugh. Michael has some advice for all of you who are in the teaching field. He says that, "Good teaching is always listening to your students and remembering that your students are there to learn how to think, not to be told how to think." After all, "creativity is the ability to bring life to your thoughts."

APPLICATION EXERCISES FOR CHAPTER 7

Application Exercise 7a. Identifying Multiple Intelligences

After rereading the Recent Perspectives section of the text chapter, identify which category of giftedness is most evident in each of the following students.

1. Jodi can't seem to sit still and tests her teacher's patience with her constant activity. She loves playing out of doors, and while many consider her a tomboy, she wins every relay race and is always chosen first for sports events.
   Category: ______________________________
2. Susie is quick to recognize what pleases both her teachers and her peers. She also recognizes when other students' actions and motives are going the wrong direction—even before the teacher notices. Her friendship is sought after and she works to make the classroom a real community.
   Category: ______________________________
3. Jack talks all the time. He loves to explain everything to everyone. Some peers call him "motormouth" while others ignore him because they don't understand the long words he uses. When he's not talking, he's writing poetry.
   Category: ______________________________
4. When the teacher needs help organizing things in the classroom, he enlists Jacob's assistance. Jacob can see how things fit. He even comes up with original and useful designs that simplify classroom layouts and events.
   Category: ______________________________
5. Darlene spends a lot of time doodling. Even when she's supposed to be taking notes, her pages are cluttered with pictures, many of which relate to the topic of the lesson.
   Category: ______________________________
6. Jimmy is the class detective. He figures out complex problems before others. He has invented his own secret code that he uses with a few buddies.
   Category: ______________________________
7. Roberta loves cars. She knows every make and model on the road. She can tell you the differences between very similar models and is always looking at car magazines.
   Category: ______________________________
8. Rachel comes to school wearing a headset and complains when she has to turn it off. Even after it's turned off, her body still seems to move with the rhythm of the last song she heard and later she sings the song for her friends.
   Category: ______________________________
9. Betsy cries every time someone gets in trouble. She is always first to offer help to someone in need. She spends more time looking out for others than attending to classwork.
   Category: ______________________________

Application Exercise 7b. IQ Scores in the Classroom

Reread the section on Identifying the Prevalence of Giftedness. Using Figure 7-6, compute how many students in a classroom of 40 students may have IQ scores similar to those below. Note that an IQ beyond 130 is very rare.

1. Sam's IQ is about 107. — Total in class with IQ range of 100–115: _____
2. Mary's IQ is about 122. — Total in class with IQ range of 115–130: _____
3. Andrew's IQ is about 136. — Total in class with IQ of 130–145: _____
4. Julie's IQ is about 148. — Total in class with IQ above 145: _____

Application Exercise 7c. Mapping Giftedness in Action

Based upon the major questions addressed in this chapter, select your favorite domain of giftedness. Create either a game or a written or visual schematic representation to summarize the major concepts affecting gifted education today.

Major Questions: Who Are Students with Giftedness? How Are Students Who Are Gifted Evaluated? How Can You Establish Effective Teaching Practices? How Can You Encourage Participation?

SAMPLE QUIZ FOR CHAPTER 7

MULTIPLE CHOICE

Circle the correct answer.

1. To establish a successful program for student with giftedness, all of the following activities would be helpful <u>except</u>:
   a. Provide activities that entice the students.
   b. Develop a program with as much pull-out time as possible.
   c. Emphasize the challenges of high capability.
   d. Affirm students' accomplishments in a newsletter.

2. While the federal definition is instrumental in guiding programs for students who are gifted, it does not address one important concern. Which concern is <u>not</u> true?
   a. Giftedness is stated as worthy of federal attention.
   b. Areas and characteristics of giftedness are described.
   c. States are required to establish programs for students who are gifted.
   d. It is stated that students who are gifted require services.

3. Although only eight years old, Tracina wins adult performing arts contests in violin. These contests are governed by official standards. Which of the following is one of Sternberg and Zhang's criteria for identifying this aspect of giftedness?
   a. Value
   b. Productivity
   c. Usefulness
   d. Demonstrability

4. Which of the following researchers has developed a model of domain-specific giftedness?
   a. Sternberg
   b. Gardner
   c. Renzulli
   d. Terman

5. Samantha's judgment seems to lag behind her development of intellect. She often struggles with authorities and questions rules, customs, and traditions. She has poor attention when bored and has a low tolerance for tasks that seem irrelevant. Which one of the following choices does this type of behavior characterize?
   a. Giftedness
   b. Attention-deficit/hyperactivity disorder
   c. A combination of both giftedness and attention-deficit/hyperactivity disorder
   d. Neither giftedness nor attention-deficit/hyperactivity disorder

6. If IQ is used as the basis for assessing giftedness, then what is the proportion of the population considered gifted?
   a. 1% to 2%
   b. 2% to 3%
   c. 3% to 4%
   d. 4% to 5%

7. The DISCOVER assessment process has evaluated a number of potentially gifted students. Which of the following students was considered a superior problem-solver and referred for placement into a gifted program?
   a. Suzy scored definite ratings in linguistic activities.
   b. Leah scored definite ratings in linguistic, logical-mathematical, and spatial activities.
   c. Tom scored definite ratings in logical-mathematical activities.
   d. Ralph scored definite ratings in spatial activities.

8. Ms. Beach recognizes that Bethany is far beyond her other students in math. In order to provide her with opportunities for more challenging projects, Ms. Beach allows Bethany to test out of the material and only do assignments she finds interesting. Which of the following methods is Ms. Beach using?
   a. Compacting the curriculum
   b. The Revolving Door Model
   c. Instructional strategies
   d. Acceleration

9. Which one of the following situations best reflects the benefits and goals of inclusion for students who are gifted?
   a. The understanding of giftedness is more easily certified.
   b. More students benefit from ability development.
   c. More help is given by the general education teacher, including "differentiated" activities.
   d. Students who are gifted can provide information for their teachers.

10. Finding the best support for children who are gifted is not always easy. What additional options are more and more parents using to help students who are gifted achieve their potential?
    a. Critical counseling
    b. Family mentors
    c. Home schooling
    d. Resource consultation

11. Three of the following categories are included in the current federal definition of giftedness. Which category of giftedness is <u>not</u> included?
    a. Intellectual
    b. Creative
    c. Intrapersonal
    d. Artistic

12. Which of the following teachers best reflects the traditional paradigm for gifted education?
    a. Ms. Jones, who uses standardized test scores to recommend students for the gifted program
    b. Mr. Samuels, who has seen Joe's remarkable ability to take machines apart and put them back together and recommends Joe for the gifted program
    c. Ms. Welch, who recognizes students for their unique abilities in diverse areas
    d. Mr. McCabe, who collaborates with other teachers to look for excellence in performance as a basis for a recommendation for the gifted program

13. Jenny demonstrates characteristics of great self-awareness, impulse control, persistence, self-motivation, empathy and social deftness. Which two researchers specifically address these characteristics in identifying giftedness?
    a. Gardner and Renzulli
    b. Sternberg and Gardner
    c. Renzulli and Sternberg
    d. Goleman and Gardner

14. Which one of the following methods builds on a talent pool and allows more students to focus on special projects or endeavors?
    a. Compacting the curriculum
    b. The Revolving Door Model
    c. Magnet schools
    d. Acceleration

15. In which of the following situations is giftedness attributed to psychosocial causes?
    a. Abby's parents provide her with many early opportunities of encouragement.
    b. Peter's parents are cautious and careful not to hurry his achievements.
    c. Joy's parents allow her to watch all the TV she wants.
    d. Tim's parents are careful not to allow him more opportunities than his brothers or sisters had.

16. Three of the following reasons underscore the benefits of formal assessment. Which one is <u>not</u> a supporting reason for formal assessment?
    a. There is more likelihood of an appropriate education for students.
    b. Schools will obtain data to validate a student's placement.
    c. Educators need test scores to validate the success of teaching.
    d. Criteria will be met to assure federal funding when available.

17. What model, structured for schools that are trying to develop the talents of all students, seeks to incorporate varied, advanced learning experiences and higher-order thinking skills?
    a. Differentiated Learning Model
    b. Renzulli's School Enrichment Model
    c. WINGS Program
    d. Project Share

18. Which type of curriculum integrates content area learning into a study of one particular topic?
    a. One that is modified according to the interest of the student
    b. One that modifies the pace of the learning
    c. One that modifies the depth of content coverage
    d. One that modifies the grading structure for the learning

19. Which one of the following students has given an example of Bloom's category of synthesis for spelling activities?
    a. Bill gave a definition in his own words.
    b. Marilyn correctly used the word in a sentence.
    c. Ann broke the words into families and identified prefixes and suffixes.
    d. Linda used word parts to create imaginary words.

20. Collaboration with the community to provide services to students with giftedness is often accomplished by utilizing which of the following?
    a. Peer assistance
    b. Involvement of teachers
    c. Mentorship programs that pair experts with students
    d. Parent volunteers

SHORT ANSWER

21. What are the five federal classifications for students who are gifted?
    a. ______________________________
    b. ______________________________
    c. ______________________________
    d. ______________________________
    e. ______________________________

22. Identify three types of curriculum modifications for students who are gifted.
    a. ____
    b. ____
    c. ____

23. State two items that could be included in a reflective learning portfolio.
    a. ____
    b. ____

ESSAY

24. Assess and prioritize different assessments used for students who are gifted according to how they build on the inherent strength of these students.

25. Compare and contrast the characteristics of program options for students who are gifted at the four different age levels. Evaluate the strengths and weaknesses at each level.

CHAPTER 8: MENTAL RETARDATION

CHAPTER OVERVIEW

Mental retardation is a social concept derived from society's views about people with intellectual challenges. This chapter explores the identification, characteristics, causes, and prevalence of mental retardation as a social construct. An overview of assessment focuses on adaptive skills to determine the presence of mental retardation, while a description of assessments establishes a means for determining the nature and extent of special education services. Setting curricular goals that address community-based instruction and authentic learning activities establish the framework for effective teaching practices. Programs that foster collaboration are presented to support the inclusion of students with mental retardation in the general education classroom. Additional program options at each level are described to provide an overview of effective practices for serving these students.

Tory Woodard's story provides an example of a three-year-old boy who is benefiting from early intervention and support from a loving family. The vignette portrays a hopeful picture: If interventions and supports are continued, Tory's developmental delays may not be a part of his life in the future. A smooth transition from the Granville County Child Development Center to preschool then elementary school may provide him with the support needed to ensure lifelong success.

CHAPTER AT-A-GLANCE

Chapter Outline	Instructional Goals	Key Concepts
WHO ARE STUDENTS WITH MENTAL RETARDATION?		
Defining Mental Retardation • Mental Retardation as a Social Construct • The Evolving Definition • The 1992 AAMR Definition	• Differentiate among models for defining mental retardation	• Definitions of mental retardation have evolved to include not only permanent intellectual impairment, but also a student's educational performance and potential, focusing on three areas: capabilities, environments, and functioning.
Describing the Characteristics • Limitations in Intellectual Functioning • Limitations in Adaptive Skill Areas • Need for Supports • Using the AAMR Approach in Schools	• Describe key characteristics of mental retardation • Identify diagnostic criteria for describing characteristics of mental retardation	• The three main characteristics of mental retardation relate to intelligence, adaptive skills, and need for support. • The diagnosis of mental retardation requires an IQ score of 70 to 75 or below.
• Identifying the Causes of Mental Retardation • Biomedical Causes • Psychosocial Disadvantage • Interaction of Biomedical and Psychosocial Causes • Preventing Mental Retardation	• Categorize causes of mental retardation • Explain levels of prevention for mental retardation	• Two ways to categorize causes of mental retardation include timing and type. • Mental retardation typically results from interactions among multiple causes. • Prevention encompasses primary, secondary, and tertiary prevention.
Identifying the Prevalence of Mental Retardation	• Recognize prevalence rates and recent trends	• Prevalence is less than 1% to 3% of the general population. • Prevalence is declining where it is increasing for students identified with learning disabilities.

HOW ARE STUDENTS WITH MENTAL RETARDATION EVALUATED?		
Determining the Presence of Mental Retardation	• Compare the characteristics of different assessment tools used to determine the presence of mental retardation	• AAMR proposes a comprehensive assessment. • The AAMR Adaptive Behavior Scale–School Edition is a frequently used assessment tool.
Determining the Nature and Extent of Special Education and Related Services	• Recognize the possibilities for developing a specialized needs based program	• Developing a profile that includes intensities of needed supports is a high priority.
HOW CAN YOU ESTABLISH EFFECTIVE TEACHING PRACTICES?		
Set Curricular Goals	• Examine curriculum options that enhance self-determination and student quality of life	• Achieve high expectations within the standard curriculum. • Adapt standard curriculum to include a life skills focus. • Identify expectations of the environment with life skills curriculum.
Implement Instruction	• Consider strategies that are effective in natural settings of everyday life	• Implement community-based instructional strategies. • Use authentic learning activities to create meaningful contexts.
Early Childhood Years	• Evaluate program at the early childhood level	• Granville County Child Development Center is designed to provide cognitive therapy, adaptive training, and collaborative support through various service agencies.
Elementary Years	• Evaluate program at the elementary level	• Cordley Elementary School offers a functional curriculum to help students generalize skills in community-based settings
Middle and Secondary Years	• Evaluate program at the middle and secondary level	• Jody's secondary level instructional goals are met through authentic activities in an inclusive school setting.
Transitional and Postsecondary Years	• Evaluate program at the transition and postsecondary level	• Project TASSEL, a transition program with an interagency team, provides self-determination training to individuals so they can become competent community citizens.

HOW CAN YOU ENCOURAGE PARTICIPATION?		
Practice Inclusion	• Identify trends for inclusion of students with mental retardation	• Trends indicate that 11% of students with mental retardation receive inclusive education in general education classrooms.
Foster Collaboration	• Explore ways to collaborate on behalf of students with mental retardation	• Person-centered planning approaches bring together family, professionals, and friends for problem solving and social support.

PROJECT OPTIONS

1. Interview a general education teacher and a special education teacher in a local school system to determine what evaluation procedures are utilized to assess students with mental retardation. Find out what assessments are administered by the special education teacher and what documentation procedures he or she is responsible to complete after the process.
2. Design one authentic learning activity to be utilized with a student with mental retardation. Obtain permission to use the activity with a student in a community-based setting. Document the results and list any needed modification procedures.
3. Obtain permission from a local school system to observe an inclusive classroom where students with mental retardation are receiving services. Identify and document the curricular goals, the instructional strategies, and the specific programs used to establish effective teaching practices.
4. Observe one after-school program or one community activity to determine whether modifications are being made to accommodate students with mental retardation. Make a list of the program activities, the types of modifications observed, and what interventions could be made to improve the program.

KEY TERMS

Biomedical causes	Learned helplessness
Chromosomes	Outer-directedness
EMR classroom	Psychosocial disadvantage
Educable students	Tertiary prevention
Karyotyping	Trainable students

GUIDED REVIEW

Love Story

The Roys have been fighting for their daughter since birth. At the time she was born, her father Art said, "Everyone said, 'Don't take her home. She's not going to have a normal life.' " But the Roys were convinced that an institution was not the right place for Jennifer. "She has always been a joy and the focus of our lives," says Art. As Jennifer's graduation approached, she put the skills learned in special education classes to work labeling and mailing collection envelopes at her church. Soon the business grew and The *Special Persons Mailing Service* was created, getting half of its employees from *Skill Quest*, a Virginia Beach, Virginia, program that teaches job skills to special persons. To read more about the company see *People,* May 15, 1995, Vol. 43 Issue 19, p. 92.

Who Are Students with Mental Retardation?

1. Why is mental retardation considered a social construct? (*See* Defining Mental Retardation; Mental Retardation as a Social Construct) ______________________________
2. What has been the distinguishing characteristic over the years for the AAMR's definition of mental retardation? (*See* Defining Mental Retardation; The Evolving Definition)

   ____
3. Write IDEA's definition of mental retardation and then explain how IDEA's definition of mental retardation differs from the AAMR's definition. (*See* Defining Mental Retardation; The Evolving Definition)

   IDEA's definition:

   ____

   ____

   Differences between IDEA's and AAMR's definitions:

   ____

   ____

   ____
4. Complete the following chart to demonstrate the AAMR's 1983 classification system. (*See* Defining Mental Retardation; The Evolving Definition.)

AAMR 1983 Classification	*IQ Range*	*Educational Classification*
a.		
b.		
c.		
d.		

5. The 1992 AAMR definition changed the perspective of mental retardation as an inherent trait to one that encompasses three elements. What are they? (*See* Defining Mental Retardation; The 1992 AAMR Definition.)
   a. ____
   b. ____
   c. ____

Growing Up *Down*

Buddies Jason Kingsley and Mitchell Levitz are two courageous friends who have defied Down syndrome stereotypes. Kingsley and Levitz have written a book together, *Count Us In, Growing Up with Down Syndrome* (Harcourt Brace). The book has been enthusiastically received by many people with Down syndrome. "This Down syndrome is the wrong name of our disability," says Jason. "I think Up syndrome is [more] positive." Both boys have big plans for the future. Jason wants to continue his acting career, then enter college. Mitchell, an office clerk, might enter politics. To learn more about Jason and Mitchell read *People*, May 2, 1994, Vol. 41, Issue 16, p. 120.

6. Match the definitions for identifying students with mental retardation with the source: (1) 1983 AAMR; (2) 1992 AAMR; or (3) 1997 IDEA. (*See* Defining Mental Retardation)

	(a) Recognizes both intellectual and adaptive behavior limitations and their effects on the person
	(b) Mental retardation means significantly subaverage general intellectual functioning existing concurrently with deficits in adaptive behavior and manifested during the developmental period that adversely affects a child's educational performance.
	(c) Holds the environment responsible for providing needed support for greater inclusion of individuals with disabilities.
	(d) Mental retardation refers to significantly subaverage general intellectual functioning existing concurrently with deficits in adaptive behavior and manifested during the developmental period.
	(e) Includes the four levels of mild, moderate, severe, and profound.
	(f) Includes four assumptions essential to its application: cultural and linguistic diversity, assessing adaptive behavior within typical environments, recognizing strengths as well as needs, and expressing great expectations for people with mental retardation.

7. What component has been added to the AAMR definition that reflects the new understanding of mental retardation? (*See* Defining Mental Retardation; The 1992 AAMR Definition)

____

____

In The Cards

Down syndrome hasn't kept Carrie Clise from creating a booming business. Search the Internet and you will find *Carrie's Cards* by Carrie Clise, featuring black-ink drawings. Carrie's meticulously detailed angels, brides, and other figures attract international clientele. "I think of her as the Grandma Moses of her generation," declares customer Gem Bordages of Galveston, Texas. It was Carrie's special education teacher, Sue Rundborg, who first noticed Carrie's talent. "I realized she could really do this as her life's work," she says. Carrie is a productive citizen who does something she really enjoys.

See *People,* November 30, 1998, Vol. 50 Issue 20, p. 142.

8. What are the three main characteristics of mental retardation? (*See* Describing the Characteristics of Mental Retardation)
   a. ____
   b. ____
   c. ____

9. Regardless of IQ score, what two areas are affected in students with mental retardation? (*See* Describing the Characteristics of Mental Retardation; Limitations in Intellectual Functioning)
   a. ____
   b. ____

10. Identify the four areas of difficulty for each limitation in intellectual functioning and the main identifying characteristics. (*See* Describing the Characteristics of Mental Retardation; Limitations in Intellectual Functioning)

Area of Difficulty in Intellectual Functioning	***Identifying Characteristic***
a.	
b.	
c.	
d.	

The Special Needs Collection

Children with Mental Retardation: A Parents' Guide, Woodbine House, 1993, is one book in a collection of guides (edited by Romayne Smith, M.A., CCC-SLP) designed to assist parents in their search for knowledge as they become advocates for children with special needs. Using new 1992 AAMR terminology, this book's intended readership is primarily parents of children with mental retardation who need intermittent to limited support. Background information, the evaluation process, coping with feelings about diagnosis, and practical strategies for helping your child succeed are covered using statements made by real-life parents of children with mental retardation.

11. Students with mental retardation often lack motivation. Identify how to help students to learn through The Efficacy Model. (*See* Describing the Characteristics of Mental Retardation; Limitations in Intellectual Functioning)
    a. Decrease learned helplessness or outer-directedness:
    ____
    ____
    b. Increase learned capacity or inner-directedness:
    ____
    ____

12. In addition to significant subaverage intelligence, how many adaptive skill areas must be significantly affected before a student can be identified as having mental retardation? (*See* Describing the Characteristics of Mental Retardation; Limitations in Adaptive Skill Areas)
    ____

13. What are the four areas in which students may need varying systems of support? (*See* Describing the Characteristics; Limitations in Intellectual Functioning)
    a. ______________________________
    b. ______________________________
    c. ______________________________
    d. ______________________________

14. Four levels of intensities of support have been identified. First, identify the four levels. Second, identify the variables that must be considered within each level. (*See* Describing the Characteristics; Need for Support)
    a. Levels: __________ __________ __________ __________
    b. Variables: ______________________ ______________________
    ______________ ______________ ______________________

15. How many causes of mental retardation have been identified? (*See* Identifying the Causes of Mental Retardation.)__________________

16. How does the AAMR categorize causes of mental retardation? (*See* Identifying the Causes of Mental Retardation.)

Timing	***Type***
a.	a.
b.	b.
c.	

What Will Happen When I Die?

Despite laws such as IDEA and ADA, many adults with mental retardation continue to depend on their parents to care for them. Many of these parents are at a stage in their life when they need the type of nurturing and care they have bestowed on their children. For these elderly parents, the strain can be enormous. "I worry all the time," one parent shares. "What will happen when I die?"

Adults with mental retardation find financial and housing obstacles to achieving independence. For example, a parent who loved her son and wanted him to gain the independence he was capable of achieving had to disown him, the only way he could receive Medicaid and afford to live in an apartment with a roommate. Her son who is deaf and mentally retarded signed, "All of this has helped me to have good goals and to be successful in independent living."

Many adults with mental retardation have been on waiting lists for over a decade to be placed in group homes that could provide them with independence and opportunities for meaningful employment. Instead of planned, careful, individualized placement of these adults, much of the placement in group homes has been crisis-oriented, based on who is most desperate for care, usually when a caregiver becomes extremely ill or dies.

One major cause for the lack of group homes is neighborhood resistance. Why do neighbors resist? Part of it is fear and part of it is financial (concern about property values). How would you feel about a group home being constructed in your neighborhood?

See *Cleveland Jewish News*, May 16, 1997.

17. Chromosomal disorders and oxygen deprivation are associated with which type of causes? (*See* Identifying the Causes of Mental Retardation)

____

18. What is the frequency of occurrence for Down syndrome, one of the most common chromosomal disorders? (*See* Identifying the Causes of Mental Retardation; Biomedical Causes)

____

19. How are chromosomal disorders identified? Name and describe the process. (*See* Identifying the Causes of Mental Retardation; Biomedical Causes)

____

____

20. Name the most common cause of mental retardation, and list at least three possible influencing factors. (*See* Identifying the Causes of Mental Retardation; Psychosocial Disadvantage)

Most common cause: ____

Influencing factors: ____

____

21. Out of a school of 500 students, probably ________ to ________ would have mental retardation. (*See* Identifying the Prevalence of Mental Retardation)

22. Why are more students being diagnosed with learning disabilities than mental retardation? (*See* Identifying the Prevalence of Mental Retardation)

____

23. List the three levels of prevention, the time of intervention, and at least one example of each. (*See* Identifying the Causes of Mental Retardation; Psychosocial Disadvantage.)

Level	*Time of Intervention*	*Example*
a.		
b.		
c.		

How Are Students with Mental Retardation Evaluated?

24. An important type of evaluation for students who might have mental retardation is the ________________________, which is completed by parents, teachers, or others who work closely with the student. (*See* How Are Students with Mental Retardation Evaluated?)

Include Us

Christy Johnson searched diligently and in vain for an entertainment video that featured children with disabilities like her daughter Tiffani, who has mental retardation. When Christy attended the National Down Syndrome Congress's annual conference in 1995, she shared her frustration with Lou Shaw, a Hollywood producer whose daughter Hillary also has mental retardation. Together, they formed TiffHill Productions, named for their daughters, and created the video *Include Us*, which features children at a playground, forming a rainy-day band from kitchen utensils, and enjoying a magic show. Some national video store chains now carry *Include Us*, and sales have been strong. An educator's guide comes with the video, in case you want to purchase it for your classroom.

Christy cried when she learned that one five-year-old had befriended a classmate with Down syndrome after watching the video. "It's so important for typical children to know they can have friendships with people like my daughter," Christy says.

See *Good Housekeeping*, June 1997, p. 36, and the Internet site http://IncludeUs.com for more information.

How Can You Establish Effective Teaching Practices?

25. Identify two long-term curricular goals for students with developmental disabilities and two areas on which to focus for students with mental retardation. (*See* How Can You Establish Effective Teaching Practices?; Set Curricular Goals)

	Curricular Goals
a.	
b.	

The Rehabilitation Research and Training Center on Improving Community Integration for Persons with Mental Retardation is located at the University of Minnesota. Its goal is to improve community integration by conducting applied research, training, and dissemination activities in each of five areas: community living arrangements, financial support, extended service options and opportunities for community integration, social skills and interpersonal relationships, and personal independence and choice. A wealth of useful and relevant material is available by contacting the Center at 612-624-6328 or 612-625-6619 (fax).

26. Two instructional strategies that apply particularly to students with mental retardation are ____________ and ____________. (*See* How Can You Establish Effective Teaching Practices?; Implement Instruction)

27. With authentic instruction the teacher has to walk in the shoes of the students. List the three steps of authentic instruction. (*See* How Can You Establish Effective Teaching Practices?; Authentic Instruction)
    a. ____________
    b. ____________
    c. ____________

28. List key features for each of the following programs. (*See* How Can You Establish Effective Teaching Practices?; Observe Programs in Practice)

Program	***Key Features***
Early Childhood Years: Granville County Child Development Center	
Elementary Years: Cordley Elementary School	
Middle and Secondary Years: Jody's Program	
Transitional and Postsecondary Years: Project TASSEL	

How Can You Encourage Participation?

29. Match the percentages of students with their education placements. (*See* How Can You Encourage Participation?; Practice Inclusion)

a. _____ 28%	1. Separate class
b. _____ 54%	2. Residential facility
c. _____ 0.5%	3. Resource room
d. _____ 11%	4. Regular class
e. _____ 0.5%	5. Separate school
f. _____ 6%	6. Home/ hospital

30. What preparation and training must be provided to educators to ensure that schools can effectively include students with developmental disabilities in the general education classroom? (*See* How Can You Encourage Participation?; Practice Inclusion)

____

31. How can the practice of inclusion increase success for students with mental retardation? (*See* How Can You Encourage Participation?; Practice Inclusion)

____

The Most Valuable Player on Stallings' Team

Retired University of Alabama coach Gene Stallings hoped for a son who could play football. Instead, his son Johnny was born with Down syndrome in 1963, twelve years before IDEA was enacted in 1975. Johnny's doctors recommended institutionalization, and the family received little support when they decided to take Johnny home with them. Johnny could not even attend public school until he was ten.

Despite the challenges the family faced, they believe that Johnny provided them with something far more valuable than the ability to play football. "Johnny has given us love—total, unconditional love—and joy," Gene Stallings said in an interview with *People* magazine. Johnny attended games with his father and spent time with the players, teaching them to do their best with what they have. You can read more about Johnny and his family in Gene Stallings' book, *Another Season: A Coach's Story of Raising an Exceptional Son.*

People, February 2, 1998, pp. 40–45.

APPLICATION EXERCISES FOR CHAPTER 8

Application Exercise 8a. Identifying Limitations in Intellectual Functioning

Identify which area related to intellectual limitations is affected in the following situations:

1. Judy does not recognize her name when it is announced at the conclusion of the class performance. ________________
2. Dan has learned how to count the money in his pocket, but he can't figure out how much change to give the bus driver. ________________
3. Pamela has no hobbies or personal interests. ________________
4. James can add single digit numbers one day, but forgets the process while completing the next assignment. ________________

Application Exercise 8b. Adaptive Behavior Limitations

Identify which adaptive behavior limitation is being remediated in the following situations:

1. Amy is learning to check the water temperature before getting into the bathtub. ____________________________
2. Lynn is learning not to grab food off other people's plates. ________________________
3. Ed can identify and appropriately respond to the stop sign at the street corner. ____________________________
4. Sue is learning to speak in complete sentences. ______________________________
5. Allan is learning how to comb his hair. ____________________________________

Application Exercise 8c. Obstacles to Learning Challenge

Based upon the major questions (listed below) addressed in this chapter, summarize the concepts concerning mental retardation. For the third and fourth questions, describe how you would deal with problems associated with (a) attention, (b) memory, (c) generalization, and (d) motivation.

Major Questions: Who Are Students with Mental Retardation? How Are Students with Mental Retardation Evaluated? How Can You Establish Effective Teaching Practices? How Can You Encourage Participation?

SAMPLE QUIZ FOR CHAPTER 8

MULTIPLE CHOICE

Circle the correct answer.

1. Which of the following is the new phrase in the title of the AAMR's recent manual that reflects a new perspective in the definition of mental retardation?
   a. Definition
   b. Classification
   c. Characteristics
   d. Systems of support

2. Sharla, a student with mental retardation, often experiences frequent failure. In order to prevent future failure she sets low goals. Which of the following is <u>not</u> true about Sharla?
   a. She distrusts her own solutions.
   b. She seeks cues from others.
   c. She lacks motivation to learn or act.
   d. She is inner-directed.

3. A person identified with mental retardation must have limitations in how many of the ten adaptive skill areas essential for daily functioning?
   a. A minimum of two
   b. A minimum of three
   c. A minimum of four
   d. A minimum of five

4. Bill has difficulty distinguishing and paying attention to relevant cues in a social situation. Which characteristic of mental retardation is associated with this limitation?
   a. Limitations in intellectual functioning
   b. Limitations in academic functioning
   c. Limitations in adaptive skill areas
   d. Need for support

5. Which of the following is <u>not</u> associated with biomedical causes of mental retardation?
   a. Oxygen deprivation
   b. Chromosomal disorders
   c. Usually originate later in the child's development
   d. Usually require extensive support

6. Which of the following represents the current prevalence rate for mental retardation?
   a. 10 to 15 %
   b. 3 to 5 %
   c. 8 to 16 %
   d. 1 to 3 %

7. Which of the following is <u>not</u> an example of a primary prevention for mental retardation?
   a. Early intervention programs
   b. Vaccines
   c. Prenatal testing
   d. Educational programs to reduce the abuse of drugs

8. Which of the following is <u>not</u> true about Down syndrome?
    a. Trisomy 21 is the most common form.
    b. Karyotyping shows that the individual has 46 chromosomes.
    c. It can be identified as early as the first few hours after birth.
    d. Three separate chromosomal aberrations are associated with Down syndrome.

9. Jimmie's curriculum focuses on basic academic and social skills. He receives intensive programming in reading, math, and language arts. Which type of curriculum option is this?
    a. Remedial
    b. General classroom support
    c. Adult outcomes
    d. Life skills preparation

10. Which of the following most accurately portrays the ideal order, from most desirable to least desirable, of service delivery for students with mental retardation if inclusion is the ultimate goal?
    a. Separate school, separate class, resource room
    b. Separate class, resource room, inclusive classroom
    c. Inclusive classroom, resource room, separate class
    d. Resource room, inclusive classroom, separate class

11. To emphasize the need to improve understanding of the new definition, AAMR revised the title of its manual. Which new word(s) illustrate(s) this new component of the definition?
    a. Mental Retardation
    b. Systems of Support
    c. Definition
    d. Classification

12. Which of the following is <u>not</u> a perinatal cause of mental retardation?
    a. Premature labor
    b. Meningitis
    c. Head trauma at birth
    d. Maternal malnutrition

13. Juana's IQ has been found to be between 70 to 75. How might you expect her to intellectually function in school?
    a. Similar to students with a lower IQ
    b. Similar to students with learning disabilities
    c. Similar to students with average ability
    d. Similar to students with physical disabilities

14. Joseph, a student with mental retardation, often misses social cues that tell him to stop a certain behavior. Which area of impairment in the learning process is most in focus when missing such a cue?
    a. Attention
    b. Memory
    c. Generalization
    d. Motivation

15. Which of the following is associated with psychosocial disadvantage?
    a. Chromosomal disorders
    b. Down syndrome
    c. Oxygen deprivation
    d. Late or absent prenatal care

16. Which level of support is characterized by consistency over time, is time-limited, but is not of an intermittent nature?
    a. Pervasive
    b. Extensive
    c. Limited
    d. Intermittent

17. Which one of the following four domains is used to determine the presence of mental retardation?
    a. Intellectual functioning and adaptive skills
    b. Psychological and emotional considerations
    c. Physical and health considerations
    d. Environmental considerations

18. Authentic instruction includes all of the following except:
    a. Assessing student strengths and needs
    b. Teaching an authentic activity
    c. Determining the functional priority of strengths and needs
    d. Developing an assessment to be completed in written format

19. Which group of students is least likely to be included in a general education classroom for instructional purposes?
    a. Students with learning disabilities
    b. Students with giftedness
    c. Students with mental retardation
    d. Students with an attention deficit disorder

20. Which is not an example of an authentic learning activity that ties curriculum content to culture in a community?
    a. Reading about ranching practices in a Colorado community
    b. Native American students preparing a traditional dish for a class banquet
    c. African American students making a presentation about a Martin Luther King Jr. celebration
    d. Susan sharing in show and tell about her great grandmother's trip from Ireland to the United States

SHORT ANSWER

21. What are the four areas of impairment in the learning process that students with mental retardation typically experience?

    a. ____________________ c. ____________________

    b. ____________________ d. ____________________

22. Students with mental retardation need varying intensities of support. Identify the four levels of intensities and explain each one briefly.

    a. ____

    b. ____

    c. ____

    d. ____

23. Why is there an increasing curricular emphasis on a life skills orientation from the early years?

    ____

    ____

ESSAY

24. Explain the changes in the definition of mental retardation over time. Discuss how the latest changes offer new benefits to students like Tory.
25. Describe how curricular goals are established for students with mental retardation utilizing community-based and authentic instructional practices.

CHAPTER 9: SEVERE AND MULTIPLE DISABILITIES

CHAPTER OVERVIEW

Students with severe and multiple disabilities typically have severe mental retardation and other accompanying disabilities. This chapter examines the categories of characteristics of these students in relationship to the causes and prevalence as understood today. Various evaluation tools are explored, with a particular focus on Making Action Plans (MAPs). Innovative curriculum and methods are examined to see what possibilities are being utilized for students with severe and multiple disabilities. Important aspects of inclusion and collaboration are presented in the context of real life applications. Some strong program options tie together the chapter's contents, demonstrating that students with severe and multiple disabilities have many options and possibilities.

The life of Joshua Spoor provides an illustration of a student with very severe disabilities who has the benefit of attending one of the country's premier inclusion programs—the Johnson City, New York, school program. Joshua's story also illustrates that special challenges can arise within families that require them to find additional support in order to meet the 24-hour needs of their children. In Joshua's case, he lives at a residential center, but he still has the opportunity to be included in one of his community's schools.

CHAPTER AT-A-GLANCE

Chapter Outline	Instructional Goals	Key Concepts
WHO ARE STUDENTS WITH SEVERE AND MULTIPLE DISABILITIES?		
Defining Severe and Multiple Disabilities	• Recognize that the term defines a very diverse group of people	• IDEA has two separate definitions, one for multiple disabilities and one for severe disabilities.
Describing the Characteristics of Severe and Multiple Disabilities • Intellectual Functioning • Adaptive Skills • Motor Development • Sensory Impairments • Health Care Needs • Communication Skills	• Describe key characteristics of severe and multiple disabilities	• Two indications of intellectual function include limited academic skills and levels of awareness. • Deficits in adaptive behavior include a lack in self-care skills, a lack of typical social interactions, and challenging behaviors. • Delayed motor development often results in abnormal muscle tone. • Two out of five students with severe and multiple disabilities typically have sensory impairments. • Health care needs include procedures such as clean intermittent catheterization, gastrostomy tube feeding, and respiratory ventilation. • The critical factor in communication is to identify and interpret a student's particular method of communication.
Identifying the Causes of Severe and Multiple Disabilities • Genetic Metabolic Disorders • Disorders of Brain Formation • Preventing Severe and Multiple Disabilities	• Identify causes of severe and multiple disabilities • Explain ways to prevent severe and multiple disabilities	• Etiology is unknown in 40% of this population. • Most known causes are due to prenatal biomedical factors. • Some severe and multiple disabilities are preventable through medical technology, maternal education, and genetic counseling.

Identifying the Prevalence of Severe and Multiple Disabilities	• Recognize prevalence rates	• Prevalence for multiple disabilities is 0.17% of all students between 6 and 21 who are served in IDEA programs. • No data is provided on prevalence for severe disabilities
HOW ARE STUDENTS WITH SEVERE AND MULTIPLE DISABILITIES EVALUATED?		
Determining the Presence of a Disability	• Identify the different assessment tools used to determine the presence of severe and multiple disabilities	• Screening tests such as the Apgar determine the type and extent of the disability. • While controversial, IQ tests and adaptive behavior scales are most often used to make classification decisions.
Determining the Nature and Extent of Special Education and Related Services • Ecological Assessment • Making Action Plans	• Compare the characteristics of different approaches for determining special education and related services	• Approaches to assessing skills for curriculum and program development, including the developmental model, the ecological model, assessment of behavioral states, and Making Action Plans, offer different perspectives.
HOW CAN YOU ESTABLISH EFFECTIVE TEACHING PRACTICES?		
Set Curricular Goals	• Differentiate curriculum options available for use with students with severe and multiple disabilities	• Increase priority skills related to the results of an ecological assessment. • Expand relationships with school mates, and foster school and community memberships.
Implement Instruction	• Examine effective methods for teaching students with severe and multiple disabilities	• Utilizing a "universal design," adapt skill sequences and rules through the use of personal assistance and technology. • Use such state-of-the-art strategies as partial participation and adaptations, cooperative learning, and peer tutoring.
Early Childhood Years	• Identify effective characteristics of effective childhood programs	• The Circle of Inclusion Program offers a desirable social and communicative environment.
Elementary Years	• Identify effective elementary programs for students with severe and multiple disabilities	• One elementary school uses a collaborative problem-solving process and a "critical friend" to facilitate the action research process.
Middle and Secondary Years	• Identify effective characteristics of effective programs for middle and secondary students	• A middle school adopted a mission statement, "All Means All," that values academic excellence, acceptance of diversity, and respect of all students.
Transitional and Postsecondary Years	• Identify effective program options for adults with severe and multiple disabilities	• Asbury College permits students to receive college credit while attending high school.
HOW CAN YOU ENCOURAGE PARTICIPATION?		
Practice Inclusion	• Identify appropriate settings for students with severe and multiple disabilities	• Students with severe or multiple disabilities are taught in a variety of settings, from totally segregated to fully inclusive classrooms.

Foster Collaboration • Professional-to-Professional Collaboration • Family and Professional Collaboration	• Explore ways to collaborate for students with severe and multiple disabilities	• Because of medical and health care needs, families, educators, physicians and occupational therapists, speech and language pathologists, and medical personnel must work collaboratively.

PROJECT OPTIONS

1. In a local school or institution, get to know one student and do a case study using an ecological inventory. Include a "Vision for the Future" statement to summarize your findings.
2. Do a library search of children's literature to find as many books as possible that relate to students with severe and multiple disabilities. Classify the books according to the amount of inclusion in typical settings experienced by the individuals with disabilities.
3. Design your own evaluation for students with severe and multiple disabilities based on the best aspects of the models presented in this chapter.
4. Research different support systems and organizations available in your community. Based on all you learn, create a plan for one student that would incorporate the best advantages offered within your community.

KEY TERMS

Action research

Augmentative and alternative communication

Authentic assessment

Clean intermittent catheterization

Ecological assessment

Ecological curriculum

Encephalocele

Enzymes

Functional academic skills

Gastrostomy tube feeding

Metabolism

Muscle atrophy

Partial participation

Reciprocal friendship

Respiratory ventilation

Task analysis

GUIDED REVIEW

Silent Spirit

After a difficult birth, Marshall Stewart Ball failed to gain weight and suffered from seizures before his first birthday. At age three, when he could not walk or talk, doctors were baffled. They told his parents that he was probably profoundly retarded and would likely die before the age of ten. But his parents, who would not give up on him, read to him constantly and tried to teach him the alphabet. "We tried not to focus on his physical limitations," his mother said. Ignoring the grim prognosis, his parents started using an alphabet board with Marshall when he was five. Testing at the University of Texas a year later confirmed that he had third grade reading skills. By age nine he was functioning at the level of a high school senior. At the age of thirteen, he published a book that sold more than 80,000 copies. To read more about Marshall, *see People*, December 1999, *52*(23), pp. 203–205.

Who Are Students with Severe and Multiple Disabilities?

1. According to the definitions discussed for severe and multiple disabilities, list five types of disabilities that are included in this category. (*See* Who Are Students with Severe and Multiple Disabilities?; Defining Severe and Multiple Disabilities)
   a. ______________________________
   b. ______________________________
   c. ______________________________
   d. ______________________________
   e. ______________________________

2. What two characteristics pervade these different definitions? (*See* Defining Severe and Multiple Disabilities)
   a. ______________________________
   b. ______________________________

3. The vast majority of students who are served in programs for students with severe and multiple disabilities have which level of mental retardation? (*See* Defining Severe and Multiple Disabilities)

   ____

4. Identify the six categories of characteristics that help describe students with severe and multiple disabilities. Then describe key identifying features of each category. (*See* Describing the Characteristics of Severe and Multiple Disabilties)

Characteristic Category	*Key Identifying Features*
a.	
b.	
c.	
d.	
e.	
f.	

5. What are the two indicators of intellectual functioning in students with severe and multiple disabilities? (*See* Describing the Characteristics of Severe and Multiple Disabilities)
   a. ______________________________
   b. ______________________________

6. What two adaptive behaviors are especially relevant for individuals with severe and multiple disabilities? (*See* Describing the Characteristics of Severe and Multiple Disabilities)
   a. ______________________________
   b. ______________________________

I Have Something to Say!

Elizabeth is nonverbal and has never had the opportunity to sing the words to wish her sister a happy birthday. With the touch of a switch, a voice output communication aid (VOCA) has changed all that by providing a recorded voice. Just before a birthday celebration for Elizabeth's sister Kaitlin, another sister recorded "Happy Birthday" on Elizabeth's voice output communication aid. When children like Elizabeth can communicate basic wants and needs, express feelings and emotions, and share information, opportunities for inclusion, independence, and participation are greatly enhanced. For more information, recommended books, resources, and websites see *Exceptional Parent*, December 1998, *28*(12), pp. 56–58.

7. Hearing and vision impairments are so common among individuals with severe and multiple disabilities that __________ out of every ____________ students have sensory impairments. (*See* Describing the Characteristics of Severe and Multiple Disabilities)
8. What are three examples of health care needs of students with severe and multiple disabilities that now are being met by teachers and other school staff? (*See* Describing the Characteristics of Severe and Multiple Disabilities)
   a. ______________________________
   b. ______________________________
   c. ______________________________
9. The majority of known causes for severe and multiple disabilities relate to prenatal biomedical factors. Give four examples of these factors. (*See* Identifying the Causes of Severe and Multiple Disabilities)
   a. ______________________________
   b. ______________________________
   c. ______________________________
   d. ______________________________
10. Abnormalities in a parent's genes can cause a disorder in a child's metabolism. The two types of hereditary genetic transmissions discussed in the chapter are ________________ and ________________. In recessive disorders, when both parents have the gene, the children have a __________ percent chance of being affected by the disorder. In dominant disorders, when a carrier and a noncarrier have children, the children have a ________ percent chance of developing the disorder. If both the parents have the dominant gene, the disease can be ____________ for a child. (*See* Identifying the Causes of Severe and Multiple Disabilities)

11. Identify and explain with examples current techniques to identify and possibly prevent multiple disabilities. (*See* Identifying the Causes of Severe and Multiple Disabilities)

Technique	*Explanation and Examples*
a. Prenatal fetal therapy	
b. Routine postnatal screenings	
c. Maternal education	

12. The prevalence of severe and multiple disabilities appears to be between _________ percent and ______________ percent. (*See* Identifying the Prevalence of Severe and Multiple Disabilities)

How Are Students with Severe and Multiple Disabilities Evaluated?

13. Newborns are screened with a(n) ___________________ test, which measures the following five physical traits. (*See* How Are Students with Severe and Multiple Disabilities Evaluated?; Determining the Presence of Severe and Multiple Disabilities)
    a. ______________________________
    b. ______________________________
    c. ______________________________
    d. ______________________________
    e. ______________________________

14. What two approaches can be used to assess a student's skills for specific curriculum goals and instructional development? (*See* How Are Students With Severe and Multiple Disabilities Evaluated? Determining the Nature and Extent of Special Education and Related Services)
    a. ______________________________
    b. ______________________________

We encourage you to contact The Association for Persons with Severe Handicaps (TASH), a professional organization that advocates inclusion for people with severe disabilities into family, educational, and community settings. TASH sponsors conferences, a journal, a newsletter, and a range of educational opportunities. They can be reached at 11201 Greenwood Avenue North, Seattle, WA 98133, 206-361-8870.

How Can You Establish Effective Teaching Practices?

15. Explain the emphasis of the ecological curriculum approach. (*See* How Can You Establish Effective Teaching Practices?; Set Curricular Goals)

____

____

____

16. Name and describe the two ways of adapting the general education curriculum so students with severe and multiple disabilities can participate fully. (*See* How Can You Establish Effective Teaching Practices?; Set Curricular Goals)

Curriculum Adaptation	***Identifying Characteristic***
a.	
b.	

17. ______________________ ______________________ is a research-validated instructional strategy to use with students with severe and multiple disabilities. (*See* How Can You Establish Effective Teaching Practices?; Implement Instruction)

18. In the table below, list the components of cooperative learning and provide a description of each. (*See* How Can You Establish Effective Teaching Practices?; Implement Instruction)

Components	***Description***
a.	
b.	
c.	
d.	
e.	
f.	

19. List and define the six types of partial participation that students with severe and multiple disabilities may learn. (*See* How Can You Establish Effective Teaching Practices?; Implement Instruction)
    a. ____
    b. ____
    c. ____
    d. ____
    e. ____
    f. ____

The Research and Training Center on Improving Supported Employment Outcomes for Individuals with Developmental and Other Severe Disabilities is located at Virginia Commonwealth University in Richmond, Virginia. The goal of this center is to increase employment options for individuals with severe disabilities. This center serves as a national clearinghouse of research and best practice information. Their telephone number is 804-367-1851. Their fax number is 804-828-2521.

20. Match the four instructional strategies for individualized adaptations for students with severe and multiple disabilities to examples of adaptations. (*See* How Can You Establish Effective Teaching Practices?; Implement Instruction)

Instructional Strategy	***Examples of Adaptations***
a. Adapting Skill Sequences	1. ________ Allowing a longer lunch period so student who has difficulty eating quickly can eat with peers in cafeteria
b. Adapting Rules	2. ________Asking a friend to help turn pages for a student who has poor fine motor skills
c. Utilizing Personal Assistance	3. ________ Using color-coded home phone numbers for a student who has low reading ability
d. Materials and Devices	4. _________Sitting on floor before picking up puzzle pieces from the floor for a student who is unable to balance when bending and reaching
	5. _________Using enlarged game pieces for a student with poor fine motor skills
	6. _________Asking someone to push out-of-reach elevator button for a student in a wheelchair
	7. _________ Writing name with a rubber stamp for a student unable to write name
	8. _________Tagging clothes that match with coded labels for a student who has difficulty matching colors

21. List key features for each of the following programs. (*See* Observe Programs in Practice)

Program	***Key Features***
Circle of Inclusion Program	
Collaborative Problem-Solving and "Critical Friend"	
"All Means All" Mission Statement	
High School Credit through Asbury College	

How Can You Encourage Participation?

22. At the present time, students with severe and multiple disabilities are taught in a _________________ of settings. (*See* How Can You Encourage Participation?; Practice Inclusion)

23. There are six themes related to the successful inclusion of students with disabilities. List and explain your ranking for these six themes as they apply to students with severe disabilities. (*See* How Can You Encourage Participation?; Practice Inclusion)
    a. ______________________________
    b. ______________________________
    c. ______________________________
    d. ______________________________
    e. ______________________________
    f. ______________________________

24. Explain the different roles for each of the following collaborators in the life of a student with severe and multiple disabilities. (*See* How Can You Encourage Participation?; Foster Collaboration)
    Professional Collaborator: ______________________________
    ____
    Family Collaborator: ______________________________
    ____
    Student and Community Collaborator: ______________________________
    ____

Consider the community in which you are living. What are some of the recreational opportunities in which you think Joshua Spoor and his family could participate as a family unit? What changes do you think might be made in community services and support so that they might be more responsive to him and his family?

APPLICATION EXERCISES FOR CHAPTER 9

Application Exercise 9a. Determining the Likelihood of a Disability in a Newborn

Based on Apgar evaluations, identify which infants are at risk for disabilities. Rank the infants in order of risk and defend your ranking.

	Heart Rate		***Respiratory Effort***		***Muscle Tone***		***Gag Reflex***		***Color***	
	1 min	5 min	1 min	5 min	1 min	5 min	1 min	5 min	1 min	5 min
1. Miguel	2	2	2	2	2	2	2	2	1	2
2. Susannah	1	1	1	1	0	0	0	0	1	1
3. Vishnu	2	2	2	2	2	2	1	2	2	2
4. Felicia	0	1	0	1	0	0	0	0	0	1
5. Chin-Cheng	2	2	1	1	2	2	1	1	2	2

Application Exercise 9b. Assessment Methods for Student Learning and Performance

Identify which assessment method is being used for the students described below.

Assessment Model	***Student's Performance Activity***
a. Developmental Model	1. _____ Zubaidah is putting pegs in a pegboard to demonstrate eye-hand coordination.
b. Ecological Model	2. _____ Khaldoun is learning to dance to popular music, thus learning to spend time after school with friends.
c. Behavior States	3. _____ Daniela is vocalizing when asked direct questions in order to stay alert for 10 minutes.
d. Making Action Plans	4. _____ Janis is locating an item on a grocery shelf to demonstrate a knowledge of shopping.

Application Exercise 9c. Concept Application in Context

Discuss the life of Joshua Spoor as you summarize each of the major questions addressed in this chapter. Summarize the major concepts concerning severe and multiple disabilities as you integrate your knowledge about Joshua with the chapter contents for students with severe and multiple disabilities.

Major Questions: Who Are Students with Severe and Multiple Disabilities? How Are Students with Severe and Multiple Disabilities Evaluated? How Can You Establish Effective Teaching Practices? How Can You Encourage Participation?

SAMPLE QUIZ FOR CHAPTER 9

MULTIPLE CHOICE

Circle the correct answer.

1. Key instructional strategies for students with severe and multiple disabilities include all of the following <u>except</u>:
    a. Parental assistance
    b. Partial participation
    c. Cooperative learning
    d. Peer tutoring

2. Which of the following is <u>not</u> mentioned by the authors as a category of characteristics that describes students with multiple and severe disabilities?
    a. Health care needs
    b. Sensory functioning
    c. Adaptive behavior
    d. Functional needs

3. For what percentage of children born with severe or multiple disabilities is there no identifiable cause?
    a. 25%
    b. 40%
    c. 55%
    d. 70%

4. What are the four intensity levels of support for students with multiple and severe disabilities?
    a. Intermittent, limited, extensive, pervasive
    b. Minimal, maintenance, major, intensive
    c. Minimal, limited, profound, extensive
    d. Episodic, transitional, constant, permanent

5. Which assessment method for educational program development uses a "bottom-up" approach that uses sequenced skills checklists?
    a. Behavior states
    b. Ecological model
    c. Developmental model
    d. Environmental model

6. What is the major difference between an ecological approach to curriculum and a life skills approach to curriculum?
    a. Focusing on basic skills that are broken down into discrete steps
    b. Adapting rules to individualize the curriculum
    c. Organizing community collaboration
    d. Completing a comprehensive analysis of the disability and how it can be overcome

7. What is the level of the prompt that occurs when the teacher positions Kasey's hand directly over the correct silverware bin?
    a. Gestural
    b. Full physical
    c. Minimal physical
    d. Partial physical

8. Devon has poor motor skills and cannot handle a broom. He is allowed to use a cordless vacuum cleaner instead. What adaptation has occurred?
    a. Adapting rules
    b. Using materials and devices
    c. Adapting skill sequences
    d. Incorporating personal independence

9. Since the passage of IDEA, where is the largest percentage of students with multiple disabilities now placed?
    a. Regular classroom
    b. Separate class
    c. Residential facility
    d. Homebound

10. Through problem-solving and action research, the Johnson City Schools provide an excellent example of what?
    a. Peer mentoring
    b. Community outreach
    c. Teacher preparation
    d. Inclusion and collaboration

11. When is the Apgar screening test, used by physicians to determine the type and extent of the disability for students with severe and multiple disabilities, usually begun?
    a. At three years of age
    b. Right before birth
    c. Right after birth
    d. Only if the parent makes a request

12. What are two indicators of intellectual functioning in students with multiple and severe disabilities?
    a. Communication and adaptive behavior
    b. Levels of awareness and academic skills
    c. Sensory functioning and literacy
    d. Eye contact and communication

13. To ensure that students with severe and multiple disabilities receive sufficiently intense instruction in the general education classroom, collaboration between general educators and special educators should focus on all of the following <u>except</u> which concept?
    a. Cooperative learning and peer tutoring
    b. Daily pull-out programs
    c. Collaboration among all the staff members, peers, and volunteers
    d. Classroom structure to support diverse learning styles

14. What is the cause of the congenital defects that most commonly lead to severe and multiple disabilities?
    a. Viral infections
    b. Disruptions in the development of the brain and spinal cord
    c. Rubella
    d. Exposure to lead

15. Dr. Feldman is checking a newborn. Which of the following is <u>not</u> included in a normal screening process?
    a. Checking for potential developmental problems
    b. Checking for intellectual aptitude
    c. Checking for observable disabilities
    d. Checking for genetic and metabolic disorders

16. Elizabeth had an Apgar score of 4 at one minute after birth and has now received a score of 0 at five minutes after birth. What can her physician deduce from this information?
    a. She is crying.
    b. She has some flexion.
    c. She is limp and blue.
    d. She is at risk for irregular heartbeat.

17. Seven-year-old Antonio has been declared "untestable" by the school counselor due to severe disabilities. What can be concluded from this event?
    a. Antonio will need to attend a residential or separate school rather than a regular classroom.
    b. Antonio is too severely affected by his disabilities to communicate.
    c. The counselor is probably inexperienced in testing students with severe and multiple disabilities.
    d. A developmental model will be most appropriate for his assessment.

18. A special education teacher at a residential facility, Polly individualizes each of her student's educational programs by focusing on vision, strengths, preferences, and needs. What kind of assessment method is she using?
    a. Behavior states
    b. MAPs
    c. Developmental model
    d. Ecological model

19. Sue has moved from "passivity to participation" and her joy in learning the casual connections between her using speech and the response of the TV/videotape and radio is obvious. What type of technology is she using?
    a. Speech-recognition technology
    b. Assistive technology
    c. Computer technology
    d. Speak technology

20. Which of the following is <u>not</u> one reason why the "Circle of Inclusion" Program is effective?
    a. Value-based commitment to including children with significant disabilities
    b. Collaboration among parents and professionals
    c. Participation of physicians in classrooms
    d. Commitment to child-centered education

SHORT ANSWER

21. What two major characteristics pervade the definitions of multiple and severe disabilities?
    a. ______________________________
    b. ______________________________

22. List four approaches that can be used to assess a student's skills for specific curriculum goals and program development.
    a. ______________________________
    b. ______________________________
    c. ______________________________
    d. ______________________________

23. Identify three problems that occur when using the developmental model of assessment with students who have severe and multiple disabilities.
    a. ______________________________
    b. ______________________________
    c. ______________________________

ESSAY

24. Compare and contrast the benefits to students for the four approaches used to assess a student's skills for specific curriculum goals and program development: developmental model, the ecological model, the behavior states, and Making Action Plans (MAPs).
25. Describe the factors that make the Circle of Inclusion Program effective. Compare these factors with those of other program options described in this chapter.

CHAPTER 10: AUTISM

CHAPTER OVERVIEW

Autism, the disability that affects verbal and nonverbal communication and social interaction, was not recognized as a separate IDEA disability until 1991. This chapter examines how our understanding of autism has changed in many areas. It traces how autism's definition has emerged and the typical characteristics, causes, and prevalence rates associated with people with this disability. Various evaluation procedures are explored as well as successful curriculum and methods. Special attention is given to the methods of positive behavioral support and social stories. Issues surrounding successful inclusion and collaboration on behalf of students with autism are also discussed, with several important strategies highlighted. Key factors of successful program options for students with autism are also presented.

This chapter examines autism through the life of thirteen-year-old Jeremy Jones. Jeremy's middle school teachers, together with a team of researchers at the University of Kansas, have been working with Jeremy to help him develop the skills needed to ensure positive educational experiences in a safe, inclusive environment. With the help of his family and school, he is learning how to manage his own behavior through positive behavior support and student-specific assistance. His future looks bright because of the collaborative support system that has been established for him.

CHAPTER AT-A-GLANCE

Chapter Outline	Instructional Goals	Key Concepts
WHO ARE STUDENTS WITH AUTISM?		
Defining Autism	• Recognize the diverse factors defining autism	• Autism is a developmental disability significantly affecting verbal and nonverbal communication and social interaction.
Describing the Characteristics • Language Development • Social Interaction • Repetitive Behavior • Impeding Behavior • Need for Environmental Predictability • Sensory and Movement Disorders • Intellectual Functioning	• Identify the key characteristics of autism • Explain the role of facilitative communication	• The seven main characteristics of autism are listed in the first column. • Two language impairments associated with autism are delayed language and echolalia. • Facilitative communication is a training method that involves supporting a person who does not speak or has highly repetitive speech to use a facilitator and keyboard to communicate. • People with autism often have fewer and weaker social skills. • Stereotypical behaviors (inappropriate and repetitive acts are displayed) are typical. • Behavioral challenges include self-injurious behavior, aggression, tantrums, and property destruction. • Predictability and structure are important sources of security. • Sensory disorders often result in under- or over- responsiveness to sensory stimuli. • The majority of people with autism function in the IQ range of mental retardation.

Identifying the Causes of Autism • Historical Perspective on Causes • Biomedical Causes	• Trace the changes in explanations for causes of autism • Explain biomedical causes	• Although parents have historically been seen as the cause of their child's autism, this viewpoint is totally unwarranted. • Autism is biologically caused, but the specific biological trigger is unknown at this time.
Identifying the Prevalence of Autism	• Recognize prevalence rates for people with autism	• The prevalence of autism is approximately 1 person per 1,000.
HOW ARE STUDENTS WITH AUTISM EVALUATED?		
Determining the Presence of Autism	• Explain how major assessment tools are used to determine the presence of autism	• The Autism Diagnostic Interview—Revised is a diagnostic tool that is used to detect the presence of autism.
Determining the Nature and Extent of Special Education and Related Services	• Recognize the possibilities for developing a functional assessment with tailored intervention	• A functional assessment identifies specific relationships between environmental events and a student's problem behavior and tailors intervention accordingly.
HOW CAN YOU ESTABLISH EFFECTIVE TEACHING PACTICES?		
Set Curricular Goals	• Differentiate among domains of curricular options for students with autism	• The typical curriculum domains include life skills for integrated community living, vocational preparation, and functional academics.
Implement Instruction	• Evaluate different methods that are effective for varied student needs	• Positive behavioral support seeks to create a personally tailored responsive environment. • Social stories describe social situations in terms of important social cues and appropriate responses to those cues.
Early Childhood Years	• Describe characteristics of effective childhood programs for students with autism	• Individualized Support Project combines positive behavioral support with a family center plan.
Elementary Years	• Describe characteristics of effective elementary programs for students with autism	• TEACCH model uses a holistic view to provide support from preschool to adulthood that is tailored to specific needs.
Middle and Secondary Years	• Describe characteristics of effective programs for middle and secondary students with autism	• Middle school utilizes a schoolwide model of positive behavioral supports to address individual needs.
Transitional and Postsecondary Years	• Describe characteristics of effective program options for adults with autism	• Community Services for Autistic Adults and Children (CSAAC) provides state-of-the-art vocational training and community co-worker support.

HOW CAN YOU ENCOURAGE PARTICIPATION?		
Practice Inclusion	• Examine how inclusion is viewed for students with autism	• There are many different viewpoints on the appropriateness of inclusion for students with autism.
Foster Collaboration • Professional-to-Professional Collaboration • Family and Professional Collaboration • School, Student, Family, and Community Collaboration	• Explore ways to collaborate on behalf of students with autism	• Collaboration with professionals, families, students, and communities can significantly increase successful inclusion for individuals with autism.

PROJECT OPTIONS

1. Based on the characteristics of as many successful program models for students with autism that you can find, create the ideal program for a student with autism. Describe this program at each of the four levels: early childhood, elementary, secondary, and postsecondary years.
2. Investigate how your school system educates students with autism. Describe and then evaluate how this schooling lines up with the six values guiding special education.
3. Interview a family with a member who has autism. Get to know each member of the family and ask each to help you draw up a plan for this student that will emphasize the place of the six values guiding special education.

KEY TERMS

Asperger's syndrome

Echolalia

Facilitated communication

Obsessions

Pervasive developmental disorder

Positive behavioral support

Savant syndrome

Social stories

Stereotypical behaviors

Theory of mind

Tics

GUIDED REVIEW

Who Are People with Autism?

We experience things holistically. The sight, sound, smell, feel, and emotional tone of a situation hits us all at once. It's hard to filter anything out. Sometimes one sensation seems to trigger all our senses, making it difficult to tell where the real signal came from. We may be alert to information others miss, but the task of processing and dealing with it can be overwhelming.

We are visual learners with good memories. We tend to notice and remember visual details. Often this is very useful, but we may need help to separate what's important from what is not. While others see larger patterns emerge from details, for us these are like hidden pictures that *stay* hidden. The unseen future is difficult to grasp.

We are straightforward and honest. We expect people's words and behavior to mean exactly what they seem, and not to have multiple or covert meanings. The language of emotions can prove especially tricky.

We have specialized interests. We avidly pursue and thoroughly enjoy what appeals to *us*, not just the latest style or fad.

We prefer routines. Sudden changes are too unnerving. You might say we are traditionalists.

Our friends are very important to us. Being a friend takes a lot of effort and energy. Some people think we don't care about having a social life, but we do.

From *Look Again: An Inside View of Autism/PDD* by The Autism National Committee.

Who Are Students with Autism?

1. When autism was first identified, why was this condition called early infantile autism? (*See* Defining Autism)

   ____

2. Autism is a severe form of a broader group of disorders referred to as ______________________ ______________________ ______________________. (*See* Defining Autism)

3. Name and describe two common forms of language impairments experienced by students with autism. (*See* Describing the Characteristics; Language Development)

   a. ____

   b. ____

4. Complete the following chart to demonstrate your knowledge of the major characteristics of autism. (*See* Describing the Characteristics)

Area Affected	***Identifying Characteristics***	***Appropriate Responses to Students with These Characteristics***
a. Language development		
b. Social interaction		
c. Stereotypical behavior		
d. Behavioral challenges		
e. Need for environmental predictability		
f. Sensory and movement disorders		
g. Intellectual functioning		

5. When is language intervention most successful for students with autism? (*See* Describing the Characteristics; Language Development)

____

6. Facilitated communication is a training method that involves using a human facilitator and keyboard to communicate. Match the element of facilitated communication with its identifying characteristics. (*See* Describing the Characteristics; Language Development)

1. Physical support	a. _____ Provides emotional support or encouragement, knowing the person's thinking and literacy will reveal themselves over time
2. Initial training/ introduction	b. _____ Reminds student to keep eyes on the communication aid, use index finger for pointing, reduce extraneous actions, and type what he or she intends to communicate
3. Maintaining focus	c. _____ Helps student isolate index finger and stabilize student's hand or arm during typing
4. Avoiding competence testing	d. _____Works on fading physical support as student becomes more independent
5. Generalization	e. _____ Provides encouragement and repeated attempts to generalize to more facilitators
6. Fading	f. ______Provides initial activities with fairly predictable answers and encourages progress to open-ended conversation

7. Define *echolalia* and then tell why children and youth with autism may use echolalia. (*See* Describing the Characteristics; Language Development)

____

____

8. List the four categories of behavioral challenges encountered by students with autism and the identifying characteristics for each one. (*See* Describing the Characteristics; Impeding Behavior)
   a. ____________________ ______________________________
   b. ____________________ ______________________________
   c. ____________________ ______________________________
   d. ____________________ ______________________________

What Is It Like to Have Autism?

Imagine that you enter your classroom and your teacher tells you that you will have only three things to do to get along well in your new room: sit still in your seat, follow simple directions, and be reasonably quiet. It sounds simple, but in a simulation experience designed by Susan Moreno, a parent of a child with autism, these three tasks become very difficult. Participants are in a room where all lights are turned out except a strobe light. A radio is blaring white noise (static). The teacher wears a cotton glove while shaking hands to greet students and varies his voice pitch and volume while speaking. He stands uncomfortably close to each student while conversing. When a student responds by pulling away or making noise, the teacher pats her face with a dampened luffa sponge and screams, "It's all right! Don't be so nervous!"

Students with autism, according to current theory, are overstimulated or understimulated by information they receive through their senses. Thus, a gentle touch could be painful for these students. Words spoken softly may seem loud or not be heard at all. As you continue this review, think about the challenges these students are facing and how you might try to make their school environment more conducive to learning.

9. Name and describe two variations of intellectual function associated with students with autism. (*See* Describing the Characteristics; Intellectual Functioning)
   a. ______________________________________
   b. ______________________________________

10. How has the perception of the causes of autism changed over time? (*See* Identifying the Causes of Autism; Historical Perspective on Causes)

____

____

11. If a school district has 40,000 students, how many are likely to have autism? __________ How many of those students with autism would be male? ___________ (*See* Identifying the Prevalence of Autism)

How Are Students with Autism Evaluated?

12. What four areas are most frequently assessed to determine eligibility for the diagnosis of autism? (*See* How Are Students with Autism Evaluated?; Determining the Presence of Autism)
   a. ______________________________
   b. ______________________________
   c. ______________________________
   d. ______________________________

13. What is the name for one of the most frequently used diagnostic scales? How many areas of behavioral observations does it require? (*See* How Are Students with Autism Evaluated?; Determining the Presence of Autism)
   a. Name: ______________________________
   b. Number of areas: ______________

14. One kind of ecological assessment is functional assessment. Identify the five steps for conducting a functional assessment. (*See* How Are Students with Autism Evaluated?; Determining the Nature and Extent of Special Education and Related Services)
    a. ______________________________
    b. ______________________________
    c. ______________________________
    d. ______________________________
    e. ______________________________

15. List examples of circumstances that influence problem behaviors associated with autism. Then propose modifications for intervention. (*See* How Are Students with Autism Evaluated?; Determining the Nature and Extent of Special Education and Related Services)

Factors	***Circumstances***	***Proposed Modifications***
Physiological factors		
Classroom environment		
Curriculum and instruction		

How Can You Establish Effective Teaching Practices?

16. What is the key to appropriate, beneficial education for students with autism? (*See* How Can You Establish Effective Teaching Practices?; Set Curricular Goals)

    ____

17. Compare and contrast how curriculum options differ for students who function at higher cognitive levels from those who have mental retardation. Give specific examples appropriate to each one. (*See* How Can You Establish Effective Teaching Practices?; Set Curricular Goals)

Curriculum for Students at Higher Cognitive Levels	***Curriculum for Students Who Have Mental Retardation***

18. What three areas are typically included in a curriculum for students with autism who also have mental retardation? (*See* How Can You Establish Effective Teaching Practices?; Set Curricular Goals)
    a. ______________________________
    b. ______________________________
    c. ______________________________

Social Skills for Social Ills

Reflections of a parent of a young person with Asperger's syndrome provide an introduction to this article. The authors then share some educational principles and strategies that they have found to be effective with adolescents with Asperger's syndrome. An overview of the syndrome, challenges faced, and strengths exhibited by these students are covered as well as how to build specific social skills and positive outcomes. To read more, see *Teaching Exceptional Children, November/December 1999, 32*(2), pp. 56–61.

19. Identify and briefly describe two frequently used instructional methods for students with autism. (*See* How Can You Establish Effective Teaching Practices?; Implement Instruction)
    a. ____
    ____
    b. ____
    ____

20. Describe how social stories can decrease aggressive behavior and help students with autism learn how to handle specific social situations. (*See* How Can You Establish Effective Teaching Practices?; Implement Instruction)
    ____
    ____

21. Compare and contrast the characteristics, goals, and outcomes of the two programs below. (*See* Observe Programs in Practice)

	CSAAC (Rockville, MD)	***Individualized Support Project***
Characteristics		
Goals		
Outcomes		

22. Identify the five characteristics of the TEACCH model for elementary students with autism. (*See* Observe Programs in Practice)
    a. ____
    b. ____
    c. ____
    d. ____
    e. ____

23. The success of individuals involved with Community Services for Autistic Adults and Children can be traced to several key factors. Identify at least three factors leading to the success of individuals with autism. (*See* Observe Programs in Practice; Transitional and Postsecondary Years)
    a. ______________________________
    b. ______________________________
    c. ______________________________

> "When people with autism succeed, it's not because some professor's theory worked to a 't', but because real-life people with real-life common sense did what they had to do with what they got. And no theory can replace that."
>
> KL, a person with autism

How Can You Encourage Participation?

24. What percentage of students with autism are educated in separate environments? (*See* How Can You Encourage Participation?; Practice Inclusion) ______________ percent

25. What percentage of students with autism receive the majority of their education in a general education classroom? (*See* How Can You Encourage Participation?; Practice Inclusion) ________________ percent

26. Identify at least four characteristics of successful inclusion programs for students with autism. (*See* How Can You Encourage Participation?; Practice Inclusion)
    a. ______________________________
    b. ______________________________
    c. ______________________________
    d. ______________________________

27. Describe at least three things each different collaborator can do to encourage the success of students with autism in a school inclusion model. (*See* How Can You Encourage Participation?; Foster Collaboration)

Collaborator	*Contributions to Encourage Student Success*
Professional collaborators	1. 2. 3.
Family collaborators	1. 2. 3.
Student and community collaborators	1. 2. 3.

Mother Seeks Medical and Educational Assistance for Son

The mother of Umair Choudhry, a ten-year-old boy with autism, sought medical treatment for her son in the U.S. last year. Farah Choudhry left her husband, country, and life in Pakistan to live in a modest two-bedroom apartment in Chicago so her son could benefit from classes with a 1:1 student-teacher ratio at the New Horizon Center. She feared that in Karachi, Pakistan, as Umair got older, he would be taken to a *pagal khana* (mad house) where he would spend his days in a cage.

Umair has no understanding of the legal issues surrounding his situation, but he knows to wait for the bus at 7:40 a.m. On Saturdays he picks up his lunchbox and backpack, ready to go out the door. Farah says, "He can't talk, but I know he's asking, 'Why can't I go to school?'"

See *Time*, October 16, 2000, pp. 90–92.

APPLICATION EXERCISES FOR CHAPTER 10

Application Exercise 10a. Identifying Characteristics of Autism

Identify which characteristic of autism is in focus for the following students:

a. Language development	1. ______ Bob frequently rocks back and forth, attempting to communicate his boredom with certain situations.
b. Social interaction	2. ______ Malik experiences great anxiety whenever his expected television shows are not on.
c. Stereotypical behavior	3. ______ Shan is in the majority of students with autism, in that her IQ registers below 50.
d. Behavioral challenges	4. ______ Julian screams whenever he has to wear formal clothes to church because they feel scratchy and different.
e. Need for environmental predictability	5. ______ Marga's family saw significant changes in her communication with the use of facilitated communication.
f. Sensory and movement disorders	6. ______ Jimmy has a pattern of not making eye contact with others and chooses to spend large amounts of time alone.
g. Intellectual functioning	7. ______ Eduardo demonstrates aggressive behavior that, without positive behavioral support, is potentially harmful to others.

Application Exercise 10b. Functional Assessment: Matching Situation and Intervention

Identify which intervention is most suited to the situation described.

a. Intersperse an easy activity with the more difficult activity	1. ______ Jemima demands her own way during reading circle and will kick and bite to sit by the teacher.
b. Make sure she eats breakfast and/or has an early snack.	2. ______ Shanti cries when she is asked to complete a fairly lengthy assignment.
c. Give her a specific place to sit all her own and you, the teacher, change places each time.	3. ______ Alvara is off task for most of the science class assignment.
d. Ask her to monitor her own corrections or give her an easier assignment.	4. ______ Emily slaps her arm and sometimes others around 10:30 every day because she is hungry.
e. Give her clear instructions about a select portion of the work she is to complete.	5. ______ Samantha argues with the teacher about correcting her mistakes and then refuses to make corrections on daily worksheets.

Application Exercise 10c. Social Stories to Convey Conceptual Understanding

Based upon the major questions addressed in this chapter, summarize the major concepts concerning autism. For each major chapter question, create a social story to explain the main concepts in that section.

Major Questions: Who Are Students with Autism? How Are Students with Autism Evaluated? How Can You Establish Effective Teaching Practices? How Can You Encourage Participation?

SAMPLE QUIZ FOR CHAPTER 10

MULTIPLE CHOICE

Circle the correct answer.

1. Autism is a severe form of what broader group of disorders?
   a. Pervasive Developmental Disorders
   b. Rett's Disorder
   c. Childhood Disintegrative Disorder
   d. Pervasive Developmental Syndrome

2. A. J. participates in a general education fourth-grade classroom for part of the day. Why do his mother and teachers feel this is not an ideal situation?
   a. He doesn't like to be with other students with disabilities.
   b. He thinks the other fourth graders are too rough on the playground.
   c. The classroom is not predictable enough for him to feel comfortable.
   d. He does not have enough opportunities to develop his potential.

3. Sarah, age seven, has autism. Which of the following is most probably true of her?
   a. She runs to her mother for a hug and bandage when she skins her knee.
   b. She does not like to spend time alone.
   c. She always takes her teddy bear with her whenever she leaves the house.
   d. She greets strangers without prompting but keeps shaking their hand too long.

4. Jim is a five-year-old boy with autism who is very sensitive to sensory stimuli. How can his mother best help Jim when she takes him grocery shopping?
   a. Calmly describe everything he sees.
   b. Let him know in advance that a shopping trip will occur.
   c. Provide him with headphones and a favorite cassette.
   d. Let him choose a favorite treat to distract him.

5. Your friend Kristen, who is talented both in athletics and in the fine arts, is thinking about working with children with autism, but she does not want to be a classroom teacher. What might be another appropriate career option you might suggest to her?
   a. Music therapist
   b. Lovaas therapist
   c. CSAAC staff worker
   d. Bettelheim Project employee

6. Which of the following most commonly provides security for many individuals with autism?
   a. Cattle squeeze chutes
   b. Security blankets
   c. Rigid routines and patterns
   d. Loving support of peers

7. Which of the following is <u>not</u> a major benefit derived from utilizing social stories with students with autism?
   a. They help them focus on relevant social cues.
   b. They help them achieve better scores on tests and evaluations.
   c. They help them learn new routines and rules.
   d. They help them expand social skills.

8. Rocking back and forth and hand flapping are examples of what behavioral challenge?

   a. Stereotypical behavior
   b. Aggression
   c. Tantrums
   d. Self-injury

9. Laurie, a ten-year-old with autism, has just finished the school year. Her family is packing for a vacation to Disney World. What is Laurie most likely to exhibit?

   a. Anxiety
   b. Sensory disorders
   c. Nonchalance
   d. Happiness

10. What is savant syndrome?

    a. An individual with autism who displays extraordinary ability in one area
    b. An individual with autism who has an IQ above 90
    c. An individual with autism who has Asperger's disorder
    d. An individual with autism who has higher-functioning autistic disorder

11. Using functional assessment to pinpoint the reasons for problem behavior is an example of which procedure?

    a. Positive behavioral support
    b. Facilitated communication
    c. CARS
    d. Language Intervention Program

12. The following are good suggestions for conversing with people who are nonverbal or have delayed language, <u>except</u> which one?

    a. Be spontaneous
    b. Use a monotone voice
    c. Develop a special handshake
    d. Use familiar phrases

13. Which of the following is <u>not</u> a typical characteristic of autism?

    a. Echolalia
    b. Abnormal physical appearance
    c. Delayed language
    d. Behavioral challenges

14. Stereotypical behaviors are used by persons with autism to accomplish all of the following <u>except</u>:

    a. To communicate boredom
    b. To communicate agitation
    c. To regulate level of awareness
    d. To bother the teacher

15. For what is Leo Kanner well known?

    a. He first identified autism.
    b. He founded the TEACCH model.
    c. He proposed IDEA.
    d. He developed facilitated communication.

16. What type of support has been used at the Tiffany Park Elementary School in Seattle to promote model elementary school practices that help students with autism in the school and outside of the school setting?

    a. Collaborative support
    b. Parent and teacher support
    c. Positive behavioral support
    d. Community support

17. What did researchers at the University of Kansas develop to help a young boy with autism learn how to wash his hands?

    a. An audiotape
    b. A demonstration of the technique
    c. A social story and a movie
    d. A best practices display

18. What type of assessment of students with autism leads to an individually tailored intervention plan aimed at helping them function as successfully as possible?

    a. Formal assessment
    b. Informal assessment
    c. Portfolio assessment
    d. Functional assessment

19. Which of the following would not be part of a nondiscriminatory evaluation for a student with autism?

    a. Physical examination
    b. Individualized intelligence test
    c. Anecdotal records
    d. Classroom grades

20. What is higher-functioning autistic disorder?

    a. Condition in which individuals with autism have an IQ above 70
    b. Another name for savant syndrome
    c. Condition in which individuals with autism show no movement disorders
    d. Another name for delayed neuromotor communication

SHORT ANSWER

21. Name two common language impairments in students with autism.

    a. ______________________ b. ______________________

22. What is a neuromotor impairment? ______________________

    ____

23. What is CARS and how is it used? ______________________

    ____

ESSAY

24. Discuss principles of positive behavioral support.
25. How has IDEA helped students with autism?

CHAPTER 11: OTHER HEALTH IMPAIRMENTS

CHAPTER OVERVIEW

The category of other health impairments includes disabilities with many diverse characteristics that can be either easy or difficult to identify. The factors common to all health impairments include limitations in strength, vitality, or alertness. Students served under IDEA are those whose educational needs have been adversely affected by the condition. This chapter investigates the multifaceted characteristics, causes, and prevalence of six specific health impairments. Different evaluation processes that can be used for determining the presence of health impairments and the nature and extent of special education needed are discussed. Use of service dogs, handling insensitivity, and coping with grief are topics covered in this chapter that apply to other exceptionalities as well. The place of inclusion and collaboration for students with a chronic illness in the classroom is described, followed by a discussion of various program options currently available in schools and communities today.

The life of Jacob Empey helps demonstrate and clarify issues revolving around students with other health impairments. Jacob has epilepsy. His condition is classified as "other health impairment" under IDEA because his alertness, vitality, and strength are adversely affected. Jacob frequently experiences generalized tonic-clonic and absence seizures at school. His family, teachers, paraprofessionals, and peers work closely to provide Jacob with an inclusionary school environment that is accommodated to meet his needs.

CHAPTER AT-A-GLANCE

Chapter Outline	Instructional Goals	Key Concepts
WHO ARE STUDENTS WITH OTHER HEALTH IMPAIRMENTS?		
Defining Other Health Impairments	• Clarify distinctions in defining health impairments	• The conditions and definitions in this category vary widely in symptoms and prognosis.
Describing the Characteristics • Human Immunodeficiency Virus • Asthma • Cancer • Diabetes • Epilepsy	• Describe key characteristics of other health impairments • Recognize unifying criteria for inclusion as a health impairment	• Students with health impairments have limitations in strength, vitality, or alertness. The condition can be chronic or acute. • To be served under IDEA, educational needs must be adversely affected by the condition. • The conditions vary widely and are condition-specific, but their unifying criteria are limits in strength, vitality, and/or alertness.
Identifying the Causes of Other Health Impairments • Infections • Genetic Factors • Environmental Influences	• Explain causes of other health impairments	• Health impairments can be caused by infections, genetic factors, and environmental factors, including prenatal teratogens and postnatal influences.
Identifying the Prevalence of Other Health Impairments	• Identify prevalence figures for other health impairments and where these students are served	• 0.31% of school-age (6–21 year-olds) children are served • 315% increase between 1987 and 1988, largely resulting from the inclusion of students with AD/HD.
HOW ARE STUDENTS WITH OTHER HEALTH IMPAIRMENTS EVALUATED?		
Determining the Presence of Other Health Impairments	• Recognize who determines the presence of other health impairments	• A physician usually makes a diagnosis.
Determining the Nature and Extent of Special Education and Related Services	• Identify who decides the nature and extent of special education and how it is decided.	• School personnel have to decide if the student can be served under IDEA evaluation measures.

HOW CAN YOU ESTABLISH EFFECTIVE TEACHING STRATEGIES?		
Set Curricular Goals	• Explain how curriculum needs are met for students with other health impairments	• Curricular needs vary depending on the type and/or severity of the condition, but are similar to those for students without disabilities.
Implement Instruction	• Evaluate effective methods for students with other health impairments	• Standard methods work for students with other health impairments, though the teacher should make accommodations as necessary. • When a student is dying, teachers should provide honesty and support to the students, family, and classmates. • Accommodations should be made to prevent the student from lagging behind academically because of absence due to illness.
Early Childhood Years	• Describe characteristics of effective childhood programs	• Kids On The Block, Inc., utilizes puppet theater to share stories of children with health impairments.
Elementary Years	• Describe characteristics of effective elementary programs	• Walt Disney Memorial Cancer Institute prepares children for school reentry while still attending home/hospital school.
Middle and Secondary Years	• Describe characteristics of effective programs for middle and secondary students	• Meeting the Challenge was developed to improve five social skills of adolescents with health impairments: self-awareness, social imitation and conversational skills, assertion or direct communication, empathy or active listening, and conflict resolution and problem solving.
Transitional and Postsecondary Years	• Describe characteristics of effective program options for adults with other health impairments.	• HIV University provides emotional support and eliminates barriers to participation for students with other health impairments.
HOW CAN YOU ENCOURAGE PARTICIPATION?		
Practice Inclusion	• Summarize importance of inclusion for students with other health impairments	• The least restrictive environment for most students with other health impairments is the general education classroom. • Accommodating the setting and providing proper support services are important as well as considering the possibility of home-bound teaching.
Foster Collaboration • Professional-to-Professional Collaboration • Family and Professional Collaboration • Collaboration with Peers	• Explore how collaboration benefits students with other health impairments	• Close communication among all collaborators promotes learning and wholeness for students with other health impairments.

PROJECT OPTIONS

1. Select one of the health impairments discussed in this chapter and research options in your community that specifically work with and help people with this impairment. Prepare a descriptive brochure highlighting your findings.
2. Visit a local nursing home and interview three people older than seventy five about people they have known with health impairments (which might include the people you're interviewing). Ask each person to describe the difficulties these people overcame and the positive contributions they made to their families, schools, friends, and communities. Then compare and contrast findings from the three people you interviewed.
3. Write a case study and design an activity around it that demonstrates the importance of strength, vitality, and alertness to all of life and how people with health impairments are affected by their absence. Show how these three characteristics are tied to the six values guiding special education.

KEY TERMS

Absence seizure

Acquired Immune Deficiency Syndrome (AIDS)

Acute condition

Asymptomatic or latency stage

Chronic condition

Focal sensory seizures

Generalized seizures

Health care plan

Hyperglycemia or ketoacidosis

Hypoglycemia

Myclonic seizures

Opportunistic infections

Other health impairments

Partial seizures

Symptomatic stage

Temporal lobe or psychomotor seizure

Tonic-clonic or grand mal seizure

GUIDED REVIEW

Undiagnosed with Myoclonic Seizures

H. D. and J. D. Merrick have been looking for a diagnosis for their son since he was six months old. He has severe hypotonia, global developmental delays, and myoclonic seizures during sleep. Adam, their four-and-a-half-year-old, was also having the same seizures. At first they thought the seizures were voluntary movements or perhaps responses to gas. After some testing, he was also diagnosed with myoclonic seizures. A support network was then formed of professionals, parents, friends, and family who continue to see the family through the triumphs and setbacks. To read more, see *Exceptional Parent*, November, 1998, p. 12.

Who Are Students with Other Health Impairments?

1. How does IDEA define other health impairments? (*See* Defining Other Health Impairments)

   ____

   ____

   ____

2. What three limitations are central to the other health impairments category? (*See* Defining Other Health Impairments)
   a. ______________________________
   b. ______________________________
   c. ______________________________

3. The IDEA definition emphasizes that conditions can be chronic or acute. Explain the differences between these two conditions. (*See* Defining Other Health Impairments)
   Chronic condition: ______________________________
   Acute condition: ______________________________

Human Immunodeficiency Virus

4. HIV gradually infects and destroys important cells in the ______________ system. T4 ______________ cells are a major target of HIV. (*See* Describing the Characteristics; Human Immunodeficiency Virus; What Is HIV?)

5. People with HIV are susceptible to ____________________ infections that generally do not affect otherwise healthy people. (*See* Describing the Characteristics; Human Immunodeficiency Virus; What Is HIV?)

6. Name and describe the stages of HIV. (*See* Describing the Characteristics; Human Immunodeficiency Virus; What Is HIV?)

Stage	*Symptoms*

A New Face

"This is the new face of AIDS," comments correspondent Leslie Stahl. Magic Johnson, after living with HIV for years, is robust, healthy, and vigorous. In 1998, the virus was virtually undetectable in his bloodstream. Hoping that his exercise regime and positive attitude were the causes of his progress, Magic was inconsistent with his medication for a time. The result? The virus made a comeback. Realizing his need to continue taking his medication cocktail, Magic now has the energy and health to continue his work improving the quality of life for people in poor neighborhoods. He comments, "I'm not cured, I'm healed."

See "60 Minutes" transcript, May 10, 1998.

7. A person has AIDS when he or she is in the ______________________________ stage. The CDC identifies AIDS as when a person has a T4 cell count less than _____________ and has developed one or more specified ___________________________ infections. (*See* Describing the Characteristics; Human Immunodeficiency Virus; What Is HIV)

8. Describe the two issues involved with HIV in the classroom. (*See* Describing the Characteristics of Other Health Impairments; Human Immunodeficiency Virus; HIV and the Classroom)
   a. Transmission and spread of HIV in schools:

   ____

   ____

   b. How the condition can affect learning and behavior of students with HIV:

   ____

   ____

Asthma

9. How often does asthma begin before age three? ______________________________ What is the ratio of boys to girls with asthma?________________________________ (*See* Describing the Characteristics; Asthma; What Is Asthma?)

10. List the three primary features of asthma. (*See* Describing the Characteristics; Asthma; What Is Asthma?)
    a. ____
    b. ____
    c. ____

11. Describe the circumstances when medical help should be sought for students with asthma. (*See* Describing the Characteristics; Asthma; What Is Asthma?)

    ____

    ____

    ____

12. Identify four preventions and treatments that you as a teacher need to know to help students with asthma. (*See* Describing the Characteristics; Asthma; What Is Asthma?)
    a. ____
    b. ____
    c. ____
    d. ____

Cancer

13. Cancer is a condition that causes ____. In 1993, approximately _____________children and adolescents died from cancer, with ____________ of those from leukemia. Approximately __________ percent of all children survive cancer today. (*See* Describing the Characteristics; Cancer; What Is Cancer?)

14. Why should all children reentering school after cancer have an IEP completed? (*See* Describing the Characteristics; Cancer; Cancer and the Classroom)

____

____

The Jester Has Lost His Jingle

Not long after his twenty-third birthday and soon after graduating from Yale with honors in art and English, David Saltzman died from Hodgkin's Disease. Before his death, he wanted to leave a legacy. Combining his love for words and art, David wrote and illustrated a children's book titled *The Jester Has Lost His Jingle* (call 800-9-JESTER or contact your local bookseller to order). In the story, the Jester looks for someone who can still laugh, despite the difficulties of life. He finds the laughter from a little girl with cancer. You can read more about David and his book at www.chnms.com/jester/index.html.

David wrote, "The best we can do is live life, enjoy it and know it is meant to be enjoyed—know how important and special every time . . . moment . . . person is."

Diabetes

15. Diabetes results when the ____________________ stops producing or produces too little of the hormone ________________. Diabetes (Type I) begins before age ____________, and onset is most common in young people between _________ and _________. (*See* Describing the Characteristics; Diabetes; What Is Diabetes?)

16. Describe the two serious medical conditions that can occur in the classroom if the student's diabetes is not under good control. (*See* Describing the Characteristics; Diabetes; Diabetes and the Classroom)

Name of Condition	***Medical Description and Symptoms***	***Treatment***
Hyperglycemia/ Ketoacidosis		
Hypoglycemia		

Epilepsy

17. How can students usually reduce the number of seizures? (*See* Describing the Characteristics; Epilepsy; Epilepsy and the Classroom)
    a. ____
    b. ____

18. Students sometimes experience a(n) ________________ that lets them know that they are about to have a seizure. After a seizure, a student often needs to __________________. (*See* Describing the Characteristics; Epilepsy; Epilepsy and the Classroom)

19. Fill in the information about the types and subtypes of seizures associated with epilepsy (*See* Describing the Characteristics; Epilepsy; What Is Epilepsy?)

Types	*Characteristics*	*Subtypes*	*Characteristics of Subtypes*
Generalized seizures		a. b.	a. b.
Partial seizures		a. b. c.	a. b. c.

Identifying the Causes of Other Health Impairments

20. Three causes of other health impairments include ______________________________, ______________________________, and ______________________________. (*See* Identifying the Causes of Other Health Impairments)

21. Approximately _______ percent of students have health impairments, though only _______ percent are served under IDEA. (*See* Identifying the Prevalence of Other Health Impairments)

How Are Students with Other Health Impairments Evaluated?

22. Perhaps the most important part of the diagnostic procedure is to__________________ ______________________________. Following this, the student should receive an IEP if ____. An attached ______________________________ allows coordination and dissemination of essential medical information among family and medical and school staffs. (*See* How Are Students with Other Health Impairments Evaluated?; Determining the Presence of Other Health Impairments)

How Can You Establish Effective Teaching Strategies?

23. Teachers can modify curriculum for students who must be absent often by asking what three questions? (*See* How Can You Establish Effective Teaching Strategies?; Accommodating Curriculum)
    a. ____
    b. ____
    c. ____

What's So Funny?

How do you handle disability humor? Where do you draw the line between finding a joke amusing and being appalled by it? Robin Smith, who uses a wheelchair because of her disability, asks these questions in her article "Offensive Humor: Can I Handle It?" (*Tuesday's Child Magazine*, March/April 1998, pp. 30–31). Robin suggests asking yourself: "Does this joke laugh at or with? Is there a cost? Is it exploitative? Who benefits?" She also discusses ways to confront inappropriate jokes. We highly recommend that you read this article.

24. Describe three important methods associated with helping students with other health impairments discussed in this chapter. Describe classroom benefits for each method. (*See* How Can You Establish Effective Teaching Strategies?; Implement Instruction)

Method	*Key Characteristics*	*Classroom Benefits*
Including service dogs		
Handling insensitive comments and teasing		
Understanding the grief process		

25. When a student is dying, teachers need to develop support systems for whom? (*See* How Can You Establish Effective Teaching Practices?; Grief in the Classroom)

a. ____________________ c. ____________________

b. ____________________ d. ____________________

26. Describe key characteristics of successful program options available for individuals with health impairments at each of the four life-span stages described in the textbook. (*See* Observe Programs in Practice)

Life-Span Stage	***Key Characteristics***
Early Childhood Years	
Elementary Years	
Middle and Secondary Years	
Transitional and Postsecondary Years	

How Can You Encourage Participation?

Ending the Isolation

What would you do if your children had a rare disorder and research was limited because of the unavailability of people with the condition? Patrick and Sharon Terry, whose two children have pseudoxanthoma elasticum, decided to be proactive. They formed an international PXE registry, linked together by the Internet. Thanks to their efforts, medical researchers now have ready access to blood samples and people willing to participate in studies. Recently, the gene that causes PXE was identified. Moreover, people with the condition no longer feel isolated; they support each other through an e-mail forum. Their informal dialog is also providing new insights into the condition.

27. Why are inclusion and collaboration inseparable issues for students with health impairments? (*See* How Can You Encourage Participation?; Practice Inclusion)

____

____

28. What are the three primary educational placements for students with other health impairments? List them from greatest to least placements. (*See* How Can You Encourage Participation?; Practice Inclusion)
   a. ____
   b. ____
   c. ____

29. Identify key collaborators and the contribution they can make when collaborating on behalf of students with other health impairments. (*See* How Can You Encourage Participation?; Foster Collaboration)

Collaborator	***Contributions***

The Poison Within

About 900,000 children in the United States have high levels of lead in their blood, according to the Centers for Disease Control. One family thought they had found the perfect place to live, but their son, Owen, had a test that revealed a high blood lead level (BLL). After doing what they could to reduce his exposure, another test revealed an even higher blood lead level. The long process of reducing their son's exposure to lead involved even relocating the family for a period of time. Now they continue to watch as he grows older and wonder: Were his outbursts, terrible tantrums, and unbearable stubbornness due to the lead that was poisoning his system? If you would like information on signs of lead poisoning, how to test for lead, and how to protect children and families, read more in *Parenting*, March 2000, p. 129–136.

APPLICATION EXERCISES FOR CHAPTER 11

Application Exercise 11a. Identifying Conditions and Symptoms of Health Impairments

Try to match the physical symptoms experienced with the associated health impairment.

a. Stage 2 of HIV	1. _______ Khaldoun often feels dizzy, sweaty, and shaky when he forgets to take his medicine. Sometimes he has blurred vision and headaches, too.
b. Prenatal substance exposure	2. ________ Josephina's treatment has many side effects, and may even lower her white cell count, but the survival rate is 72 percent.
c. Hypoglycemia	3. ________ Jamie's tiredness is accompanied by frequent fevers. Just recently her glands have been swelling and she has had night sweats.
d. Asthma	4. ________ Maria has a low tolerance for change, cannot read social cues, and has not developed good friends. She also experiences poor ability to pay attention and concentrate.
e. Temporal lobe or psychomotor seizure	5. ________ Joan picks at her clothes and repeats a sentence several times, but has no memory of doing these things.
f. Stage 3 of HIV	6. _________ Tomatillo is extra sensitive to physical changes. He takes medication daily to maintain routine activities and to help him when he has difficulty breathing.
g. Hyperglycemia	7. _________ Steve is experiencing thirst, excessive urination, and blurred vision. He appears to be drunk.
h. Childhood leukemia	8. _________Elissa is critically ill. Eating is not only difficult, but her body isn't able to obtain nutrients from food. She's lost much weight and therapies have only minimal effect.

Application Exercise 11b. Developmental Responses to Death

See if you can match the child's understanding of death with the appropriate age range.

a. Newborn to age three	1. __________ Omar thinks he can handle the grief himself so doesn't express his feelings to anyone, but he really needs help from adults.
b. Ages three to six	2. __________ Rebecca understands that death is final, but needs a detailed explanation of how the person died.
c. Ages six to nine	3. __________ Olga thinks she is responsible for the death.
d. Ages nine to twelve	4. __________ Wanda shows more anger, guilt, and grief than adults.
e. Teenagers	5. __________ Keith needs to have his routine maintained as much as possible and be given extra affection and attention.
	6. _________ Timothy doesn't seem affected by the death of his brother because he expects him to return.
	7. _________ Deidre needs to be reassured that it is okay to express emotions she is feeling, and that crying and feeling bad or mad are normal.
	8. _________ Darlene thinks that death is contagious and doesn't want to go to the house or funeral home.

Application Exercise 11c. Medical Vocabulary Applications

Based upon the major questions addressed in this chapter, review all the major concepts by listing and reviewing key medical vocabulary for each section. Use each medical term in a sentence to summarize the important aspect of each question and subheading.

Major Questions: Who Are Students with Other Health Impairments? How Are Students with Other Health Impairments Evaluated? How Can You Establish Effective Teaching Strategies? How Can You Encourage Participation?

SAMPLE QUIZ FOR CHAPTER 11

MULTIPLE CHOICE

Circle the correct answer.

1. Curricular goals for students with health impairments should reflect what?
   a. Future interests
   b. Energy level
   c. Physical condition
   d. Cognitive level or potential

2. Paula is in the middle stage of HIV. What is the most appropriate educational placement for her?
   a. The general classroom is always the most appropriate placement unless she has a secondary impairment causing academic limitations that cannot be met in the general education classroom, because students with HIV should be welcomed.
   b. If she is under age eight, a resource room is the most appropriate placement so that universal health precautions can be carefully observed to protect other students.
   c. If she easily contracts infections from other people, she should be educated at home or in an individualized setting.
   d. If she has been involved in drugs or sexual activity, she should be educated in a resource room so that she does not negatively influence other students who are susceptible to peer pressure.

3. Shoshanna has ADD, microcephaly, and facial deformities. Which of the following conditions does she most likely have?
   a. Ketoacidosis
   b. Fetal alcohol syndrome
   c. ARC
   d. Cerebral palsy

4. Which of the following is <u>not</u> true about asthma?
   a. About two times more boys have asthma than girls.
   b. In about half the childhood cases, asthma begins before age one.
   c. Boys are more likely to have severe asthma.
   d. Asthma is the most prevalent chronic illness of children.

5. Yang Yang died of the most common fatal disease among children ages one to fourteen. What caused her death?
   a. AIDS
   b. Asthma
   c. Heart disease
   d. Cancer

6. Usha is experiencing a dreamlike state with random actions such as picking at clothes or repeating a sentence over and over. Which of the following medical conditions might you suspect?
   a. Grand mal seizure
   b. Absence seizure
   c. Myclonic seizure
   d. Temporal lobe seizure

7. Which of the following diseases does <u>not</u> appear to have a genetic component?
   a. Diabetes
   b. Asthma
   c. Epilepsy
   d. HIV

8. What is the most common environmental disease of childhood?
   a. Radon-caused cancer
   b. Obesity
   c. Lead poisoning
   d. Fetal alcohol syndrome

9. Lidscott Elementary is in a wealthy school district but does not serve all of its students who have health impairments. What is the most likely reason?
   a. The students' conditions do not have an adverse educational effect.
   b. IDEA only funds school districts where at least 10 percent of the students are below the poverty line.
   c. Parents who are from higher socioeconomic levels do not want IEPs attached to their children.
   d. IEPs are not necessary for children with chronic illnesses.

10. Rhett, a student in your class, has died of cancer. Identify the appropriate response to students after informing them of his death.
   a. Focus their attention on schoolwork so they do not dwell on morbid thoughts.
   b. Express your own grief and answer questions.
   c. Do not directly talk about it so emotions have a chance to heal.
   d. Use euphemisms to get it out in the open.

11. Which of the following children is not a possible candidate for services under the IDEA category of OHI?
   a. Jeri, who has sickle cell anemia
   b. Ulan, who has nephritis
   c. Roger, who has tuberculosis
   d. Ellyn, who has muscular sclerosis

12. What is useful to attach to IEPs for students with other health impairments?
   a. Lesson plans
   b. Functional behavioral assessment
   c. Health care plan
   d. Behavioral intervention plan

13. Six-month-old Nat, who had prenatal substance exposure to alcohol, is very irritable and difficult to handle. Although he has no physical deformities, for what is he at risk?
   a. Abuse from caregivers
   b. Asthma
   c. Teratogens
   d. HIV

14. Which of the following is not a primary feature of asthma?
   a. Airway linings are swollen.
   b. Airways are hypersensitive or supersensitive.
   c. Airways clogged by mucous secretions can usually be cleared by vigorous exercise.
   d. Airways narrow and breathing becomes more difficult.

15. Chemotherapy treatments for various cancers can affect what?
   a. The spinal cord
   b. The central nervous system
   c. The internal organs
   d. Blood pressure

16. Identify the medical term for "not enough sugar" that results in insulin shock.
   a. Hyperglycemia
   b. Brittle diabetes
   c. Hypoglycemia
   d. Ketoacidosis

17. Ebony has tonic seizures. What might you expect to observe?
    a. Loss of continence
    b. Sudden stiffening of the muscles
    c. Twitching movements
    d. Partial seizure accompanied by vomiting

18. Kofi was born with the abnormal gene for cystic fibrosis. What is the result?
    a. He will inherit the disease.
    b. He has a 1 in 4 chance of inheriting the disease.
    c. He will not have symptoms of the disease but will be a carrier of it to his children.
    d. He is predisposed to it and environmental factors may work in conjunction with the gene to cause the condition.

19. With whom is close collaboration essential when planning for students with a health impairment?
    a. Parents or guardians
    b. Peers or close friends
    c. Special education directors
    d. Medical personnel

20. For children and adolescents spending unending days in the hospital, what can be used to make the time pass more quickly?
    a. Computer games and chatting on the Internet
    b. Studying classroom textbooks
    c. Keeping personal diaries
    d. Completing educational workbooks

SHORT ANSWER

21. List the three major criteria of OHI according to IDEA.
    a. ______________________________
    b. ______________________________
    c. ______________________________

22. You are the teacher of Corwin, who uses an assistance dog. Briefly describe what you as a teacher could say to a parent of another student who objects to having an assistance dog in the same classroom as her child.

    ____

    ____

23. List two ways that you as a teacher can help prevent the spread of HIV.
    a. ______________________________
    b. ______________________________

ESSAY

24. Explain how the three major criteria for other health impairments are evident in HIV, asthma, cancer, and juvenile diabetes.

25. Differentiate between the characteristics of two health impairments discussed in this chapter and describe how you would support students with these impairments in the classroom.

CHAPTER 12: PHYSICAL DISABILITIES

CHAPTER OVERVIEW

Physical disabilities have the potential to severely limit an individual's mobility and ability to perform educationally. This chapter investigates the characteristics, causes, and prevalence of physical disabilities, with a detailed look at cerebral palsy, spina bifida, and muscular dystrophy. It also examines how to determine the presence of physical disabilities as well as the nature and extent of special education, with a special look at the role of the occupational therapist and physical therapist. Project MOVE represents a curriculum focused on mobility. Several assistive technologies are examined as effective methods for helping students with physical disabilities. Successful program options at four levels are highlighted for their unique contributions to students with physical disabilities.

The life of Rommel Nanasca provides an example of extraordinary team cooperation. Rommel's spinal muscular atrophy requires extensive physical supports both at home and at school. The degenerative nature of Rommel's disability along with his exemplary perseverance have special implications for classroom accommodations and emotional support.

CHAPTER AT-A-GLANCE

Chapter Outline	Instructional Goals	Key Concepts
WHO ARE STUDENTS WITH PHYSICAL DISABILITIES?		
Defining Physical Disabilities	• Examine different models for defining physical disabilities	• A physical disability is often referred to as an orthopedic impairment that affects a student's mobility and educational performance.
Describing the Characteristics • Cerebral Palsy • Spina Bifida • Muscular Dystrophy	• Describe characteristics and causes for some of the most typical physical disabilities	• Cerebral palsy describes a group of disabling conditions characterized by nonprogressive and nonhereditary brain damage; it is commonly characterized by spastic, athetoid, ataxic, or mixed movement patterns. • Spina bifida is a malformation of the spinal cord and is often accompanied by hydrocephalus. • Muscular dystrophy designates a group of nine hereditary muscle-destroying disorders. • A physical disability is caused by congenital anomaly, disease, or other causes.
Identifying the Prevalence of Physical Disabilities	• Identify prevalence rates for physical disabilities	• Approximately 1.2% of all students receiving special education services have physical disabilities.
Preventing Physical Disabilities	• Understand how physical disabilities can be prevented	• Primary prevention of physical disabilities includes educating pregnant women about risk factors. • Other types of prevention include trying to reduce the effect of a disability or trying to prevent a related disability from occurring.
HOW ARE STUDENTS WITH PHYSICAL DISABILITIES EVALUATED?		
Determining the Presence of Physical Disabilities	• Recognize the most appropriate times and ways for determining the presence of physical disabilities	• Screening may take place before or after birth or at a later date when an infant fails to meet developmental milestones.

Determining the Nature and Extent of Special Education and Related Services	• Identify principal ways to plan for special education and related services for students with physical disabilities • Describe the roles of two principal professionals in providing related services	• A functional assessment leads to a plan designed to overcome or compensate for discrepancies between student performance and performance expected from peers without disabilities. • Occupational and physical therapists play pivotal roles in the assessment of motoric abilities.
HOW CAN YOU ESTABLISH EFFECTIVE TEACHING PRACTICES?		
Set Curricular Goals	• Differentiate curriculum options available for use with students with physical disabilities	• Curriculum varies according to the students' individual strengths and needs. • Mobility should be fostered as early as possible to ensure richness of experience.
Implement Instruction	• Evaluate different methods that are effective for varied student needs	• Some students rely on assistive technology, adaptive equipment, or medical technology assistance. • Augmentative and alternative communication techniques and devices supplement students' naturally acquired speech.
Early Childhood and Elementary Years	• Describe characteristics of effective early childhood programs	• Early intervention program enhances functional mobility by utilizing technology tools such as an eye-gaze board and computer.
	• Describe characteristics of effective elementary programs for students with physical disabilities	• Elementary schools often use a buddy system to assist students with the use of adaptive equipment.
Middle Years Secondary Years	• Describe characteristics of effective programs for middle and secondary students	• A Pacific Northwest community pairs adult mentors with students to engage in learning and recreational activities.
Transitional and Postsecondary Years	• Describe characteristics of effective program options for adults with physical disabilities	• The University of California at Berkeley offers programs that assist students in gaining personal and academic independence.
HOW CAN YOU ENCOURAGE PARTICIPATION?		
Practice Inclusion	• Identify challenges for inclusion to benefit students with physical disabilities	• Inclusion challenges professionals to provide a balance between fully including students and providing them with the fundamentals they need to succeed.
Foster Collaboration • Professional-to-Professional Collaboration • Family and Professional Collaboration • School, Student, Family, and Community Collaboration	• Explore people and ways to collaborate on behalf of students with physical disabilities	• Collaboration involves the efforts of professionals, family, the student with a disability, peers, and community to work together as a team to deliver services.

PROJECT OPTIONS

1. Select the physical disability most interesting to you and interview two individuals with this disability. Use a questionnaire that you develop, based on the six values guiding special education, to ask each person. Compare and contrast your findings.
2. Compare and contrast the strengths of the four program options in this chapter with the program options available in your community. Analyze and present your findings to your local community for each of the four levels.
3. Research three forms of assistive technology. Then learn how to use one of them and write a description for others to learn how to use this type of assistive technology. Share the difficulties and joys.
4. Read at least one recent (1980–1998) adolescent or children's book dealing with one of the disabilities discussed in this chapter. Write a description of (a) what types of evaluation took place in the main character's life, (b) what types of curriculum and methods were used with him or her, and (c) the role of inclusion and collaboration in the life of the main character.

KEY TERMS

Assistive technology

Clean intermittent catheterization

Colostomy

Hypertonia

Incontinence

Intermittent Position Pressure Breathing Machine (IPPB)

Jejunum

Neonatal Intensive Care Unit (NICU)

Paraplegia

Perinatal

Postnatal

Prenatal

Pulseoximeter

Quadriplegia

Scoliosis

Speech recognition technology

Tracheostomy

Topographical classification system

GUIDED REVIEW

Maddie's Story

Trauma that Maddie suffered as a result of her premature birth left her with a diagnosis of spastic quadriplegic cerebral palsy. But Maddie is successfully integrated into a general education classroom. "Even though Maddie is confined to a wheelchair, we wanted her to grow up experiencing the same things other kids her age experience," explains Maddie's mother. Maddie's inclusion plan was designed by a team consisting of the IEP manager, the special education teacher, the classroom teacher, the gym teacher, the child psychologist, the speech-language pathologist, the occupational therapist, the physical therapist, Maddie's mother, and Maddie herself.

To review Maddie's entire intervention plan, including therapy service models, read *Teaching Exceptional Children*, November/December, 2000, *33*(2), pp. 12–18.

Who Are Students With Physical Disabilities?

1. IDEA refers to physical disabilities as orthopedic impairments. Provide IDEA's definition of "orthopedic impairment." (*See* Defining Physical Disabilities)

____

____

____

____

2. While IDEA uses the term "orthopedic impairment," educators typically use what term?
______________________________ (*See* Defining Physical Disabilities)

3. Define the terms "cerebral" and "palsy." (*See* Describing the Characteristics; What Is Cerebral Palsy?)
   a. Cerebral: ______________________________
   ____
   b. Palsy: ______________________________
   ____

4. What two characteristics distinguish cerebral palsy? (*See* Describing the Characteristics; What Is Cerebral Palsy?)
   a. ______________________________
   b. ______________________________

5. Identify the four movement terms that characterize individuals with cerebral palsy. Put an "X" after the most prevalent movement pattern. (*See* Describing the Characteristics; What Is Cerebral Palsy?)
   a. ______________ c. ______________
   b. ______________ d. ______________

A Model Child

Talent scouts said that Stephanie Hammerman, born with cerebral palsy, is a natural model. The pretty eight year old is never seen at a photo shoot without her crutches. "It's easy to model," she says, "because I like having my picture taken."

Great expectations are the rule in her family. "In this family, we try not to accept the easy way out," her mother says. When Stephanie was five, her teacher asked her mother to get her a wheelchair, but her mother refused. Stephanie could walk using a walker, but it took her longer. Mrs. Hammerman believes Stephanie is able to use crutches today because using the walker strengthened her legs. Stephanie is included in general education—even in physical education. Although Stephanie is the only student who uses crutches, she keeps up with her peers. Stephanie also insists on dressing herself each morning. Her mother says that if it takes her a half hour to button her shirt, she just determines to wake up earlier.

See "Strutting Her Stuff," by Lynda Spiegel in *Exceptional Parent* (1998), *28*(5), pp. 58–61.

6. Cerebral palsy is also characterized by the area of the brain affected. Identify each area and tell what is affected by damage to each of the three motor systems of the central nervous system. (*See* Describing the Characteristics; What Is Cerebral Palsy?)

Area of the Brain Affected	***Specific Effect on an Individual***
a.	
b.	
c.	

Making Music

Anita Gillespie, a high school student from Poca, West Virginia, has lost most of her right arm. The umbilical cord wrapped around her arm and cut off the circulation. But Anita has not let her disability stop her from playing in the band. The talented and well-liked teenager plays the trumpet with her left hand. Not only does she play solos, she is first chair All County and second chair All Area. Matthew Shank, one of her peers, says, "Anita has overcome her disability without a doubt!"

7. Match the form of cerebral palsy with its primary characteristics. (*See* Describing the Characteristics; What Is Cerebral Palsy?)

1. Spastic, or hypertonic, form	a. _____ Abrupt involuntary movements of the head, neck, face, and extremities, particularly the upper ones.
2. Athetoid, or low-tone, form	b. _____ Spastic muscle tone and the involuntary movements of athetoid cerebral palsy.
3. Ataxic form	c. _____Tightness in one or more of the muscle groups, which causes limited movement.
4. Mixed form	d. _____ Unsteadiness, lack of coordination and balance, and varying degrees of difficulty with standing and walking.

8. Cerebral palsy is also classified by referring to the area of the body that is affected. Name each, then describe the seven areas of the body that are affected. (*See* Describing the Characteristics; What Is Cerebral Palsy?)

Classification	***Area of Body Affected***
1.	
2.	
3.	
4.	
5.	
6.	
7.	

9. What are some identified causes of cerebral palsy? (*See* Describing the Characteristics; What Is Cerebral Palsy?)
   a. ____________________
   b. ____________________
   c. ____________________

10. Spina bifida refers to a(n) ____________________ or ____________________ spine. In a person with spina bifida, the spinal column does not ____________________ ____________________. The higher the spinal defect, the more ____________________ is the loss of function. (*See* Describing the Characteristics; What Is Spina Bifida?)

Second Chance For Baby Ethan

Ethan is one of 2,000 American children born each year with spina bifida. Manifesting itself within a month after conception, spina bifida consists of a congenital hole in the spine that allows the spinal cord to protrude and the fluid that directs brain development to leak out. This can cause extensive damage to the brain and the body.

In the mid-1970s, neurosurgeons started operating on newborns, closing the spinal column and allowing many to survive into adulthood. But the surgery did not undo the disabilities that can be wrought during months in the womb. Ethan may be spared from most of these challenges due to innovative surgery that a decade ago seemed like science fiction. Ethan underwent corrective prenatal surgery at Vanderbilt University Medical Center in Nashville, Tennessee, before his actual birth. A doctor removed his mother's uterus, placed it on her abdomen, and made an incision in the womb. Then another doctor closed the hole at the base of Ethan's spine. The womb was then sewn closed and reinserted into the mother's abdomen. The doctor advised the parents to be restrained in their optimism, predicting that Ethan would probably walk with braces.

Now at almost four months old, Ethan's recent MIR indicated only mild hydrocephalus, meaning he won't need the dreaded shunt. "He's my miracle baby," his mother says. "Ethan is beautiful."

See *People*, May 8, 2000, *53*(18), pp. 60–66.

11. Identify the three most common forms of spinal bifida, then describe their degree of severity and typical characteristics. (*See* Describing the Characteristics; What Is Spina Bifida?)

Form of Spina Bifida	***Degree of Severity***	***Typical Characteristics***
a.		
b.		
c.		

12. To date, what is known about the causes of spina bifida? (*See* Describing the Characteristics; What Is Spina Bifida?) ____

____

13. What does the term "muscular dystrophy" designate? (*See* Describing the Characteristics; Muscular Dystrophy)

____

____

14. By what is spinal muscular atrophy characterized? (*See* Describing the Characteristics; Muscular Dystrophy)
    a. ____
    b. ____

15. Three types of spinal muscular atrophy have been identified. Identify each type and list the accompanying symptoms. (*See* Describing the Characteristics; Muscular Dystrophy)
    a. ____
    b. ____
    c. ____

16. What is the cause of spinal muscular atrophy? (*See* Describing the Characteristics; Muscular Dystrophy)____

17. Identify three conditions that often accompany spinal muscular atrophy and describe how these conditions can be treated or prevented. (*See* Describing the Characteristics; Muscular Dystrophy)

Conditions Accompanying Spinal Muscular Atrophy	***Treatment and/or Prevention***
1.	
2.	
3.	

18. What percentage of all students who receive special education services have physical disabilities? (*See* Identifying the Prevalence of Physical Disabilities) ______________________ percent

19. Identify at least two ways physical disabilities can be prevented. (*See* Preventing Physical Disabilities)
    a. ____
    b. ____

How Are Students with Physical Disabilities Evaluated?

20. At what times can screening take place for physical disabilities? (*See* Determining the Presence of Physical Disabilities)

    ____

21. Two professional disciplines are concerned with movement in the assessment of students with physical disabilities. Identify them and describe each one's role in intervention. (*See* Determining the Nature and Extent of Special Education and Related Services)

Professional Discipline	***Intervention Role of This Professional Discipline***
a.	
b.	

22. Explain how to carry out an ecological inventory for a student with physical disabilities and how it can enhance this student's daily living experiences. (*See* Determining the Nature and Extent of Special Education and Related Services)

    ____
    ____
    ____

How Can You Establish Effective Teaching Practices?

23. List five goals that lead to the ultimate outcomes desired for students with physical disabilities. (*See* How Can You Establish Effective Teaching Practices?; Set Curricular Goals)
    a. ______________________________
    b. ______________________________
    c. ______________________________
    d. ______________________________
    e. ______________________________

24. Identify examples for three different assistive technologies/methods and tell how they enable students with physical disabilities to be full participating members of their schools. (*See* How Can You Establish Effective Teaching Practices?; Implement Instruction)

Type of Assistive Technology	***Example***	***How It Accommodates the Student***
a. Adaptive equipment		
b. Augmentative and alternative communication		
c. Medical technology assistance		

25. Identify some of the complicated issues raised by the use of medical technology assistance. (*See* How Can You Establish Effective Teaching Practices?; Medical Technology Assistance)
____
____
____

26. To what does "augmentative and alternative communication" refer? (*See* How Can You Establish Effective Teaching Practices?; Augmentative and Alternative Communication)
____
____

Why Do You Use a Wheelchair?

John Dybala, who has spondiloephiphysial dysplasia, is a junior at Colorado State University. John has had over 40 operations in his lifetime. But that hasn't stopped him from having great expectations for himself. He is preparing to be a teacher. He shares the following advice about how you can help students feel comfortable with people who have disabilities:

As a person with a disability, I have never experienced anything other than natural curiosity from children. Answer the question "Why do you use a wheelchair?" or "Why does he walk funny?" or "What's that plastic thing in her ear?" Once that is answered, they ask other questions: "What's your favorite food?" "Did you watch TV last night?" "Do you like football?" This is more interesting to them.

We, as teachers, have a tremendous impact on students. We have the power—we really do—to show them which set of questions is more important. And we can model that.

—John Dybala

27. Describe key features of the successful programs mentioned in this chapter for students with physical disabilities. (*See* Programs in Practice)

Life-Span Stage	*Key Features*
Early childhood and elementary years	
Middle years	
Secondary years	
Transitional and postsecondary years	

How Can You Encourage Participation?

28. When assistive technology became available, what happened to students with physical disabilities who became able to independently initiate both movement and speech? (*See* How Can You Encourage Participation?; Practice Inclusion)

____

____

29. Match the percentages of students with their education placements. (*See* How Can You Encourage Participation?; Practice Inclusion)

1. Separate class	a. _____ 5%
2. Residential facility	b. _____ 2%
3. Resource room	c. _____ <1%
4. Regular class	d. _____ 31%
5. Separate facility	e. _____ 20%
6. Homebound/hospital	f. _____ 42%

30. Explain the role of the individuals who collaborate on behalf of Rommel. (*See* How Can You Encourage Participation?; Foster Collaboration)
School district resource nurse, Cathy Schmitz: ____

____

Registered nurse, Rebecca Draper: ____

____

Robin, his physical therapist: ____

____

Lorna and Romy, Rommel's parents: ____

____

Still Me

Christopher Reeve, the star of the *Superman* movies, who was paralyzed in a horseback riding accident, chose this title for his book for two reasons: he wants people to realize he is still the same person, and his paralysis causes him to live a life of physical stillness. But his life is active in other ways. Besides becoming an author, Reeve is a sought-after speaker, a film director, and an advocate for people with disabilities. When *Superman* previewed, people asked Reeve what he thought a hero was. He told them that a hero "commits a courageous act without considering the consequences." He has a new definition of hero now: "I think a hero is an ordinary individual who finds strength to persevere and endure despite overwhelming obstacles."

See Christopher Reeve, *Still Me* (Random House, 1998).

APPLICATION EXERCISES FOR CHAPTER 12

Application Exercise 12a. Identifying Forms of Cerebral Palsy by Movement Difficulties

Identify which form of cerebral palsy each individual has: spastic, athetoid, ataxic, or mixed.

1. Miguel has difficulty with coordination and balance. Often he has difficulty with standing and walking.

   ____

2. Karim has abrupt, involuntary movements of his neck and arms. Sometimes it is more frequent than other times. He does not have trouble initiating movement; rather, he has difficulty controlling movement and maintaining posture.

   ____

3. Nadia is a quadriplegic who often has involuntary movements of her upper limbs. She sometimes finds her limbs becoming rigid and tight.

   ____

4. When Abram is transferred from his bed to his wheelchair, his body straightens out and becomes extremely rigid.

   ____

Application Exercise 12b. Identifying Characteristics of Spina Bifida

Match the characteristic of spina bifida with the common forms.

1. Spina bifida occulta	a. _____ The covering of the cord protrudes through the opening created by the defect in the spine.
2. Meningocele	b. _____ This is the mildest and most common form.
3. Myelomeningocele	c. _____ More than 90 percent of people with this type of spina bifida have an inability to control their bowels or bladder.
	d. _____ In this form of spina bifida, the protrusion contains the cord's covering and a portion of the spinal cord or nerve roots.
	e. _____ The spinal cord or its covering do not protrude.
	f. _____ This form is not detectable by physical exam and is not disabling.
	g. _____ This form is the most severe form of spina bifida.
	h. _____ Four out of five children born with this kind of spina bifida also develop hydrocephalus.

Application Exercise 12c. The Conceptual Impact of Inclusion and Collaboration on Physical Disabilities

Based upon the major questions addressed in this chapter, summarize the major concepts concerning physical disabilities. Explain the role and/or impact of inclusion and collaboration as it applies to each major chapter question.

Major Questions: Who Are Students with Physical Disabilities? How Are Students with Physical Disabilities Evaluated? How Can You Establish Effective Teaching Practices? How Can You Encourage Participation?

SAMPLE QUIZ FOR CHAPTER 12

MULTIPLE CHOICE

Circle the correct answer.

1. Spinal muscular atrophy is a member of what family?
   a. Genetic family
   b. Muscular dystrophy family
   c. Congenital family
   d. Physical disability family

2. What condition can be caused by bleeding in the brain of a newborn?
   a. Spina bifida
   b. Cerebral palsy
   c. Spinal muscular atrophy
   d. Muscular sclerosis

3. Ty has spina bifida and is paralyzed from the waist down. What does this indicate?
   a. A saclike bulge occurred fairly high in his spine.
   b. He has meningocele spina bifida.
   c. He has a progressive condition.
   d. Only the covering of the spinal cord protruded.

4. What can be done for a child born with hydrocephalus?
   a. Nothing, because it is progressive and the child will die at a young age.
   b. A shunt can be implanted to remove excess fluid.
   c. Physical therapy can overcome most problems associated with hydrocephalus.
   d. Brain surgery is required to remove the frontal lobe and prevent further damage from the disease.

5. What problem associated with spinal muscular atrophy can an initial screening at birth indicate?
   a. Respiratory
   b. Vitamin deficiency
   c. Cerebral malfunctioning
   d. Incontinence

6. For what condition can electromyography and muscle biopsies establish a diagnosis?
   a. Cerebral palsy
   b. Spinal muscular atrophy
   c. Spina bifida
   d. Multiple sclerosis

7. What type of communication, developed at Emory University and at Georgia State University, can now be utilized by people like Johnny, a Vietnam vet, who had a brainstem stroke and was unable to communicate or affect his life in any way?
   a. Communication simply by thinking
   b. Communication board
   c. Assistive technology
   d. Oral communication

8. What caused educational expectations for students with physical disabilities to rise dramatically?
   a. More teachers were trained to work with children who had disabilities.
   b. IDEA mandated that all students be treated without discrimination.
   c. Assistive technology allowed students to move and speak independently.
   d. Parents demanded a role in collaboration.

9. The primary mission of which of the following is to support individuals with disabilities so they can experience self-determination as a means of enhancing their quality of life?
   a. Community centers
   b. Assisted living centers
   c. Learning centers
   d. Independent living centers

10. Identify the type of assessment that is conducted in the student's natural environment and leads to a plan designed to overcome discrepancies between actual performance and expected performance.
    a. Physical assessment
    b. Ecological assessment
    c. Functional assessment
    d. Behavioral assessment

11. Sarah has a progressive, inherited disease. Which of the following does she have?
    a. Spina bifida
    b. Muscular sclerosis
    c. Spinal muscular atrophy
    d. Cerebral palsy

12. What is the term that refers to mobility impairment of the upper and lower limb on the same side of the body?
    a. Paraplegia
    b. Diplegia
    c. Hemiplegia
    d. Monoplegia

13. What group of individuals plays a pivotal role in the assessment of motoric abilities?
    a. Medical doctors
    b. Occupational and physical therapists
    c. Special education teachers
    d. Public health personnel

14. Which of the following physical disabilities occurs during the very early days of pregnancy?
    a. Cerebral palsy
    b. Spina bifida
    c. Muscular dystrophy
    d. Scoliosis

15. What recent type of prevention enables a tiny fetus with spina bifida to have a surgical repair before being born?
    a. Preventive surgery
    b. Micro surgery
    c. Elective surgery
    d. Fetal surgery

16. What do the lumbar nerves control?
    a. The leg muscles
    b. The facial muscles
    c. The foot muscles
    d. The rectal sphincter

17. When a child presents symptoms associated with spinal muscular atrophy, what might doctors recommend?
    a. Electromyography
    b. Shunt implant
    c. IPPB
    d. Tracheostomy

18. Identify what component is most unique in determining the nature and extent of physical disabilities.
    a. Communication
    b. Muscle tone
    c. Mobility
    d. Self-help skills

19. Which of the following is not a good suggestion to enable better communication with people who use wheelchairs?
    a. Don't ask the person if he or she wants assistance.
    b. Speak directly to the person.
    c. Don't hang on the wheelchair.
    d. Don't demean the person by patting him or her on the head.

20. A program in the Pacific Northwest facilitates what type of relationship between adults with physical disabilities and students with physical disabilities to improve independent living skills?
    a. Family relationship
    b. Mentor relationship
    c. Community relationship
    d. Professional relationship

SHORT ANSWER

21. What is the term used by IDEA for physical disabilities?

____

22. List the four forms of cerebral palsy.

____

____

____

____

23. Name two professional people who are key to the assessment of students with physical disabilities but who are not as important for students with most other disabilities.

a. ______________________________

b. ______________________________

ESSAY

24. Compare and contrast the ways to classify physical disabilities as they relate to cerebral palsy, spinal bifida, and muscular dystrophy.
25. Discuss the role of inclusion and collaboration in the lives of students with physical disabilities. Include a discussion of different careers available for working with these students and their families.

CHAPTER 13: TRAUMATIC BRAIN INJURY

CHAPTER OVERVIEW

Traumatic brain injuries can cause dramatic changes in a person's intellectual, emotional, linguistic, social, and/or physical functioning. This chapter presents important information about the definition, characteristics, causes, and prevalence rates for traumatic brain injury. It describes the many dimensions of the evaluation process to determine its presence as well as the process to ensure academic and social success with appropriate special education. A discussion of the cognitive retraining curriculum and various effective methods is presented along with the place of inclusion and collaboration on behalf of these students. Emphasis is placed on the importance of collaboration between the rehabilitation program and the school for this population. This chapter concludes with a discussion describing factors critical to helping students at each age level.

The life of nine-year-old Jarris Garner demonstrates and clarifies issues revolving around students who have experienced brain injuries. As an infant, Jarris and her parents were in a serious automobile accident.. She experienced multiple seizures as well as open traumatic brain injuries, leaving her in critical condition. Jarris has recovered, but she continues to experience challenges in her intellectual, emotional, linguistic, social, and/or physical function.

CHAPTER AT-A-GLANCE

Chapter Outline	Instructional Goals	Key Concepts
WHO ARE STUDENTS WITH TRAUMATIC BRAIN INJURY?		
Defining Traumatic Brain Injury • Types of Traumatic Brain Injury • Closed Head Injury • Open Head Injury	• Differentiate among types of traumatic brain injuries	• IDEA's definition includes acquired injuries to the brain caused by an external force. It does not include brain injuries caused by anoxia or disease or congenital brain injuries. • Closed head injuries and open head injuries are the two types under IDEA.
Describing the Characteristics • Physical Changes • Cognitive Changes • Linguistic Changes • Social, Behavioral, and Personality Changes • Prognosis	• Describe key characteristics seen in students with traumatic brain injury	• Students with brain injury often experience physical, cognitive, linguistic, and social, behavioral, or personality changes. • No generalizations can be made about prognosis based on the injury's mildness or severity.
Identifying the Causes of Traumatic Brain Injury	• Identify the major causes and effects of traumatic brain injury	• Three major causes include accidents, sports and recreational injuries, and violence. • Shaken-impact syndrome is a dangerous form of child abuse that can cause brain injuries or death. • Called the silent epidemic, the effects of brain injury are widespread but often unrecognized.
Identifying the Prevalence of Traumatic Brain Injury	• Recognize prevalence rates of traumatic brain injuries	• Approximately 0.5% to 1% of school-age students have sustained a traumatic brain injury. • About 3% of adolescents have sustained head injuries that are severe enough to cause school problems.

HOW ARE STUDENTS WITH TRAUMATIC BRAIN INJURY EVALUATED?		
Determining the Presence of Traumatic Brain Injury	• Describe key characteristics in successful evaluation of brain injuries • Identify the key specialists integral to the evaluation process	• Because the needs of students with traumatic brain injury are diverse and rapidly changing, evaluation needs to be comprehensive and on-going. • The multidisciplinary team should evaluate the students in all areas of functioning, including cognitive processes such as problem solving and memory.
Determining the Nature and Extent of Special Education and Related Services	• Analyze unique education needs and services for students with traumatic brain injury	• The IEP team should update the student's document frequently, probably every six to eight weeks initially.
HOW CAN YOU ESTABLISH EFFECTIVE TEACHING PRACTICES?		
Set Curricular Goals	• Differentiate curriculum needs for students with traumatic brain injury	• Students receive three forms of cognitive retraining: component retraining, compensatory strategy training, and functional training.
Implement Instruction • Direct Instruction • Antecedent Behavior Management	• Evaluate how different methods are most effective for varied student needs • Describe how different methods address the specific needs of individuals with traumatic brain injuries	• Computer-assisted instruction helps students develop cognitive skills. • Methods for improving behavioral and social skills include identifying the cause of the behavior, allowing students to develop adaptive skills, and transferring control from teacher to student. • Professionals can improve behavior by empowering the student and his or her parents.
Early Childhood Years	• Describe characteristics of effective early childhood programs	• Since abuse accounts for 90% of brain injury in children under three, bonding with a nanny helps children make the transition. • Parent development is particularly important during these years so that they can continue any developmental program in the home.
Elementary Years	• Describe characteristics of effective elementary school programs	• Providing a structured learning environment offers access to an appropriate educational program.
Middle and Secondary Years	• Describe characteristics of effective programs for middle and secondary students	• Identifying a pattern of behavior offers an understanding of the behavior and a potential solution to decrease occurrences. • Creating social interaction opportunities is a key ingredient in developing age-appropriate behavior.
Transitional and Postsecondary Years	• Describe characteristics of effective program options for adults with traumatic brain injury	• Planning for school reentry should be determined by the degree to which the student can participate. • Vocational training and preparation for independence are key factors in the success of postsecondary students.

HOW CAN YOU ENCOURAGE PARTICIPATION?		
Practice Inclusion	• Explain the best educational placement for students with traumatic brain injury	• The general education classroom can be the least restrictive environment in most cases.
Foster Collaboration • Professional-to-Professional Collaboration • Family and Professional Collaboration • School, Student, Family, and Community Collaboration	• Explore the role of collaboration on behalf of students with traumatic brain injury	• Close collaboration among rehabilitation staff, school personnel, family, peers, and the student is essential to meet the diverse, ever-changing needs of individuals with brain injury.

PROJECT OPTIONS

1. Research the different areas of the brain that can be affected during a traumatic brain injury. Construct three creative charts comparing (a) the sections of the brain and what they control, (b) the characteristics for injuries centered in each section of the brain (including things to watch for in the classroom), and (c) the recovery prognosis for injuries in each section of the brain.
2. Find out your state's requirement for brain injury and your school district's and related medical center's means for assessment and on-going evaluation. Then interview two people with brain injury or their parents and evaluate how their experience has been coordinated with the state and local school district. From your findings, create a concept map that demonstrates how schools, communities, and parents can interact to meet the needs of students with brain injury.
3. Explore the types of brain injury programs available in your community. Then create a Power Point (or similar technology-based) presentation comparing and contrasting the local programs. Write your findings and share them with the various local programs.
4. Keep a journal for one week. For each entry, speculate about how your day would have been different if you had a brain injury.

KEY TERMS

Acquired brain injury

Aphasia

Closed head injury

Cognitive retraining

Compensatory strategy training

Component training

Congenital condition

Differential reinforcement of other behavior

Functional retraining

Open head injury

Personal intervention plan

Postconcussional syndrome, or mild traumatic brain injury (MTBI)

Traumatic brain injury

GUIDED REVIEW

I Wish I Could Go Home

In this chapter, you will learn about the changes that people with traumatic brain injury experience. In his own words, Richard Browning compares his experience to *The Wizard of Oz*:

1. Do you remember the early part of the movie? Just as the house is getting picked up by the tornado, Dorothy gets hit in the head by a storm shutter and is knocked unconscious. (*To me that sounds like a person knocked unconscious into a "coma."*)

2. When she wakes up, she is in a place she is not familiar with at all. Everything is new and different. (*That seems like after a person comes out of their coma most everything appears the same but in a different way. "Where am I?"*)

3. As she walks out of her house, she finds herself in a new and different place surrounded by many little people. [*This could be symbolic of (people with traumatic brain injury) thinking that they are bigger and better than the average person around them.*]

4. Then she starts her long walk down the yellow brick road. (*This could be the start of the long road to a complete recovery!*)

5. As she goes down the road, she meets the Scarecrow—the man with no brain. (*Or, in other words, a person with no cognitive thinking abilities!*)

6. As she goes farther down the road, she then meets the Tin Man—the man with no heart. (*To me that sounds like that could be a person that is self-centered that doesn't care for anyone else except for themselves—but as you know, the Tin Man is a very caring person.*)

7. Then she meets the Cowardly Lion. (*The person with no self-esteem afraid to do anything on his own.*)

8. As she is going along the yellow brick road, she meets the Wicked Witch. (*That is like meeting a person that wants to take advantage of you in your situation.*)

9. As she is going along the yellow brick road, she eventually makes it to Oz. (*Where they teach her what she really wants to know to get back to where she wants to be—to me, that sounds like a person going through vocational rehabilitation.*)

If you remember, throughout the entire movie all she wants to do is to go back home. (*Or become herself again.*) Then she says to herself, "I want to go home, I want to go home, etc." Then she is back where she wants to be.

But through the entire ordeal she learns love, caring, and compassion for others that are going through what she is going through.

At the end of the movie, the Wizard gives them all awards, diplomas, or medals to show that they really can do what they have been doing all along.

See *Alabama Head Injury Foundation Newsletter*, vol. 22, pp. 4–5.

Who Are Students With Traumatic Brain Injury?

1. How does IDEA define traumatic brain injury? (*See* Defining Traumatic Brain Injury)

____

____

____

2. Describe the two causes of traumatic brain injury served under the IDEA category of other health impairments. (*See* Defining Traumatic Brain Injury)

   a. Anoxia:

   ____

   ____

   b. Disease:

   ____

   ____

3. Explain the difference between an acquired brain injury and a congenital brain injury. (*See* Defining Traumatic Brain Injury)

____

____

4. Compare and contrast the two types of traumatic brain injury served under IDEA. (*See* Defining Traumatic Brain Injury; Types of Traumatic Brain Injury)

	What Causes the Brain Injury?	*What Areas of the Brain Are Damaged?*	*Resulting Behavior or Academic Problems*
Closed Head Injury			
Open Head Injury			

Much More Than a Statistic

John Dybala, whom you also read about in Chapter 12 of this study guide, shares what he experienced when his sister was involved in a car accident:

In 1990, my sister became a statistic. She was hit by a car as she tried to cross the street. My sister was but one of the many thousands of people injured in car accidents that year. Happily, she survived and is doing well.

I suspect that some people who read the brief account of the accident in the newspaper sighed and commented on what a shame it was, then went on with their day and forgot all about it. She was a number to them. A statistic. They could depersonalize it as being something that happened to someone else. It didn't affect them; therefore, it was not their concern.

For my sister, her family, and her friends, this accident was more than just one statistic. It was several frantic hours in the emergency room. It was a weekend of keeping a bedside vigil. It was a year of slow recovery, and nearly three years fighting to recover damages from the driver's insurance company.

—John Dybala

5. Even mild closed head injury, sometimes called ____________________ or ____________________ can seriously impact a person's ability to enjoy life and work and earn a living. (*See* Defining Traumatic Brain Injury; Types of Traumatic Brain Injury; Closed Head Injury)
6. The number and magnitude of changes vary according to ____________________ and ____________________ of injury, as well as the length of time the student was in a ____________________ and the student's ____________________ at the time of the injury. (*See* Describing the Characteristics)

7. Discuss the four areas of changes that are often experienced by students with traumatic brain injury by providing examples and a description of the characteristics. (*See* Describing the Characteristics)

Area of Change	***Examples of Changes***	***Characteristics/Outcomes***
1. Physical changes	a. b. c.	
2. Cognitive changes	a. b. c.	
3. Linguistic changes	a. b. c.	
4. Social, behavioral, and personality changes	a. b. c.	

Every Day Gets Better

One of the physical changes Mike Euler experienced as a result of his traumatic brain injury after being in a car accident was loss of hearing. Mike was one of the first people with traumatic brain injury to receive a cochlear implant. Now he hears sounds that are changed into electrical signals by a small speech processor. The processor sends the signals to a device that is similar to a hearing aid. When Mike was in rehab, he often spoke of when he was a "regular man" and a "normal person." Today he credits his recovery to faith in God. Mike is looking forward to the future and enjoys his hobby of bowhunting from his wheelchair. He explains, "Every day gets better, like steps on a ladder. I just gotta keep going up."

See *The Charleston Gazette*, November 24, 1994.

8. In ________________percent of traumatic brain injuries, the student experiences seizures, which often decrease or disappear with the passage of time. (*See* Describing the Characteristics; Physical Changes)
9. A student with brain injury may comprehend less of what you say with increases in (a) the rate of your speech, (b) ____, (c) abstract language, and (d) ____ (*See* Describing the Characteristics; Linguistic Changes)
10. In the 1970s, _______________percent of people with traumatic brain injury died. Currently, at least ____________percent survive. Lifetime effects are present for ________________percent of those with mild injuries, ________________ to ____________percent of those with moderate injuries, and ____________percent of those with severe injuries. (*See* Describing the Characteristics; Prognosis)

11. Identify the four major causes of traumatic head injuries and their percentages. (*See* Identifying the Causes of Traumatic Brain Injury)
    a. ____ (__________%)
    b. ____ (__________%)
    c. ____ (__________%)
    d. ____ (__________%)
12. ______________________________ accounts for the majority of infant head injuries, and more than 80 percent of deaths from head trauma in children under age two are the result of ______________________________. (*See* Identifying the Causes of Traumatic Brain Injury)
13. ______________________________________ occurs when a caretaker shakes the child violently to try to make the child stop crying. In __________percent to __________percent of these cases, the child dies. (*See* Identifying the Causes of Traumatic Brain Injury)
14. Traumatic brain injury is called the ____________________________ because it is the most common cause of death and disability in children and adults. Each year ________ out of every __________ children and adolescents will survive a head injury that requires hospitalization. (*See* Identifying the Prevalence of Traumatic Brain Injury)
15. What percentage of adolescents may have sustained a brain injury serious enough to cause school problems? ____________percent (*See* Identifying the Prevalence of Traumatic Brain Injury)

How Are Students with Traumatic Brain Injury Evaluated?

16. Name and briefly describe uses and cautions for three assessment tools that might be used to determine the presence of a traumatic brain injury. (*See* Determining the Presence of Traumatic Brain Injury)

Name of Assessment	*Uses*	*Cautions*

17. Deficits in achievement (are, are not) always present immediately after recovery. (*See* Determining the Presence of Traumatic Brain Injury)
18. What is the primary goal of programming for students with traumatic brain injury? (*See* Determining the Nature and Extent of Special Education and Related Services)

    ____

He Never Moved

Although we have presented you with a very hopeful picture of recovery for students with traumatic brain injury, there are cases in which the hoped-for recovery does not come. Jamie Butcher was in a car accident in 1977 when he was 1seventeen years old. For seventeen years, his parents watched over him tenderly, even though doctors said he "had no brain left." During that time, Jamie never moved, never heard anything, and felt nothing. Finally, in 1994, Jamie's family decided to withdraw his feeding tube. Suddenly, this grieving family became the center of controversy and media attention. You may encounter a similar situation one day that will affect one of your students. What kind of support would you offer the family?

See *U.S. News and World Report*, November 7, 1994, pp. 69–70.

19. What five decisions should the IEP team make for students with brain injuries? (*See* Determining the Nature and Extent of Special Education and Related Services)
    a. ______________________________
    b. ______________________________
    c. ______________________________
    d. ______________________________
    e. ______________________________

How Can You Establish Effective Teaching Practices?

20. Name three primary curricular goals for students with traumatic brain injury. (*See* Set Curricular Goals)
    a. ______________________________
    b. ______________________________
    c. ______________________________
21. Describe three forms of cognitive retraining that help students use residual cognitive and perceptual skills more efficiently. (*See* Set Curricular Goals)

Form of Cognitive Retraining	***Specific Areas of Retraining***
Component training	
Compensatory strategy training	
Functional retraining	

22. For students with limited attention spans and memory problems, teachers should keep instructional times ______________________ and use frequent ______________________. (*See* Implement Instruction)
23. List four intervention strategies that can help students with brain injury avoid challenging behaviors. (*See* Implement Instruction, Box 13-7)
    a. ______________________________
    b. ______________________________
    c. ______________________________
    d. ______________________________

> We've talked a lot about the value of computers for students with traumatic brain injuries, as well as other disabilities. Do you feel that people are speaking a foreign language when they are talking about computers? Do you know what a mouse or a CPU is? Then you might find the article "Getting Started with Computers" in *Exceptional Parent* (November/December 1993, pp. 27–32) contains the basic information you need to get started. By the way, *Exceptional Parent* prints one technology issue each year. *PC Novice* magazine also prints helpful guides for using computers at reasonable costs.

24. What are the five steps involved in a personal intervention plan? (*See* Implement Instruction; Antecedent Behavior Management)
    a. ______________________________
    b. ______________________________
    c. ______________________________
    d. ______________________________
    e. ______________________________

25. When using a positive reinforcement called ____, you reinforce a positive behavior that is incompatible with the undesired behavior. (*See* Implement Instruction; Antecedent Behavior Management)

26. What are two purposes that most rehabilitation centers have for students' programs? (*See* Observe Programs in Practice)
    a. ____
    b. ____

27. List characteristics leading to the success of students with traumatic brain injury at each of the four program levels. (*See* Observe Programs in Practice)

Program	***Characteristics***
Early childhood years	
Elementary years	
Middle and secondary years	
Transitional and postsecondary years	

Defining Beauty

New vistas are opening up for people with disabilities. Paula Jean Nichols-Klimin was a model before she fell ten stories in a broken elevator. The accident left her with traumatic brain injury and physical disabilities. Yet, Paula was determined to return to the career she loved. Today she wears a size 14 and is distinguished as the first woman in a wheelchair to work for a major modeling company, Ford Models, Inc. One of her fellow models noted as Paula struck a pose from her wheelchair, "She's amazing, isn't she? And she's no token."

See *Mobile Press Register*, December 12, 1994, p. 7-D.

How Can You Encourage Participation?

28. Match percentages with placements for students who are leaving rehabilitation facilities. (*See* Inclusion)

1. 10%	a. _____	Postsecondary education
2. 38%	b. _____	Institution
3. 11%	c. _____	Adult education
4. 14%	d. _____	Full-time special education
5. 8%	e. _____	General education
6. 3%	f. _____	Part-time special education

Besides the student's classroom, the planning committee will need to consider the physical layout of the entire school when planning for reentry. The student may have difficulty getting around the building without getting fatigued or confused. Open classrooms may create frustration for students who have concentration and attention problems. Also, recess, lunch, and unstructured time between classes may cause self-monitoring problems.

(Savage & Allen, 1987)

29. Name two priorities for inclusion for students with brain injury. (*See* Practice Inclusion)
    a. ______________________________
    b. ______________________________

30. Discuss the significant contributions that can be made by each of the following collaborators. (*See* Foster Collaboration)

Collaborator	*Contributions*
Professional educators	
Professional rehabilitation personnel	
Family	
Community	
Peers	

Thumbs Up!

Jim Brady's life changed dramatically after he received an open head injury from a gunshot that was meant for President Reagan. Although his rehabilitation has been challenging, he is currently active again in public service as an influential advocate for people with disabilities. As Vice Chairman of the National Organization on Disability, he comments about his perspective on the rights of people with disabilities today: "Sure, we have a long way to go before we reach our goal of full participation for people with disabilities; but, we've come a long way. We need to keep the momentum going."

See *National Community Awards Program of the National Organization on Disability.*

APPLICATION EXERCISES FOR CHAPTER 13

Application Exercise 13a. Identifying Areas of Change

You have read about how students with brain injuries vary widely in their characteristics. As you read about the following students, decide which area of change is in focus during their rehabilitation period.

1. Quimby has difficulty staying awake during rehabilitation. He finds his left arm doesn't move like it used to and he can no longer play baseball as he did before.

   Area of change: ____________________________________

2. Chin-wei only talks about himself when he's with others. When others don't listen, he becomes restless and irritable. Then he becomes sad and depressed and won't talk to anyone.

   Area of change: ____________________________________

3. Amal tends to act without thinking and he has fallen behind in his school work because he doesn't think through the instructions.

   Area of change: ________________________________

4. Samantha's headaches interfere with her ability to pay attention during class. She also now needs both glasses and a hearing aid to see and communicate with friends.

   Area of change: ____________________________________

5. Erin can't seem to think of the appropriate words when talking with her friends. When she does have the words, she finds she is slow to express them.

   Area of change: ____________________________________

6. Rosalba works hard to complete her work and when finished will loudly announce her great accomplishment to anyone around. Consequently, most of her old friends are finding it difficult to be around her.

   Area of change: ____________________________________

Application Exercise 13b. Curriculum Applications

Reread the section "Set Curricular Goals." Using descriptions of curricular options found there, identify which type of curriculum would most benefit each of the following student needs.

a. Compensatory strategy training	______ 1. Michaela has difficulty with her memory. She can't seem to remember new information from one day to the next.
b. Component training	______ 2. Lev needs to develop his reading skills through activities requiring his active involvement and commitment, such as animal training.
c. Functional retraining	______ 3. Chloe needs help to clarify and express important information.
	______ 4. Kevin has difficulty with organizing his activities and often feels confused remembering which one he needs to do.
	______ 5. Matthew has trouble paying attention and is unable to organize what needs to be done.

Application Exercise 13c. Practice Inclusion

Students with traumatic brain injury can pose a unique challenge to educators, because their injuries can result in changes in behavior, social interactions, educational performance, and classroom attitudes. Box 13-9 "Inclusion Tips" shares some practical strategies for responding to these changes, and for ensuring students with TBI are fully included into the classroom. To practice your classroom problem-solving skills and expand your repertoire of your inclusionary strategies, fill in the blank columns of the chart with additional ideas for "Alternate Responses" and "Ways to Include Peers in the Process", using the filled-in chart in the textbook as a model.

	What You Might See	What You Might Be Tempted To Do	Alternate Response	Ways to Include Peers in the Process
Behavior	The student may show behavior and personality changes, such as temper outbursts, anxiety, fatigue, or depression.	Respond with strong disapproval and discipline the student's new behavior.		
Social Interactions	The student may have forgotten social skills and experience social misunderstandings because of his new identity struggles.	Ignore the student's social difficulties and hope they go away.		
Educational Performance	Learning new information may be difficult for him, or it may take him much longer to process in formation.	Require extra work in areas of difficulty rather than focus on holding skills and what he can accomplish.		
Classroom Attitudes	He may appear easily distracted, have headaches, or show a lack of motivation during instruction.	Reprimand his apparent lack of participation. Discipline him or excuse him from class activities.		

SAMPLE QUIZ FOR CHAPTER 13

MULTIPLE CHOICE

Circle the correct answer.

1. Which of the following is a dangerous form of child abuse that can cause traumatic brain injuries or even death?
    a. Open head injury
    b. Postconcussional syndrome
    c. Shaken impact syndrome
    d. Closed head injury

2. Which of the following is <u>not</u> a symptom of a mild traumatic brain injury?
    a. Brief absence seizures
    b. Restlessness
    c. Temper loss
    d. Need for extra sleep

3. What part of the brain controls balance and coordination?
    a. Parietal lobe
    b. Frontal lobe
    c. Occipital lobe
    d. Cerebellum

4. In the 1970s, 90 percent of people with brain injuries died. What percent survive today?
    a. 30%
    b. 45%
    c. 60%
    d. 50%

5. Malcolm had a severe brain injury. What is most likely true about him?
    a. He was in a coma for twelve hours.
    b. He has a 50-50 chance of lifetime effects.
    c. He is at risk for chronic intellectual, psychological, and academic deficits.
    d. He did not receive medical care within the first three hours after the injury.

6. Emily, age eight months, died from the leading cause of infant head injuries. What is it?
    a. Motor vehicle crashes
    b. Firearms
    c. Falls
    d. Child abuse

7. What possible negative effect of a "circle of friends" is mentioned?
    a. One-sided friendships can develop.
    b. The student with the injury can depend on the circle and be reluctant to make friends with other peers.
    c. The circle can receive special treatment from the teacher.
    d. The circle can become a clique.

8. Which of the following is regarded by many educators as the most systematic approach to design and delivery procedures for building and maintaining basic cognitive skills?
   a. Large group instruction
   b. Strategy instruction
   c. Direct Instruction
   d. Whole class instruction

9. Which model, successful with children with traumatic brain injury, suggests that teachers should put more time and emphasis in preventing a behavior than correcting it after the fact?
   a. Antecedent behavior management
   b. Positive behavior supports
   c. Applied behavior analysis
   d. Direct observation

10. What is true about the brain during the elementary years?
   a. It is "supercharged."
   b. If damaged, it results in lack of bonding.
   c. Connections between and within the hemispheres become more efficient.
   d. Logical thought emerges.

11. Why are congenital and perinatal brain injuries considered in a separate category from other brain injuries?
   a. They do not disrupt the person's identity as acquired injuries do.
   b. They are generally not as severe.
   c. Because they are evident at birth, the child has already received years of service before starting school.
   d. They are generally closed head injuries and thus have different characteristics.

12. Mary Beth received a severe injury to her frontal lobe. What was most likely affected?
   a. Her vision
   b. Her sensory functions
   c. Her speech and hearing
   d. Her motor skills and personality

13. What percentage of those with traumatic brain injuries experiences seizures?
   a. 10%
   b. 20%
   c. 30%
   d. 40%

14. Jason experiences memory difficulties due to a brain injury incurred when he was nearly suffocated by a plastic bag. Why is he <u>not</u> served under IDEA's definition of traumatic brain injury?
   a. The injury was not severe enough.
   b. The injury is expected to heal within fifteen years.
   c. Suffocation by a plastic bag is not considered an external force.
   d. At least two impairments must be evident to qualify.

15. All of the following can be considered major causes of closed and open head injuries <u>except</u> which?
   a. Automobile accidents
   b. Biomedical factors
   c. Falls
   d. Violence

16. Which of the following is true about individuals with mild head injuries?
   a. There is generally little change in the effects over a three-year period.
   b. The greatest improvement takes place within six months.
   c. They are at risk for chronic psychological and academic deficits.
   d. Lifetime effects are present for 50 percent of them.

17. Which of the following does <u>not</u> apply to the assessment of students with traumatic brain injury?
    a. Evaluation needs to be comprehensive.
    b. Evaluation needs to be on-going.
    c. A nurse must complete the evaluation.
    d. Evaluation should include cognitive processes.

18. Anna's IEP team is helping her start an after-school business making and selling rubber-stamped cards. What form of cognitive retraining is involved?
    a. Component
    b. Functional
    c. Compensatory strategy
    d. Perceptual sequencing

19. The following information is being recorded for Gary: information on triggering events, types of emotional and behavioral responses, and the desired behaviors. What is being developed?
    a. Personal intervention plan
    b. TOPS
    c. Neuropsychological assessment
    d. Differential reinforcement of other behavior

20. The Children's Place in Kansas City, Missouri, uses what type of approach to serve all children with traumatic brain injury?
    a. Group therapy
    b. Peer mentoring
    c. Intense team approach
    d. Multisensory approach

SHORT ANSWER

21. List two types of brain injury not served under the IDEA definition for traumatic brain injury.

    a. ______________________ b. ______________________

22. List the three major causes of traumatic brain injuries that are currently included under the definition used in IDEA.

    a. ______________________
    b. ______________________
    c. ______________________

23. Briefly describe the three forms of cognitive retraining.

    a. ______________________
    b. ______________________
    c. ______________________

ESSAY

24. Explain the differences between open and closed head injuries. Include a discussion of the controversy over injuries that are not presently included.
25. Compare and contrast methods to improve behavior, explaining specific details of effective strategies.

CHAPTER 14: COMMUNICATION DISORDERS

CHAPTER OVERVIEW

Communication disorders can be frustrating and uncomfortable to both the speaker and the listener. This chapter examines the diverse characteristics of speech and language disorders along with recognized causes and current prevalence rates. To understand how to help students with communication disorders, several tools for determining the presence of speech and language disorders are discussed. For determining special education and related service, an analysis of how to conduct language samples is explained. The best curriculum and methods are brought into a focused discussion, followed by an evaluation of the speech-language pathologist's role in inclusion and collaboration. Exemplary program options are summarized to understand the potential for students with communication disorders.

The life of Martin Krecker highlights the importance of early identification and services for students with language disorders. Martin did not talk until he was two and one half and for several months after beginning to speak used only one- or two-word sentences. In addition, his early words were difficult for others to understand because he was unable to produce many sounds appropriately. At four, Martin was speaking in full sentences, using appropriate speech.

CHAPTER AT-A-GLANCE

Chapter Outline	Instructional Goals	Key Concepts
WHO ARE STUDENTS WITH COMMUNICATION DISORDERS?		
Defining Communication Disorders • The Distinction Between Communication Disorders: Speech and Language • Cultural Differences in Communication	• Distinguish between speech and language communication disorders • Recognize how communication differences may be related to the culture	• A speech disorder is an impairment of one's articulation of speech sounds, fluency, or voice. • A language disorder reflects a problem in receiving information, understanding it, and formulating a spoken, written, or symbolic response. • Communication differences that are related to the culture of the individual are not considered impairments.
Describing the Characteristics • Typical Speech Development • Characteristics of Speech Impairments • Typical Language Development • Characteristics of Language Impairments • Effects of Communication Disorders	• Explain the typical course of the development of speech and characteristics and effects of speech impairments • Explain the typical course of the development of language and characteristics and effects of language impairments	• Most speech disorders are articulation disorders. • Voice impairments may be noted in pitch, intensity, resonance, and vocal quality. • Language is a shared system of rules and symbols for the exchange of information and includes rules of phonology, morphology, syntax, semantics, and pragmatics. • Communication disorders can impact a student's academic, social, and emotional development.
Identifying the Causes of Communication Disorders	• Identify and evaluate the causes of communication disorders	• Causes may be functional or organic and may be further classified according to when the problem began.
Identifying the Prevalence of Communication Disorders	• Apply prevalence figures to today's population	• It is estimated that 5% to 10% of the population has a communication disorder.

HOW ARE STUDENTS WITH COMMUNICATION DISORDERS EVALUATED?		
Determining the Presence of Communication Disorders • Assessment of Students who are Bilingual or Multilingual • Assessment of Communication Skills in Infants and Toddlers • Assessment of Communication Skills During School Years	• Examine the various means used to determine the presence of communication disorders	• The speech-language pathologist is the professional most likely to determine the presence and extent of a speech and/or language impairment. • Assessments include both formal and informal measures. • Informal measures are preferable to formal ones.
Determining the Nature and Extent of Special Education and Related Services	• Analyze the nature and extent of the need for special education and related services	• Analysis of an individual's conversation can provide information to assess language development and use.
HOW CAN YOU ESTABLISH EFFECTIVE TEACHING PRACTICES?		
Set Curricular Goals	• Understand the importance of correct pragmatic skills • Understand the need for self-expression of abstract ideas	• The focus of improvement of a student's communication disorder should be appropriate social skills and should be the goal of the speech-language pathologist, classroom teacher, parents, and student.
Implement Instruction • Self-Expression • Pragmatic Skills	• Explain methods of helping students best express themselves • Explain strategies that are associated with improved social skills	• The classroom teacher is the person most responsible for implementing instruction focused on enhancing students' communication needs.
Early Childhood Years	• Describe the characteristics of an effective early childhood program and early language activities	• Early emphasis is on the development of language and its use. Therapy can occur in the day-care setting or other natural environment.
Elementary Years	• Describe the characteristics of an effective, innovative elementary school program	• Programs for elementary students focus on helping the student develop better self-expression and social skills.
Middle and Secondary Years	• Describe the characteristics of an effective, innovative middle and secondary school program	• Those students continuing therapy in middle and secondary school require much repeated practice.
Transitional and Postsecondary Years	• Describe the characteristics of effective, innovative programs for adults with communication disorders	• Postsecondary job-training programs for individuals with communication disorders sometimes include therapy.
HOW CAN YOU ENCOURAGE PARTICIPATION?		
Practice Inclusion	• Summarize benefits and problems associated with inclusion of students who have communication disorders	• Many students receive their speech-language therapy while included in their general education classrooms.

Foster Collaboration • Professional-to-Professional Collaboration • Family and Professional Collaboration • School, Student, Family, and Community Collaboration	• Explore ways parents, teachers, and speech and language pathologists may collaborate to ensure the communicative student success	• The collaborative participation of students, teachers, speech-language pathologists, and parents to enhance communicative development results in students' language objectives being targeted with a variety of people in many settings.

PROJECT OPTIONS

In a local school, work with a speech-language pathologist and evaluate how he or she differentiates instruction for students with speech disorders and those with language disorders. Construct a chart based on your observations and what you learned in this chapter that clearly identifies differences between these two groups.

Create a peer tutoring game that students with and without speech disorders can play to help overcome speech difficulties.

1. Research alternative or augmentative communication approaches, and prepare three creative and artistic advertisements for your favorite three approaches based upon the six values guiding special education.
2. Prepare and present two dramatic presentations to demonstrate inappropriate vs. appropriate ways to respond to individuals with speech and/or language impairments. Do one presentation within the classroom and one at a local school.

KEY TERMS

Aphasia

Articulation

Bidialectal

Cleft palate/lip

Dialect

Early expressive language delay

Ebonics

Echolalia

Expressive language

Fluency problems

Functional language problems

Hypernasality

Hyponasality

Language disorders

Milieu teaching

Morphology

Multilingualism

Organic language problems

Phonology

Pragmatics

Receptive language disorders

Resonance

Semantics

Social interaction theories

Specific language impairment

Speech disorders

Stuttering

Syntax

Syntax errors

Vocal nodules

GUIDED REVIEW

The Book Report

Fifth grade was one of those years when everything seemed to be changing. Even though I was a good student, I was becoming self-conscious about the impression I made on others. So when our teacher told us that next week we would have special book report presentations in the school auditorium, I was very apprehensive.

I prepared for days, memorizing what I would say and how I would say it. The day arrived too soon. When it was my turn, I floated onto the stage and somehow made it to the conclusion of my report. I had thought that the book *The Secret Garden* by Frances Hodgson Burnett was the best I ever read and planned to recommend it highly. But when I came to my concluding remarks, what I said was "This is the best book I have ever written."

My valued peers immediately burst into laughter, and I didn't have any idea why. I thought about it and concluded that I must have used the wrong part of speech. I then corrected myself with "I mean it's the best book I ever wrote." More squeals of laughter. By then I was so red in the face that I must have looked like a beet. Then, in one brief moment, I realized what I had said and felt totally humiliated. I corrected myself one final time with "This is the best book I have ever read," and sat down.

The presentations went on, but I was oblivious to them all. How could the wrong words have come out of my mouth like that? I had practiced so carefully and didn't understand how my mouth could say something I didn't mean to say. I was convinced the world was ending and that no one would ever speak to me again. Though that didn't happen, I can still feel the pain of my language failure that day.

—Dorothy Leal

Who Are Students with Communication Disorders?

1. Effective communication requires knowledge of ______________________________ and ______________________________. When an individual does not understand and follow these rules, ______________________________ may occur. (*See* Defining Communication Disorders)

2. Identify the main characteristics of the two types of communication impairments. (*See* Defining Communication Disorders; The Distinction Between Communication Disorders: Speech and Language)

   Speech disorder: ______________________________

   Language disorder: ______________________________

3. Explain cultural influences on speech and language that are reflected in the ebonics controversy. (*See* Defining Communication Disorders; Cultural Differences in Communication)

   ____

   ____

4. Children learn to produce nearly all the consonants and vowels of their native language by the age of ______________. However, a ______________ year variance between the time that some children learn a sound and the time when others learn that same sound is common. (*See* Describing the Characteristics; Typical Speech Development)

5. List the major characteristics along with examples of the following speech impairments. (*See* Describing the Characteristics; Characteristics of Speech Impairments)

Type of Speech Impairment	***Characteristics***	***Examples***
Articulation disorders		
Voice disorders		
Fluency disorders		

Keeping It Short and Simple

Young children, prior to the age of about four years, typically use a phonology rule system that allows them to reduce words so they are more easily pronounced. They may omit final sounds and say *ca* for *cat* and may also reduce the number of syllables in a word such as *amal* for *animal*. When children become older, these errors may indicate problems with the child's phonological language system. Sound substitutions can also be articulation errors. Differentiating between these errors as articulation or language impairments is sometimes difficult for speech-language pathologists.

6. Name the four types of articulation disorders and circle the two that are very common. (*See* Describing the Characteristics; Characteristics of Speech Impairments; Articulation Disorders)

   a. ______________________ c. ______________________

   b. ______________________ d. ______________________

7. What type of speech disorder is stuttering? ______________________. Approximately what percent of the population stutter? ______________percent (*See* Describing the Characteristics; Characteristics of Speech Impairments; Fluency Disorders)

"Doggie" to "Mutt"

Children typically start out with a small number of words that represent a large number of objects in their environment. For example, toddlers often label all animals as "doggie." Through the development of more precise semantic rules, they differentiate dogs from cows and elephants and eventually refine dogs to poodles, beagles, or mutts.

8. Match the developmental language characteristic with the age at which it is typically observed (*See* Describing the Characteristics; Typical Language Development)

1. Has five- to fifty-word vocabulary	a. _____ Birth to 6 months
2. Has 200- to 300-word vocabulary	b. _____ 6 to 12 months
3. Laughs	c. _____ 12 to 18 months
4. Asks "why" questions	d. _____ 18 to 24 months
5. Uses past tense	e. _____ 24 to 36 months
6. Shares personal feelings and thoughts verbally	f. _____ 36 to 48 months
7. Recognizes the names of familiar people and objects	g. _____ 4 to 5 years
8. Follows two-step directions	h. _____ 5 to 6 years

9. Name each dimension of language that is described below. (*See* Describing the Characteristics; Typical Language Development)
   a. _______________governs the structure of words and the construction of word forms.
   b. _______________ encompasses the wide repertoire of individual phonemes and how they are produced, depending on their placement in a syllable or word.
   c. _______________ refers to the use of communication in social contexts.
   d. _______________ provides rules for putting together a series of words to form sentences and defines relationships among the elements within the sentences.
   e. _______________ refers to the content and meaning of what is expressed.

10. ____________________ ____________________ theories hold that language development is the outcome of a child's drive for attachment with his or her world. (*See* Describing the Characteristics; Typical Language Development)

11. Name the language dimension in focus for each type of language impairment described below. (*See* Describing the Characteristics; Characteristics of Language Impairments)

Language Dimension	***Language Impairment***
a.	Difficulty using social cues of communication within a shared social environment
b.	Difficulty in ordering words to convey intended meaning
c.	Difficulty in using words together in sentences to show meaning
d.	Difficulty using the structure of words to get or give information
e.	Difficulty discriminating differences in sounds or sound segments that signify differences in words

12. Describe the two types of speech and language disorders according to their cause. (*See* Identifying the Causes of Communication Disorders)
    Functional disorders: ______________________________
    Organic disorders: ______________________________

> Dr. William Magee, a plastic surgeon, is helping to prevent serious speech and language impairments in children with cleft palates. Dr. Magee operates on patients as young as fifteen days old. He says that the baby "can immediately begin life with nearly normal functions . . . (and) can coo like any normal child."
>
> Michael, one of his little patients, had three surgeries for bilateral cleft palate before he was fourteen months old. The surgeries have been successful. His mother says, "He is able to say a lot of different words: *Papa, Mama, more, yes, no.*"
>
> See *People Weekly*, June 13, 1994, pp. 39-43.

13. Give causes and examples of problems associated with each of the following disorders. (*See* Identifying the Causes of Communication Disorders)

Disorder	***Cause***	***Examples of Problem***
Organic language problem		
Functional language problem		
Functional and organic problem		

14. Explain the difference between a congenital impairment and an acquired impairment. (*See* Identifying the Causes of Communication Disorders)

    ____

    ____

15. Identify the percentages of all children and youth that have the following communication disorders. (*See* Identifying the Prevalence of Communication Disorders)
    Articulation disorders: ________ percent
    Fluency disorders: _________ percent
    Voice disorders: ________ percent
    Language disorders serious enough to affect academic performance: ___________ percent

16. What education placement is used for nearly 90 percent of students with communication disorders? (*See* Identifying the Prevalence of Communication Disorders)

    ____

Helping Students Who Stutter

1. Allow the student as much time as needed to complete a thought. Be relaxed and unhurried, and avoid the impulse to finish the student's words. Remember that the student needs to feel that you value his or her participation, especially after volunteering.
2. When does the student speak most fluently? Seek to increase those circumstances. Most children who stutter are fluent under some circumstances such as singing or reading and reciting poetry. Even lines learned for plays and skits are often given fluently, as James Earl Jones, who had a stuttering problem as he was growing up, so aptly demonstrates.
3. Remind peers that everyone has areas of strengths and other areas that are challenging. Point out that some are good runners, while others are less able to run quickly. Some get assignments done faster than others. Some can talk more easily than others.

How Are Students with Communication Disorders Evaluated?

17. How are articulation problems assessed both formally and informally? (*See* Determining the Presence of Communication Disorders)

    Formally: ____

    Informally: ____

18. Fair, unbiased evaluation to determine the presence of communication disorders is difficult for a student who is ____________________, ________________________, or ____. (*See* Determining the Presence of Communication Disorders; Assessment of Students who are Bilingual or Multilingual)

19. Arena assessment for young children is recommended because ______________________________ ____. (*See* Determining the Presence of Communication Disorders; Assessment of Communication Skills in Infants and Toddlers)

20. Under IDEA, speech-language therapy is a(n) ______________ service rather than a(n) ______________ service. (*See* Determining the Nature and Extent of Special Education and Related Services)

How Can You Establish Effective Teaching Practices?

21. Name the two curricular goals with students with communication disorders. (*See* Set Curricular Goals)

    ____

    ____

22. Explain effective teacher questioning as compared to yes/no questioning. (*See* Implement Instruction)

23. Match the strategy for arranging the environment to stimulate language use with its characteristics. (*See* Implement Instruction)

1. Interesting materials	a. ____ Create an absurd situation to prompt a response.
2. Out of reach	b. ____ Set up a situation that prevents student from completing a task.
3. Inadequate portions	c. ____ Create a situation where student wants help.
4. Choice making	d. ____ Provide an insufficient amount of needed materials.
5. Assistance	e. ____ Present many options available to complete a task.
6. Sabotage	f. ____ Provide an inviting environment with things student enjoys.
7. Silly situations	g. ____ Place materials within view, but difficult to obtain.

Camp Chatterbox

How can kids learn to use augmentative and alternative communication devices (AAC) in a nonthreatening atmosphere? Send them to camp. Camp Chatterbox, located at Camp Merry Heart, the Easter Seals Camp of New Jersey, provides children ages five to sixteen the opportunity to learn and have fun at the same time. For example, one night the counselors dressed up as leprechauns for a scavenger hunt. The campers, using their AAC, had to answer questions posed by the counselors to win.

The children are not the only ones to learn from the experience. One mother comments about her tendency to translate for her son. "The camp helps kids. . . .learn how to effectively communicate for themselves without our interference."

See Joan Bruno, "Mom Went to Speech. . . .Instead of the Beach" (1998) in *Exceptional Parent, 28*(4), 48, 51.

24. Name and describe the largest national program that integrates preschoolers with disabilities into preschool classes. (*See* Early Childhood Years)

____

____

25. For therapy to be most effective for elementary age students, it is recommended that ____________________ and ____________________ approaches be combined. (*See* Elementary Years)

26. What is the focus of therapy for students who continue to receive services into the middle and secondary years? (*See* Middle and Secondary Years)

____

____

How Can You Encourage Participation?

27. Describe things collaborators can do together to facilitate students' language development and interaction. (*See* Foster Collaboration)

Professional collaborators: ____

____

Family collaborators: ____

____

Community collaborators: ____

____

28. List three changes benefiting individuals with communication disorders that resulted from ADA and IDEA. (*See* Foster Collaboration; School, Student, Family, and Community Collaboration)
    a. ______________________________
    b. ______________________________
    c. ______________________________

Does Polly Want a Cracker?

Julia Smith of Somerset, England, discovered an innovative way to help her students with speech and language impairments. Julie brings her pet cockatiel to work with her. She videotapes the students' attempts to elicit speech from the bird and then plays the tapes back to the students for analysis and discussion. The strategy is proving more effective than typical speech therapies.

See *Times Educational Supplement*, March 26, 1993, p. 4.

APPLICATION EXERCISES FOR CHAPTER 14

Application Exercise 14a. Identifying Characteristics of Typical Language Development

See if you can rank these students by language development according to age, from youngest to oldest. After you have put them in order, see if you can identify the age range for each child from birth to six years.

1. Cedric knows that when Mom says "no" she means it, even when he doesn't obey. He responds to simple commands such as "give me a kiss" and uses many sound patterns in response to others' speech.
2. Muhammad uses his vocabulary of 2,600 words in complex sentences, though may sometimes be confused. He loves to tell stories and tell you what he thought about the story. He also likes to tell simple jokes.
3. Jana's vocabulary includes over 200 words and she uses possessives, plurals, and verbs with some expertise. She listens and imitates everything and makes two- to three-word sentences.
4. Yu-chen loves to listen to stories and will often discuss them with others, recounting the events of the story. She not only follows two-step directions, but uses simple questions and pronouns.
5. Fidel has a vocabulary of about forty words when talking with people. He recognizes many words and can point to them in books as well as in the environment.
6. Thalalia's questions include *who, what, when, where, why,* and *how*. She explains and describes events with verb contractions. She has begun to identify differences and make analogies.
7. Josi laughs and coos in response to familiar situations. Her parents spend a lot of time talking to her and enjoy watching and listening to her responses to them.
8. Julienne uses past tense, but still makes some grammatical errors. She knows her first and last name and uses prepositions and conjunctions in her sentences.

Name	*Age Range*
1.	
2.	
3.	
4.	
5.	
6.	
7.	
8.	

Application Exercise 14b. Identifying Language Impairments by the Dimension of Language in Focus

Match the language dimension affected with each student's language difficulty.

1. Phonology	a.____ Anish asks questions and doesn't wait for answers or ignores them.
2. Morphology	b.____ Elissa told her six-year-old classmate "Me sick" before she went home.
3. Syntax	c.____ Amelia always says, "Give me the thing, please" instead of naming it.
4. Semantics	d.____ Ku tells long stories but won't listen to anyone else's story.
5. Pragmatics	e.____ Jim cannot auditorially differentiate between the words "fire" and "far."
	f.____ Shih Wei told his mom "Gone the boys" when his brothers left him behind.
	g.____ Lettie has difficulty in spelling and wrote "pin" for pen on a test.

Application Exercise 14c. Expanding Your Understanding of Communication Disorders

Based upon the major questions addressed in this chapter, organize your ideas similarly to the "expansion" method discussed in this chapter. Start with a simple summary statement for each of the key concepts, and then expand these into more detailed summaries. Think of different ways to word your summaries to make the concepts clearer.

Major Questions: Who Are Students with Ccommunication Disorders? How Are Students with Communication Disorders Evaluated? How Can You Establish Effective Teaching Practices? How can You Encourage Participation?

SAMPLE QUIZ FOR CHAPTER 14

MULTIPLE CHOICE

Circle the correct answer.

1. Which of the following is not a skill required for auditory processing?
   a. Blending sounds that are heard
   b. Discriminating between important and unimportant input
   c. Remembering input
   d. Articulating intelligible speech

2. Identify the name of the team approach in which the child is observed doing a wider variety of activities across many domains than would be observed in a clinical setting.
   a. Collaborative assessment
   b. Environmental assessment
   c. Arena assessment
   d. Functional assessment

3. Who is ultimately responsible for implementing strategies to help students develop communication skills in the general education classroom?
   a. Speech-language pathologist
   b. Special education teacher
   c. Paraeducator or parent volunteer
   d. Classroom teacher

4. What determines pitch?
   a. The air pressure coming from the lungs through the vocal folds
   b. The rate of vibration in the vocal folds
   c. The way in which the tone coming from the vocal folds is modified by the cavities of the throat, mouth, and nose
   d. The length of time needed for the sound to emerge from the larynx

5. As teachers consider program options, what percent of students with communication disorders can they expect to be served in the general education classroom for all or most of each school day?
   a. 50%
   b. 97%
   c. 80%
   d. 25%

6. Which one of the following is not a good strategy for arranging the environment to stimulate language use?
   a. Present two or more options for activities
   b. Create a need to communicate
   c. Do not provide assistance
   d. Provide materials that children enjoy

7. What percentage of all children and youth between birth and age twenty-one has a speech or language impairment serious enough to warrant special services?
   a. 1%
   b. 3%
   c. 5%
   d. 8%

8. Werner has a functional language problem. How does it most likely manifest itself?
   a. Articulation disorder due to cerebral palsy
   b. Acquired aphasia from meningitis
   c. Cleft palate
   d. Stuttering

9. What is the most common cause for speech and language disorders?
   a. Organic
   b. Neurological
   c. Congenital
   d. Unknown

10. When is prereferral most often used with students who might have a communication disorder?
    a. When they are bilingual
    b. When they are preschoolers
    c. When they are also mildly mentally retarded
    d. Prereferral is typically not used

11. When is a speech or language difference <u>not</u> a communication disorder?
    a. When there is steady improvement
    b. When it is due to a dialectical difference
    c. When the individual is still intelligible
    d. When it is due to congenital or hereditary causes, since it is then referred to as a handicap instead of a disorder

12. Ned, age six, has an articulation disorder. What is he most likely to say?
    a. Say "dat" instead of "that"
    b. Say "cub" instead of "cup"
    c. Say "mezur" instead of "measure"
    d. Say "half" instead of "have"

13. Which is the largest group of speech impairments?
    a. Articulation disorders
    b. Voice disorders
    c. Language disorders
    d. Resonance disorders

14. Who is the person most likely to determine the presence and extent of a speech and/or language disorder?
    a. Speech-language pathologist
    b. Special education teacher
    c. Guidance counselor
    d. Special education coordinator

15. With which type of language impairment does a student have difficulty with word meanings within a sentence?
    a. Pragmatics
    b. Morphology
    c. Syntax
    d. Semantics

16. Seven-year-old Zoe uses verb tenses incorrectly. What type of communication disorder might she have?
    a. Expressive language disorder
    b. Early receptive language delay
    c. Vygotsky's Disorder
    d. Organic language disorder

17. Helga suffered a brain injury from freestyle skiing. Although she retains her pre-injury intelligence, she now has trouble expressing herself in speech. What does she have?
    a. Milieu disorder
    b. Vocal nodules
    c. Aphasia
    d. Goldstein's syndrome

18. Quentin has a language impairment due to a congenital impairment. What is the most likely cause?
    a. Deafness due to middle ear infection
    b. Autism
    c. Meningitis
    d. Neonatal fever

19. Mrs. Richardson is reluctant to have an arena assessment conducted for her son, who has a communication disorder. What is the most likely reason?
    a. He is only three years old.
    b. He is still depending on prelinguistic communicative behaviors.
    c. He needs remediation, not compensation.
    d. He is very shy and self-conscious.

20. Melanie Waters, a speech-language pathologist in Baldwin County, Alabama, uses what techniques to serve elementary school students with communication disorders in the general education classroom?
    a. Oral presentations
    b. Phonics drills
    c. Whole language techniques
    d. Word games

SHORT ANSWER

21. List the five dimensions of language that work together to produce language.

a. ____________________ d. ____________________

b. ____________________ e. ____________________

c. ____________________

22. Explain four (of the seven) strategies used to arrange an environment that stimulates language use.

____

____

____

____

23. Explain why collaboration with a speech-language pathologist is necessary for you to help meet a student's communicative needs.

____

____

____

____

ESSAY

24. Explain how communication disorders differ in each of the five dimensions of language.

25. Discuss the different roles of the speech-language pathologist in terms of inclusion and collaboration.

CHAPTER 15: HEARING LOSS

CHAPTER OVERVIEW

In this chapter you will be studying a different culture, the Deaf culture. By your awareness and sensitivity to the unique Deaf culture, you can help build a bridge between the hearing and deaf worlds. We suggest that you see at least one film that portrays the Deaf culture. You are also provided with a case study about Heather Whitestone that asks you to consider the conflict among people with hearing loss about the use of lipreading for communication. This chapter explores many dimensions of hearing loss, including an overview of assessment possibilities and explanation of methods and curriculum that are used by people with hearing loss. Additional program options at each level are described to provide an overview of effective practices for serving these students.

The life of Amala Brown provides an illustration of a student with hearing loss who overcame a rough start in life. She has attended a public school in general education classes for much of her education and now has strong language skills in English and ASL. Amala's mother, a teacher of children who are deaf and a sign language interpreter, has provided a home environment that has been ideal for Amala to develop linguistically and socially.

CHAPTER AT-A-GLANCE

Chapter Outline	Instructional Goals	Key Concepts
WHO ARE STUDENTS WITH HEARING LOSS?		
Defining Hearing Loss	• Evaluate the issues surrounding the controversy over how to refer to people who are deaf and hard of hearing • Distinguish between definitions of deafness, hearing impairment, and hard of hearing	• Hearing loss is difficult to define because the point at which hearing stops being normal and starts being a disability cannot be stated. • Degrees of hearing loss are identified as slight, mild, moderate, severe, and profound.
Describing the Characteristics • Language and Communication • Psychosocial Dimensions • Education	• Describe key characteristics of children who are deaf or hard of hearing	• Communication with parents, peers, and teachers plays a major role in the psychological, social, and emotional development of children with hearing loss. • Achievement levels continue to be a primary concern, particularly among children from diverse racial, ethnic, and linguistic backgrounds.
Identifying the Causes of Hearing Loss • Prelingual Causes • Postlingual Causes	• Identify the major causes of hearing loss	• A conductive loss is caused by a problem in the outer or middle ear. • A sensorineural loss is caused by a problem in the inner ear or along the nerve pathway to the brain stem.
Identifying the Prevalence of Hearing Loss	• Recognize prevalence rates for individuals who are deaf or hard of hearing	• Prevalence is estimated at 1.3% of children under the age of 18. • Prelingual hearing loss accounts for 95% of students who are deaf and hard of hearing while postlingual hearing loss accounts for 5%.

HOW ARE STUDENTS WITH HEARING LOSS EVALUATED?		
Determining the Presence of Hearing Loss	• Summarize ways to determine the presence of hearing loss • Explain how an audiogram is used for assessment purposes	• Infants who fail screenings have their hearing tested using an auditory brain stem response (ABR) test. • Older students have a behavioral audiological evaluation to measure hearing levels.
Determining the Nature and Extent of Special Education and Related Services	• List the factors that are critical in determining an appropriate educational setting	• Regular reassessments of language, hearing, speech, and/or sign- or speechreading, academic achievement, and socialization are essential to provide an appropriate education.
HOW CAN YOU ESTABLISH EFFECTIVE TEACHING PRACTICES?		
Set Curricular Goals	• Describe fundamental components of the curriculum	• Language, reading, and writing form the central curriculum focus, with specialized curriculum in Deaf culture, speech, and aural habilitation.
Implement Instruction	• Identify the communication modes used in classrooms • Explain helpful instructional strategies	• Communication methods include oral/aural, bilingual-bicultural and total communication. • Instructional strategies are particularly effective when they emphasize experiential learning, build on the students' current knowledge and skills, require them to interact with peers, capitalize on the visual medium, and reduce environmental distraction.
Early Childhood Years	• Distinguish characteristics of effective early childhood programs for students who are deaf or hard of hearing	• It is important for early identification programs to have a direct connection to early intervention programs
Elementary Years	• Distinguish characteristics of effective elementary programs for students with hearing loss	• A top priority in elementary programs is English language acquisition.
Middle and Secondary Years	• Distinguish characteristics of effective programs for middle and secondary students	• During the secondary years, the priority is to maintain high academic standards and expectations.
Transitional and Postsecondary Years	• Distinguish characteristics of effective program options for adults with hearing loss	• The U.S. Congress funds six postsecondary programs for students who are deaf and hard of hearing. • Transition programs recognize that difficulties with English-based communication are the most significant obstacle to successful transition.

HOW CAN YOU ENCOURAGE PARTICIPATION?		
Practice Inclusion • Regular Classroom • Resource Room • Separate Class • Special School	• Provide arguments for both sides of the controversy over the least restrictive environment for students who are deaf or hard of hearing	• Most educators favor inclusion while members of the Deaf community advocate for placement in schools for the deaf. • More than 80% of students with hearing loss are being served in the public schools.
Foster Collaboration • Professional Collaboration • Student and Family Collaboration • Community Collaboration	• Identify the professionals who should collaborate to meet the educational needs of a child with hearing loss.	• The needs of individuals with hearing loss are accommodated through family members as well as through sign language interpreters, special text telephones, telephone relay services, captioned television and real time graphic display, and the Internet.

PROJECT OPTIONS

1. Interview a person who is deaf or hard of hearing that you meet through a deaf club or the organization Self-Help for the Hard of Hearing. Ask this person questions about LRE, cochlear implants, and the role of ASL in the education of children with hearing loss. Present your findings in chart form.
2. Record and watch a television comedy or drama with the sound off and the captions activated on your TV. Write about your response to the experience. Then watch the same show with the sound on. Summarize the differences and identify what would have made the first experience more comfortable for you.
3. Teach yourself American Sign Language well enough to carry on a brief conversation with someone who is deaf or hard of hearing. Prepare what you will say and questions you will ask. Then enjoy the conversation and have the person you converse with evaluate the strengths and weaknesses of your ASL.
4. Investigate program options and typical placements in your community. Ask the person in charge at each place how the six values guiding special education are operative in the programs. Using the responses, prioritize where you would place Amala and other students you know who have hearing loss.
5. Research available technology for those who are deaf, such as captioned TV and TDDs. Evaluate the benefits and drawbacks for each one. Then interview two or three people who have hearing loss to find out what needs are not yet being met that could be met by technology. Summarize your findings and submit them to a national technology corporation.

KEY TERMS

American Sign Language (ASL)

Audiogram

Audiologist

Cochlear implant

Conductive hearing loss

Deaf culture

Deafness

Fingerspelling

Hearing aid

Interpreters

Prelingual hearing loss

Postlingual hearing loss

Sensorineural hearing loss

TT (Text Telephone)

GUIDED REVIEW

Giving Pride

Curtis John Pride is the first deaf baseball player in the major leagues for fifty-three years. Curtis's disability became apparent to his parents at an early age. He yelled instead of babbled when he was six-months old and did not flinch or startle when a door slammed. Curtis was diagnosed with sensorineural deafness at ten months. His father says he felt very negative about his son's future at that time. Then he realized, "As parents, it was our responsibility to give him a chance." They enrolled him in a preschool program that used oral communication and increased their efforts to teach him orally and through pictures at home. Although Curtis knows sign language, he relies on lipreading and speaking. His parents also helped him become as independent as possible by teaching functional skills, like going to the restaurant counter alone and ordering pizza for his family. Curtis attended a school for the deaf in elementary school, but once he reached seventh grade, he pleaded with his parents to return to his neighborhood school. They agreed. "Attending the neighborhood school was a big turning point in Curtis's life," his mother says. "From then on, he just blossomed."

See "Brave Hearts: Giving Curtis Pride," by Bridget Lyne in *Exceptional Parent* (1998), *28*(5), pp. 26–34, 50.

Who Are Students with a Hearing Loss?

1. Why is hearing loss difficult to define? (*See* Defining Hearing Loss)

   ____

2. Give three problems with categorizing hearing. (*See* Defining Hearing Loss)
   a. ______________________________
   b. ______________________________
   c. ______________________________

3. Audiologists evaluate hearing in terms of ____________ and ____________.
   The results are then charted on a(n) ____________. (*See* Defining Hearing Loss)

4. List the five terms used to identify degree of hearing loss. (*See* Defining Hearing Loss)
   a. ______________________________
   b. ______________________________
   c. ______________________________
   d. ______________________________
   e. ______________________________

5. In this chapter you read about the diversity of terms used in identifying students with hearing loss. List and explain at least three terms used with a people-first approach. (*See* Defining Hearing Loss)

People-first Term	***What Does This Term Communicate?***
a.	
b.	
c.	

6. The single greatest challenge for children who are deaf or hard of hearing is ______________________________
   ______________________________. (*See* Describing the Characteristics; Language and Communication)

7. Contrast earlier and recent perceptions about the social and emotional development of children and adolescents who are deaf and hard of hearing. (*See* Describing the Characteristics; Psychosocial Dimensions)
   Earlier beliefs: ______________________________
   Recent beliefs: ______________________________

8. Describe the educational issues surrounding the academic achievement of students with hearing loss. (*See* Describing the Characteristics; Education)

____

____

9. How is the ear like a radio? (*See* Identifying the Causes of Hearing Loss)
   a. Inner ear: ____
   b. Middle ear: ____
   c. Outer ear: ____

10. Describe the types of hearing loss and identify in which part of the ear they occur. (*See* Identifying the Causes of Hearing Loss)

    Conductive hearing loss: ____

    ____

    Sensorineural hearing loss: ____

    ____

11. Match the cause of hearing loss to the percentage and time of onset associated with it. (*See* Identifying the Causes of Hearing Loss)

1. Prelingual cause (95% of all students)	a. _____ Meningitis
2. Postlingual cause (5% of all students)	b. _____ Infants born prematurely
	c. _____ Recurring otitis media
	d. _____ Side effects from medications
	e. _____ Genetic deafness
	f. _____ Maternal rubella
	g. _____ The virus known as congenital cytomegalovirus

12. What percentage of all students experience hearing loss? (*See* Identifying the Prevalence of Hearing Loss)

    ________________ percent

How Are Student with a Hearing Loss Evaluated?

13. Determining the presence of hearing loss requires various assessments, depending on the age of the individual. Describe the evaluation for an infant and for an older child. (*See* Determining the Presence of Hearing Loss)

    Infants: ____

    Older Children: ____

14. What does an audiogram record? (*See* Determining the Presence of Hearing Loss)
    a. ______________________ or pitch, the number of vibrations in one second;
    b. ______________________ or loudness;
    c. pressure of sound rather than its movement, as measured by ____________________.

15. An audiogram, found in a student's file, provides much useful information. You can tell many things by where the Xs and Os were on the audiogram. Identify two useful things you can learn from the audiogram. (*See* Determining the Presence of Hearing Loss)
    a. ____
    b. ____

16. In determining the appropriate education setting and related services and supplementary aids for a child with hearing loss, six areas are considered. Identify those six areas and explain who is involved and what information they may provide in determining the needs in this area. (*See* Determining the Nature and Extent of Special Education and Related Services)

Area Assessed to Determine Appropriate Education	***Contributing Participants and Their Input***
a.	
b.	
c.	
d.	
e.	
f.	

Babbling in Sign Language

Deaf children often go through a babbling stage as they learn sign language, similar to the vocal babbling of hearing children. The hand movements of deaf children of deaf parents who use sign language meet the criteria of babbling 71 percent of the time. The hand movements of children with hearing parents meet the criteria only 15% of the time. The criteria for babbling is the incorporation of sounds (movements) of the parents' language, repetition of those sounds or movements, and the use of those in the first meaningful words used by the infant.

See *Kansas City Star*, April 14, 1991.

How Can You Establish Effective Teaching Practices?

17. What are the two schools of thought about curriculum for students who are deaf and hard of hearing? (*See* Set Curricular Goals)

    a. ______________________________

    b. ______________________________

18. Explain the purpose and characteristics of curriculum for the four identified areas for students who are deaf and hard of hearing. (*See* Set Curricular Goals)

Curricular Area	***Purpose***	***Characteristics or Components***
a. Language, reading, and writing		
b. Deaf culture		
c. Speech		
d. Aural habilitation		

19. Match the methods of communication in educational programs used by individuals who are deaf and hard of hearing with the characteristics of the methods. (*See* Implement Instruction; Instructional Conversations)

1. Oral/aural	a. _____ Instruction in ASL
2. Bilingual-bicultural	b. _____ The expectation that the students use ASL for communication and teaching of English through written form
3. Total communication	c. _____ Instruction in spoken English, curriculum in speech and aural habilitation, and the expectation that students use speech, speechreading, and auditory skills
	d. _____ Instruction with speech and a manually coded English
	e. _____ Incorporates curriculum in speech and aural habilitation

20. With children who are deaf and hard of hearing, English is sometimes introduced as the second language. What is typically taught as the child's first language? (*See* Implement Instruction; Bilingual/Bicultural)

____

21. Describe key characteristics and examples of five effective instructional strategies for students with hearing loss. (*See* Implement Instruction; Classroom and Instructional Design Modification)

Instructional Strategy	***Characteristics and Examples***
a.	
b.	
c.	
d.	
e.	

Visual Teaching Strategies

How do you enhance communication and instruction for students who are deaf or hard of hearing? Do you need some general visual techniques, including task organizers and daily schedules? To obtain this information as well as a sample lesson, See *Teaching Exceptional Children*, January/February, 2001, *33*(3), pp. 38–44.

22. List key features for each program mentioned in this chapter at each of the life-span levels. (*See* Observe Programs in Practice)

Program	***Key Features***
Dallas Regional Day School Program for the Deaf	
Northwest Regional Program	
Utah Extension Consultant Division	
Universities conduct needs assessments and design accommodations	

How Can You Encourage Participation?

Would you know what to do if a student's hearing aid stopped working? If you have a student who is deaf or hard of hearing in your class, you will want to talk to an audiologist or teacher of the deaf to find out how to do minor repairs. Generally, a battery replacement will be all that's needed. It will be a good idea to have a battery tester on hand as well as a supply of extra batteries. The batteries need to be disposed of properly.

23. What is the stand of virtually all professional and parent organizations involved in the field of deafness regarding educational options for children who are deaf and hard of hearing? (*See* Practice Inclusion)

    ____

24. Why is appropriateness of placement, instead of the least restrictive environment, more desirable for students who have a hearing loss? (*See* Practice Inclusion)

    ____

25. What percentage of students who have hearing loss are being served in the public schools? ___________% What percentage of these students are fully included in regular classrooms? __________________% (*See* Practice Inclusion)

26. Compare and contrast characteristics for how different school placements serve students with different needs. (*See* How Can You Encourage Participation?; Practice Inclusion)

Placement	***Characteristics***
a. Regular Classroom	
b. Resource Room	
c. Separate Class	
d. Special School	

The Power of Community Influence

King Jordan is the first deaf president of Gallaudet University. Referring to the student/faculty strike in March 1988 that helped him become elected, Jordan stated that it required a revolution for him to become president of Gallaudet. Making sure that Gallaudet had a deaf president was only one important outcome of the Deaf President Now movement, however. President Jordan emphasized that the movement said to the world, "You can no longer pretend we are not as capable as you. You must allow us to shape our own lives."

See *Perspectives on Deafness*, Vol. 41, No. 1-2, pp. 75–78.

27. Using information and boxes from the chapter, identify ways different collaborators can contribute to the success of students with hearing loss. (*See* Foster Collaboration)

Professional: ______________________________

Student and family:

____

Community:

____

28. "TT" stands for ______________ ______________ and can be used for some of the following purposes:

____

____

____

(*See* Foster Collaboration; Special Telephones)

Education and Deafness

Understanding the past and the needs of the present enables a better tomorrow, according to this article. For a clear definition of deafness and finding an identity in the hearing and nonhearing worlds, as well a thorough coverage of public laws that affect the education of students who are deaf or hard of hearing, read "Education and Deafness" in *Exceptional Parent*, September 1998, *28*(9), pp. 40–46.

APPLICATION EXERCISES FOR CHAPTER 15

Application Exercise 15a. Identifying Levels of Hearing Loss

Place in order the following students according to their level of hearing loss, listing the student with the greatest hearing difficulty first. You may want to use Figure 15-2 in your textbook, "Frequency Spectrum of Familiar Sounds," to help you.

1. Jaime has difficulty hearing things like waterfalls.
2. Summea is not able to hear the lawn mower outside her bedroom window.
3. Pedro cannot hear the sounds "j" and "n" "ng" and "d" and "b."
4. Najee is able to identify the "f" and "s" sounds, but he struggles to hear the "ch" and "sh" sounds.
5. Juliana can hear the phone ring and can even hear occasional trucks, but is not able to hear rock bands playing.
6. Sammie loves to watch the jets at the airport, but cannot hear the sounds they make.

Greatest amount of hearing loss	1.
	2.
	3.
	4.
	5.
Least amount of hearing loss	6.

Application Exercise 15b. Differentiating Means of Communication

Read the different ways students communicate, then identify the communciation mode being used.

1. Sully relies on her minimal hearing abilities and speechreading abilities.

   ____

2. NamPrik tells his friends "I have too much homework" by speaking these words at the same time as using a sign for each word and inflection.

   ____

3. Griffin wants to tell a friend that he is going to a movie. He first signs the location ("movie theater"), then signs who is gong ("me") and then finally the signs the verb ("going").

   ____

4. Sharon receives instruction in spoken English, though her curriculum is in speech and aural habilitation.

   ____

5. Memo receives instruction in ASL.

   ____

6. Kunti receives instruction through the use of speech and manually coded English.

   ____

Application Exercise 15c. Interpreting Key Components of Hearing Loss

Based upon the major questions addressed in this chapter, summarize the major concepts concerning hearing loss. For each major chapter question, use what you know about Amala or another individual highlighted in this chapter to explain the key concepts involved in answering each question.

Major Questions: Who Are Students with Hearing Loss? How Are Students with a Hearing Loss Evaluated? How Can You Establish Effective Teaching Practices? How Can You Encourage Participation?

SAMPLE QUIZ FOR CHAPTER 15

MULTIPLE CHOICE

Circle the correct answer.

1. Identify the name of the visual, on-line community where students are brought together for instructional conversations monitored by an on-line teacher.
    a. Schoolhouse Palace
    b. Children's Chat
    c. Internet Discussion Board
    d. Group Chat

2. What does an audiogram measure?
    a. Frequency and pitch
    b. Frequency and intensity
    c. Intensity and loudness
    d. Intensity and movement

3. Karl's hearing is at the 80 decibel level. What can he hear?
    a. A baby crying
    b. The phone ringing
    c. A cat purring
    d. A dishwasher in operation

4. What percent of children who are deaf have hearing parents?
    a. Under 50 percent
    b. About 60 percent
    c. About 75 percent
    d. Over 90 percent

5 All of the following form the central curricular goals for students who are deaf or hard of hearing <u>except</u> which?
    a. Language
    b. Social studies
    c. Reading
    d. Writing

6. Which of the following is <u>not</u> true about hearing aids?
    a. They can correct hearing loss only up to 40 decibels.
    b. There is always some distortion with hearing aids.
    c. The amplifier is worn inside the ear, but the microphone and receiver can be worn on the body.
    d. They are electroacoustic devices that make sounds louder.

7. What is the most common cause of hearing loss in children?
    a. Heredity
    b. Meningitis
    c. Premature birth
    d. Unknown

8. To what does intensity refer?
    a. The number of vibrations in a second
    b. The pitch of a sound
    c. The pressure of a sound
    d. The cycles of frequency

9. Under IDEA, what is the most important criterion for determining program placement?
   a. Meeting students' needs
   b. Least restrictive environment
   c. Student choice
   d. Parental collaboration

10. Why do many educators and members of the Deaf community oppose the use of manually coded English systems?
    a. They take longer to sign than ASL.
    b. They are not true languages, but distortions, of ASL.
    c. They are being introduced by the younger generation, and older deaf people cannot understand them.
    d. They are not understood overseas, which presents problems at international conferences of the Deaf.

11. What is the speech banana?
    a. The range of frequencies and decibel levels found in speech sounds
    b. The shape on a chart that shows the most common areas of deafness
    c. The width of an individual's mouth at its widest points, measured in millimeters
    d. The ratio of decibels to intensity

12. Which of the following is not a responsibility of an audiologist?
    a. Identify and evaluate hearing loss
    b. Select and evaluate hearing aids and other amplification devices
    c. Interpret for a student in a general education classroom
    d. Rehabilitate individuals with hearing loss

13. For children who are deaf, what modality is the one through which language must largely be acquired?
    a. Sensorimotor
    b. Palatal
    c. Visual
    d. Cognitive

14. Prelingual hearing loss, at birth or before learning language, accounts for what percent of students who are deaf and hard of hearing?
    a. 75 percent
    b. 95 percent
    c. 25 percent
    d. 50 percent

15. What is the range of hearing levels?
    a. 125 to 8,000 cycles per second
    b. 100 to 350 cycles per second
    c. 0 to 110 dB
    d. 20 to 800 dB

16. In hearing, to what does frequency refer?
    a. The decibels of a sound
    b. The loudness of a sound
    c. The intensity of a pitch
    d. The number of vibrations per second

17. Where do the fewest placements occur for students who are deaf or hard of hearing?
    a. Resource room
    b. Separate class
    c. Regular class
    d. Residential facility

18. What early childhood program, mentioned in the textbook, is family-centered and provides parent advisors who make home visits at least weekly to provide services to the Deaf and encourage the development of language?
    a. Texas School for the Deaf
    b. Texas Childhood Development Center
    c. Early Childhood Community Center
    d. Dallas Regional-Day School Program

19. Why is the Deaf community concerned over the declining role that schools for the deaf play in the lives of children and youth?
    a. Loss of quality education
    b. Loss of access to best practices
    c. Loss of the sense of community shared by students
    d. Loss of Deaf culture being passed to succeeding generations

20. What is the major challenge faced by college or university students who are deaf or hard of hearing?
    a. Socialization
    b. Collaboration
    c. Individualization of instruction
    d. Evaluation

SHORT ANSWER

21. What are four factors that play a significant role in a child's psychosocial development?
    a. ______________________________
    b. ______________________________
    c. ______________________________
    d. ______________________________

22. Name three ways in which deaf people typically communicate and three methods of communication used in educational programs.
    a. ______________ d. ______________
    b. ______________ e. ______________
    c. ______________ f. ______________

23. Name three ways instructional strategies for students with hearing loss can be made particularly effective.
    a. ______________________________
    b. ______________________________
    c. ______________________________

ESSAY

24. You are a teacher and will have a deaf student in your class this year. Describe the classroom design and visual aid modifications you can make to enhance learning for this student.

25. Present a rationale for both sides of the controversy of the least restrictive environment and appropriate placement for students with hearing loss in schools today. Explain the role of Deaf culture in the controversy.

CHAPTER 16: BLINDNESS AND LOW VISION

CHAPTER 16 OVERVIEW

This chapter provides an understanding of both the legal definition and IDEA's definition of visual impairment. It describes the characteristics, causes, and prevalence rates associated with this disability and explains how low vision and blindness affect learning. It notes that because of a visual impairment, students may experience limitations in the range and variety of experiences, in the ability of getting around, and in interactions with the environment. It explains that once the presence of a visual impairment has been determined, it is important that teachers assess how a student uses vision in order to determine the nature of special education for students who are blind or who have low vision. Two broad areas of academic and functional curricula are described as equally important for the future success of these students. A history of inclusion and collaboration gives the background for understanding placement options available today. This chapter concludes with characteristics of program options that demonstrate the best practices for different age students with visual impairments.

The life of high school freshman Elexis Gillette is a good example of a student with a significant visual impairment for whom the system worked. His mother, who is also blind, has modeled self-sufficiency for him. The school system has responded to meet Elexis's needs by providing him with qualified and knowledgeable teachers and orientation and mobility specialists. He has been encouraged to do for himself and to be an equal participant in his home and his school. "Special" considerations were provided only to equalize his knowledge of the world and accessibility to it, not to make life at home or school "easier."

CHAPTER AT-A-GLANCE

Chapter Outline	Instructional Goals	Key Concepts
WHO ARE STUDENTS WITH VISUAL IMPAIRMENT?		
Defining Visual Impairment	• Explain how blindness and visual impairment are defined	• Legal blindness is defined as a central visual acuity of 20/200 or less in the better eye (with corrective lenses) or central visual acuity of greater than 20/200 if the field of vision is less than 20 degrees. • Within education, visual impairment is an impairment in vision that adversely affects a student's educational performance.
Describing the Characteristics • Limitations in the Range and Variety of Experiences • Limitations in the Ability to Get Around • Limitations in Interactions with the Environment	• Describe key characteristics of visual impairment	• Students with visual impairments and blindness have a limited ability to model visually and learn incidentally from the environment. • Students with visual impairments are at risk of being experientially deprived because they are not able to learn about the world from a distance.

Identifying the Causes of Visual Impairment • Transmission of Light Energy • Conversion of Light to Electrical Impulse • Transmission and Interpretation of Electrical Impulses by the Brain	• Inventory causes and influences of visual impairments	• There are many factors that influence the process of what we refer to as seeing. Damage to or malfunction of any part of the visual system can lead to a significant loss of visual functioning. • Types of visual impairment can be classified as being related to transmission of light energy, conversion of light to electrical impulse, and transmission and interpretation of electrical impulses by the brain. Also key is then the impairment occurred.
Identifying the Prevalence of Visual Impairment	• Identify prevalence estimates for individuals with visual impairments	• The best estimates for prevalence state that approximately one student in 1,000 has a visual disorder that interferes with learning. • Visual impairment accounts for less than 1% of the total special education population.
HOW ARE STUDENTS WITH VISUAL IMPARMENTS EVALUATED?		
Determining the Presence of a Visual Impairment	• Identify how visual impairment is determined	• Medical specialists determine the presence of a visual disorder. • Optometrists and low vision specialists determine if the visual disorder can be corrected through lenses or other optical devices.
Determining How a Student Uses Vision	• Differentiate between a clinical examination and a functional vision evaluation	• While a medical exam reports findings in clinical terms (such as 20/120), a functional vision exam reports findings in concrete observable ways.
Determining the Appropriate Reading Medium	• Identify appropriate reading media for students with visual impairments	• A Learning Media Assessment helps determine the most efficient mode of reading and learning: braille, using optical aids, large print, etc.
Determining the Nature and Extent of Special Education and Related Services	• Recognize areas that need to be considered in determining the nature and extent of special education and related services	• Educators determine the effects of the visual impairment on the student's development of academic, communication, social/emotional, sensorimotor, orientation and mobility, daily living, and career/vocational skills.
HOW CAN YOU ESTABLISH EFFECTIVE TEACHING PRACTICES?		
Setting Curricular Goals	• Differentiate among different curricula in order to evaluate the essentials of facilitating a comprehensive education for students who are blind or visually impaired	• In addition to overcoming problems related to accessing the general academic curriculum, students must develop functional skills that are typically learned incidentally by students with good vision.

Implement Instruction • Accessing the General Academic Curriculum • Learning Functional Life Skills • Integrating the Academic and Functional Skills Curricula	• Describe the activities of teachers as they facilitate the development of academic and functional skills in students with visual impairments.	• Professionals meet the academic needs of students through providing meaningful, concrete experiences, alternative skills to access print, instruction in assistive technology, and specialized instruction and materials. • Professionals meet the functional life skills needs of students with visual impairments by providing specialized instruction in the areas of potential unique need, including activities of daily living, orientation and mobility, and skills of self-advocacy.
Early Childhood Years	• Describe characteristics of effective early childhood programs	• The focus of early intervention and preschool education is to help parents understand the effects of visual impairment on learning and to present effective methods that reduce the impact of these effects on development.
Elementary Years	• Describe characteristics of effective elementary programs	• Effective programs help students learn to read and write with appropriate media, participate in orientation and mobility training, do physical education, and develop friendships with sighted and blind peers.
Middle and Secondary Years	• Describe characteristics of effective programs for middle and secondary students	• In middle and secondary programs, students' self-confidence, self-esteem, and social skills are especially important in addition to all their sighted peers learn with regard to transitioning to postsecondary environments.
Transitional and Postsecondary Years	• Describe characteristics of effective program options for adults with visual impairments	• In postsecondary education, students continue to receive orientation and mobility training along with skills that prepare them for work or college and independent living.
HOW CAN YOU ENCOURAGE PARTICIPATION?		
Practice Inclusion	• Summarize benefits and problems associated with inclusion for students with visual impairments	• Inclusion means support for individualized services designed to meet individualized needs, taking place in the environment that best facilitates learning for each student.
Foster Collaboration • Professional-to-Professional Collaboration • Family and Professional Collaboration • School, Student, Family, and Community Collaboration	• Explore ways to collaborate on behalf of students with visual impairments	• Professional, family, community, and peer collaboration each contribute much toward successful student learning.

PROJECT OPTIONS

1. Research and find at least five children's books with students who are blind or visually impaired as primary characters. Provide complete biographical information for these five books. Then read at least three of these books and compare and contrast the characters' visual characteristics, their curriculum and methods in school, and the collaborative nature of their relationship to their peers and families.
2. Keep a list of the places you travel in a week. For each trip you make, note the amount of time it took you to make the trip and the mode of transportation you used. Then, pick a day on which you made several trips and determine how you would have managed the travel without using a personal automobile or a friend to drive you. Call bus, cab, and paratransit agencies to determine cost and availability of services to your destinations. Finally, interview a person who is blind or who has low vision to determine the impact of nondriving on housing, home management, vocational, and recreational options. Prepare a paper describing what you have learned about the transportation issues of people with visual impairments.
3. Investigate what curriculum and methods are most common in your local school district for students with low vision. Interview two teachers who work with these students. Evaluate the strengths and weaknesses of the curriculum and methods in use and tell how you would change or adapt them based on what you have learned in this chapter.
4. Research available technology for those who are visually impaired, such as TV and movies which describe the action on the screen, or issues involving computer use. Evaluate the benefits and drawbacks for each one. Then interview two or three people who are visually impaired to find out what needs are not yet being met that could be met by technology breakthroughs. Summarize your findings and submit them to a technology corporation.

KEY TERMS

Adventitious

Albinism

Anterior visual pathway

Cataracts

Congenital

Cortical visual impairment

Field of vision

Fovea

Functionally blind

Glaucoma

Legal blindness

Low vision

Macula

Macular degeneration

Myopia

Optic nerve atrophy

Optic nerve hypoplasia

Reading medium

Retina

Retinitis pigmentosa

Retinopathy of prematurity

Totally blind

Tunnel vision

Visual acuity

Visual disability

GUIDED REVIEW

That's Not Right!

Becca Caroline and her family have learned to accept her blindness with a sense of humor. Becca's mom, Sally, also has a disability—dyslexia—which makes for some interesting interactions between mother and daughter. Once when Becca was looking for a hole punch, she asked her mom to tell her where to find it. Her mother told her that it was on the floor about five steps to her left.

The problem was that Sally and Becca were facing each other. Sally realized her mistake but forgot the term for the opposite of left. She told Becca, "I mean your . . .uh . . .uh . . . your other left."

Becca grinned and replied patiently, "Would that be the 'left' that the rest of us call 'right,' Mom?"

See *Exceptional Parent* (July 1994, pp. 20-22) for more anecdotes about Becca.

Who Are Students with Visual Impairments?

1. What criteria are used for the two different definitions for visual impairment? (*See* Defining Visual Impairment)
   a. ______________________________
   b. ______________________________

2. What constitutes tunnel vision? (*See* Defining Visual Impairment)
   ____
   ____

3. How does IDEA define visual disability, including blindness? (*See* Defining Visual Impairment)
   ____
   ____

4. Describe the three classifications educators use to classify students with visual impairments. (*See* Defining Visual Impairment)

Classification	*Identifying Characteristics*
Low vision	
Functionally blind	
Totally blind	

Did you realize that people who are blind or have visual impairments are perfectly comfortable when others use words like "look" and "see"? As a teacher, you will want to teach your students by your own comfort level that it is fine to respond to people with disabilities as they do to others.

See *When You Have a Visually Handicapped Child in Your Classroom: Suggestions for Teachers* (I. Torres & A. Corn) for other suggestions for accommodating students with visual impairments.

5. List terms to use and terms to avoid, identified by the National Federation of the Blind, that refer to individuals with visual impairment. (*See* Box 16-1)

Terms to Use	***Terms to Avoid***

6. What is the one characteristic shared by all individuals with visual impairment? (*See* Describing the Characteristics)

____

____

7. Describe areas affected by limitations in the range and variety of experiences for students with visual impairments. (*See* Describing the Characteristics; Limitations in the Range and Variety of Experiences)
   a. ______________________________
   b. ______________________________
   c. ______________________________

8. Explain how limitations in the ability to get around affect everyday life for students with visual impairments. (*See* Describing the Characteristics; Limitations in the Ability to Get Around)

____

____

9. Identify some consequences of not being able to monitor the environment. (*See* Describing the Characteristics; Limitations in Interactions with the Environment)
   a. ______________________________
   b. ______________________________
   c. ______________________________

10. Thus, students with visual impairments face ______________________ and ______________________ deprivation. (*See* Describing the Characteristics; Limitations in Interactions with the Environment)

11. List the four leading causes of visual impairment. (*See* Identifying the Causes of Visual Impairment)
   a. ______________________________
   b. ______________________________
   c. ______________________________
   d. ______________________________

Two high school students have invented a vest that contains infrared light sensors to signal the location of obstacles. The battery-operated vest uses a device fitted to the back of the hand to alert the wearer.
See *Design News*, June 7, 1993, pp. 87–90.

12. There are many factors that influence the process of what we refer to as *seeing*. Identify the area of the eye in focus and resulting conditions when there are problems in this area. (*See* Identifying the Causes of Visual Impairment)

Category	*Area of Eye Affected*	*Resulting Conditions*
Transmission of light energy		
Conversion of light to electrical impulse		
Transmission and interpretation of electrical impulses by the brain		

13. An adventitious visual occurs ______________________, while a congenital visual impairment occurs ____________________. Which of these two conditions is most likely to cause problems with learning about the world? ___________________. (*See* Identifying the Causes of Visual Impairment)

14. The best estimates for prevalence state that approximately one student in __________has a visual disorder that interferes with learning. (*See* Identifying the Prevalence of Visual Impairment)

15. Visual impairment accounts for less than _________________ percent of the total special education population. (*See* Identifying the Prevalence of Visual Impairment)

How Are Students with Visual Impairments Evaluated?

16. The results of a medical examination may be reported in ________________________ terms, while the results of a functional vision examination are reported in language that ____________________. Functional vision evaluations describe a student's use of vision in a variety of ___________________ environments. (*See* Determining the Presence of a Visual Impairment)

17. Why is it important for the student to be evaluated in these types of environment?

    ____

    ____

    (*See* Determining How a Student Uses Vision)

18. Ideally, when should a functional vision evaluation occur?

    ____

    Why?____

    (*See* Determining How a Student Uses Vision)

19. Identify some common reading media for students with visual impairments. (*See* Determining the Appropriate Reading Medium)

    a. ______________________________ c . ______________________________

    b. ______________________________ d. ______________________________

A Garden For Peter

Gardening is Roger Bossley's favorite leisure activity. His older son Benjamin readily participated in this activity with his father, but Roger hesitated to let his younger son Peter, who is blind, become involved in this activity. However, he decided one day that he would try to find ways to include his son, who was becoming increasingly more curious about the activity. That was the beginning of Peter's 12-square-foot garden. Roger involved Peter in planning, planting, and maintaining the garden.

What was the result? "His gardening experiences have led to an increased enjoyment of the outdoors and greater knowledge of plants and plant growth." Roger says the most valuable part of the experience, though, is that it is "an activity we can enjoy together."

See *Exceptional Parent*, May 1994, pp. 22–26, to learn more about Peter's garden.

20. What are the seven areas to be evaluated when determining the nature and extent of special education and related services needed? (*See* Determining the Nature and Extent of Special Education and Related Services)
    a. ______________________________
    b. ______________________________
    c. ______________________________
    d. ______________________________
    e. ______________________________
    f. ______________________________
    g. ______________________________

Closed captioning has made television accessible to people with hearing impairments, but how can a blind person *watch* TV? Audetel, an audio description of TV, provides a running commentary of a television program along with the soundtrack. Similar audio description devices are being made available in some theaters. The person uses a headset so they can listen without disturbing others.

How Can You Establish Effective Teaching Practices?

21. Curricular goals for students with visual impairments focus on developing skills to ______________ and skills related to ______________. (*See* Setting Curricular Goals)

22. For the following sentences taken from an early reading book, indicate what concrete activity would be necessary for the visually impaired child to have experienced to get full meaning from a sentence. (*See* Implement Instruction)

Sentence	***Concrete Activity***
The wind looked down on a boat.	
"The fox in the boat can't go", said the wind.	
"I will blow to make the boat move."	
The wind blew.	
Next to the water was a little crab.	

23. Would the child with good vision need to have had these same concrete experiences to understand this well-illustrated story? ________ Why or why not? (*See* Implementing Instruction) ______________
____

24. Braille is a(n) ______________________ method of reading. Describe some of the primary characteristics of this reading code. (*See* Implement Instruction; Access to Print)
____

____

25. For each of the following activities listed below, indicate which might be the most appropriate type of assistive technology for the visually impaired individual described.

Student and Activity	***Assistive Technology to be Used***
Heather, who has low vision, needs to use a computer to prepare a report.	
Elexis, who is totally blind, needs to use a computer to prepare a report.	
Elexis, who is totally blind, needs to create a braille copy of his report so he can check it for errors.	
Heather, who has low vision, needs to look at a map.	
Elexis, who is totally blind, needs to take lecture notes in his history class.	
Both Elexis and Heather, need to copy a document and incorporate it into a report they are writing.	

26. Students with good vision learn many functional life skills through ____________________ learning, which can be defined as ____. (*See* Learning Functional Life Skills)

27. In addition to having high expectations, teaching strategies that are effective with students with visual impairments include the following five components: (*See* Implement Instruction; Managing Daily Living Skills)
    a. ____
    b. ____
    c. ____
    d. ____
    e. ____

28. When students learn orientation and mobility skills, they are learning ______________________________________ and ____. (*See* Implement Instruction; Orientation and Mobility)

29. Identify three situations where an adult with a visual impairment might need to use self-advocacy skills learned while in school. (*See* Implement Instruction; Self-Advocacy)
    a. ____
    b. ____
    c. ____

The National Federation of the Blind has introduced skill development centers in Colorado, Louisiana, and Minnesota. The centers use blind instructors who have already reduced the impact of blindness in their lives to the level of nuisance. Besides learning blindness skills like braille reading and writing, participants learn a sense of personal worth and pride in accomplishment through activities like rock climbing and river rafting.

Can Residential Placements Be Least Restrictive?

Placement at a school for the blind with a residential option sometimes is considered the least restrictive environment for a student with a severe visual impairment. Such a placement gives these youngsters the opportunity to learn the skills necessary to eventually access the general curriculum environment.

Michael, who has low vision, became unmotivated and found it easy to get by using his impairment as an excuse in his local school. His mother also realized the challenge she faced of breaking her habit of doing too much for Michael. She thought Michael would learn skills of independence more readily at the residential school. Now, after two years, when Michael comes home on weekends, he demonstrates his pride in doing the laundry and some of the cooking for both of them. His confidence in his academic work also has improved. She believes that after another year, Michael's needs will have changed enough so that his local school will once again be able to serve him appropriately.

30. The focus of early intervention and preschool education is to help parents understand ______________________________ and to ______________________________. (*See* Observe Programs in Practice; Early Childhood Years)

31. Elementary school is a key time for ______________, ______________, and ______________. (*See* Observe Programs in Practice; Elementary Years)

32. Transition to work and community living are important activities for students with visual impairments at the ______________________ level (*See* Observe Programs in Practice; Middle and Secondary Years)

33. Programs like The Living Skills Center for the Visually Impaired in San Pablo, California, provide what opportunities for some young adults with visual impairments? ______________________________. (*See* Programs in Practice; Transitional and Postsecondary Years)

How Can You Encourage Participation?

34. Identify different placement options that have been used for students with visual impairments since 1900. Each of these may be appropriate, depending on the student's needs. Give the percentage of students in these placements today. (*See* Practice Inclusion)
    a. ______________________________ ______________%
    b. ______________________________ ______________%
    c. ______________________________ ______________%
    d. ______________________________ ______________%
    e. ______________________________ ______________%
    f. ______________________________ ______________%

35. What are some major roles of collaborators for students with visual impairments? (*See* Foster Collaboration)

Collaborator	***Roles***

Guiding Future Generations

Blake Lindsay, who became blind when he was nine months old as a result of a cancerous tumor that destroyed his retinas, is a radio disk jockey with a booming voice. As if one job weren't enough, he is also a customer service representative at a bank in Dallas, Texas.

Despite his fifty-hour-per-week schedule, he still finds time to speak to students at local public schools. He answers their questions about his blindness honestly. Blake views these students as future employers. He hopes that by letting them get to know him, they will be more open to contacts with people with disabilities once they are out of school. "I want society to know, in fact, how normal we are. We desire opportunities as much as anyone else."

See *The Mobile Press*, November 12, 1994, pp. 1D and 4D.

APPLICATION EXERCISES FOR CHAPTER 16

Application Exercise 16a. Identifying Causes of Visual Impairment

Match the category of the cause of visual impairment with the type of resulting disorder.

1. Transmission of light energy through the cornea, iris, pupil, lens, aqueous, vitreous	a. _____ Johann has cataracts.
2. Conversion of light to electrical impulse in the fovea, retina, macula	b. _______ Bill has an adventitious visual impairment.
3. Connection to the brain through the optic nerve, visual cortex	c. _____ Habb has tunnel vision and cannot see at night.
4. Timing of the impairment to any part of the eye	d. _____Christina has severe myopia.
	e. _____ Josephina has cortical visual impairment.
	f. _____ Singh has macular degeneration and cannot distinguish colors.

Application Exercise 16b. Matching Educational Needs with Appropriate Teaching

Match the educational need with the appropriate curriculum or method. Some descriptions have more than one answer. List all appropriate answers for each one.

1. Orientation and mobility training	a. _____ Anita is functionally blind and needs access to the academic curriculum.
2. Learn to use a cane	b. _______ TsangYao, who has low vision, was assigned homework with average size print which he will do using his hand-held magnifier.
3. Instruction in self-advocacy	c. _____ Jenawik has just moved into a new home and is unfamiliar with the layout.
4. Use of braille	d. _____Susie needs to convince a prospective employer that she has the abilities to do the job with adaptations.
5. Direct instruction in difficult or highly visual academic areas	e. _____ Kunti is learning new math skills for which she does not have the background experience.
6. Additional time to complete or more opportunities to practice	f. _____ Otis wants to cross the street but cannot clearly see the traffic.
7. Adapted materials or techniques	g. ______ Mina has a medical problem but doesn't know who to talk to about it.

Application Exercise 16c. Seeing Beyond the Content

Most adults, including educational administrators, think of congenital visual impairment primarily as a problem related to access of printed materials, and not as a problem related to access to information about the world (because of the lack of incidental learning). Given this fact, for each of the major issues addressed in this chapter, summarize the concepts by telling how you would convince an administrator that specialized instruction may be necessary for these students, in addition to the instructional activities related to the general education classroom.

Major Issues: Who Are Students with Visual Impairments? How Are Students with Visual Impairments Evaluated? How Can You Establish Effective Teaching Practices? How Can You Encourage Participation?

SAMPLE QUIZ FOR CHAPTER 16

MULTIPLE CHOICE

Circle the correct answer.

1. Identify the definition of legal blindness.
   a. Central visual acuity of 20/100 or less in the better eye
   b. Central visual acuity of 20/150 or less in the better eye
   c. Central visual acuity of 20/200 or less in the better eye
   d. Central visual acuity of 20/250 or less in the better eye

2. Which of the following is <u>not</u> a limitation imposed on an individual by a significant visual impairment?
   a. Limitation in the ability to get around
   b. Limitation in the range and variety of experiences
   c. Limitation in interactions with the environment
   d. Limitation in academic ability

3. Amanda is two years old and has significant visual impairment. What is a likely result of her limitation in movement?
   a. Psychosis
   b. Passivity
   c. Inability to speak
   d. Increased risk of mental retardation

4. Students who acquire a visual loss after having normal vision are said to have what type of visual impairment?
   a. Cortical visual impairment
   b. Functional blindness
   c. Adventitious visual impairment
   d. Congenital visual impairment

5. What is the leading cause of visual impairment among young children?
   a. Cortical visual impairment
   b. Retinopathy of prematurity
   c. Glaucoma
   d. Myopia and cataracts

6. What is affected with visual disorders such as optic nerve hypoplasia and optic nerve atrophy?
   a. The interpretation of what is viewed by the brain
   b. The transmission of light energy
   c. The conversion of light energy to electrical nerve impulses
   d. Color blindness

7. Which of the following is <u>not</u> included in the list of suggestions for working with students with visual impairments?
   a. Keep students actively involved in tasks.
   b. Teach functional tasks in natural environments.
   c. Assume that prior learning has occurred.
   d. Use real objects.

8. Why do braille readers have difficulty with some tests?
   a. Feeling the raised dots becomes painful to the touch after about 30 minutes of use.
   b. They tend to get mixed up in their numbering order, although their answers are correct.
   c. The tests are usually composed with a slate writer, which is more difficult to read than commercially prepared braille products.
   d. Scanning is difficult with braille.

9. What special opportunities are provided to students with visual impairments by the Living Skills Center for the Visually Impaired, located in San Pablo, California?
   a. Special assistance from a team of experts
   b. Autonomy and independence without the demands of a structured high school
   c. Transitional plans
   d. Individualized education programs

10. Orientation and mobility training is an example of which type of training that students with visual impairments must master?
    a. Regular academic curriculum in physical education
    b. Skills learned incidentally by sighted students
    c. Specialized study skills
    d. Skills to access the academic curriculum

11. Greg is having his visual acuity checked. How will it be determined?
    a. By checking to see if his field of vision is 360 degrees
    b. By having him look at the Snellen Chart from a distance of twenty feet
    c. By giving him a Learning Media Assessment
    d. By giving him a tunnel simulator to look through

12. What are the three broad categories into which educators classify students with visual impairments?
    a. Low vision, functionally blind, totally blind
    b. Assisted vision, print vision, braille vision
    c. Minimally impaired vision, severely impaired vision, profoundly impaired vision
    d. Visually challenged, visually impaired, blind

13. For visually impaired students, what can be a result of limitations in interaction with the environment?
    a. Tendency to stay in one familiar room and not leave the house, with resulting obesity
    b. Overreliance on the audio portion of television
    c. Inability to play
    d. Anxiety

14. Legal blindness is a measurement that is used primarily for what reason?
    a. To entitle people to government or private assistance programs
    b. To set curricular goals
    c. To assist classroom teachers
    d. To design educational programs

15. For which is there a significant correlation to blindness and visual impairment?
    a. Gender
    b. Race or ethnic background
    c. Poverty
    d. Asthma

16. What is affected when an individual has myopia?
    a. The transmission of light energy
    b. The interpretation of what is viewed by the brain
    c. Light-to-electrical impulse conversion
    d. The density of the vitreous fluid

17. Ideally, when should a functional vision evaluation occur?
    a. At birth if the child is born with a visual impairment
    b. Before and after an examination by a low vision specialist
    c. At the same time as the prereferral
    d. When access to print occurs

18. It has been determined that braille is the best reading medium for Seung, age six, who has low vision. How was this decision reached?
    a. In a Learning Media Assessment conducted by a teacher
    b. In an Optical Motor Evaluation conducted by an optometrist
    c. In an Ophthalmology Orientation Test conducted by an ophthalmologist
    d. In an Academic Medium Evaluation conducted by a low vision specialist

19. A nondiscriminatory evaluation is being conducted for Dean, age six. Who should be on the team?
    a. An ophthalmologist
    b. A representative from the National Federation of the Blind
    c. An orientation and mobility specialist
    d. An optometrist

20. What was a major impetus for the establishment of programs for the blind in local school districts in the 1950s?
    a. Residential schools were being closed down.
    b. After World War II, families wanted to remain united and keep their blind children at home.
    c. There was a rise in the incidence of blindness in premature babies.
    d. Helen Keller became a symbol of inspiration to the nation.

SHORT ANSWER

21. How does IDEA define visual disability?

____

____

22. List the three components of the process referred to as seeing.

a. ____

b. ____

c. ____

23. What is the position of the National Federation for the Blind on labeling?

____

____

ESSAY

24. Summarize the differences among these terms: low vision, functionally blind, and totally blind. Explain how you will assess the nature of special education and related services for students in each of these classifications.
25. Discuss how limitations with the environment influence both the curriculum and methods that must be used to help students who are visually impaired learn. Apply what you learned from the various program options in this chapter to add additional insights.

ANSWER KEY: APPLICATION EXERCISES FOR CHAPTER 1

Application Exercise 1a. Dignifying Labels: Possible Alternatives:

Words to Avoid	***Words with Greater Dignity***
Cripple/invalid	Person with a disability Disabled
Handicapped	Person with a disability Disabled
Birth defect	Disabled since birth/born with
Victim	Person who experienced or who has
Normal (referring to persons without disabilities as "normal" infers that those with disabilities are abnormal)	Nondisabled
Deaf mute/Deaf and dumb	Person who is deaf Person without speech, nonverbal
Crazy/Insane	Person with an emotional disorder Person with mental retardation
Slow	Person with a developmental delay Person with a learning disability
Confined to a wheelchair	Uses a wheelchair

Some Potential Guidelines to Consider in Labeling: Taken from "Portrayal Issues" *in Guidelines for Reporting and Writing About People with Disabilities*, Fifth Edition, (1996). Lawrence, KS: Research and Training Center on Independent Living.

- Do not focus on disability.
- Do not portray successful people with disabilities as superhuman.
- Do not sensationalize a disability.
- Do not use generic labels.
- Put people first, not their disability.
- Emphasize abilities, not limitations.
- Do not imply disease when discussing disabilities.
- Show people with disabilities as active participants of society.

Application Exercise 1b. IDEA's Six Principles

1. e	4. f	7. e	10. c	13. f
2. b	5. d	8. b	11. e	14. b
3. c	6. c	9. a	12. d	15. d

Application Exercise 1c. Assessing What You've Learned

Representations will vary according to the student applications.

ANSWER KEY: APPLICATION EXERCISES FOR CHAPTER 2

Application Exercise 2a. Identifying Stages of a Nondiscriminatory Evaluation

1. Referral
2. Screening
3. Prereferral
4. Prereferral
5. Referral

Application Exercise 2b. IQ Scores in the Classroom

1. b	5. h	9. c	13. i
2. d	6. f	10. g	
3. f	7. d	11. e	
4. a	8. i	12. a	

Application Exercise 2c: Assessing What You've Learned

Tests will vary according to each student's individual applications.

ANSWER KEY: APPLICATION EXERCISES FOR CHAPTER 3

Application Exercise 3a. Identifying Placements for Students with Disabilities

1.	Setting: Residential facility	Percentage: 0.7%
2.	Setting: Resource room	Percentage: 27%
3.	Setting: Regular class	Percentage: 46%
4.	Setting: Homebound/ hospital	Percentage: 0.7%
5.	Setting: Separate school	Percentage: 3%
6.	Setting: Separate class	Percentage: 22%

Application Exercise 3b. Matching Collaborators with Professional Roles

Definitions:

a. Supportive role: Caring and being there for your colleagues to share in times of need and in times of joy.
b. Facilitative role: Helping your colleagues develop a capacity to solve problems, engage in tasks, or deal independently with professional challenges.
c. Information-giving role: Providing direct assistance to your colleagues so they are better equipped to deal with problems on an on-going basis.
d. Prescriptive role: Prescribing a path of action to your colleagues.

Professional Roles of Listed Collaborators: Answers may vary depending on the collaborator's experience. Some probable suggestions include:

1. c
2. c, d
3. a, b, c, d
4. a, b, c, d
5. b, c
6. a, c
7. a, c, d
8. a, b, c, d

Application Exercise 3c. Collaborating for Success

Representations will vary according to each student's participation and collaboration.

ANSWER KEY: APPLICATION EXERCISES FOR CHAPTER 4

Application Exercise 4a. Identifying Characteristics of Learning Disabilities

1. Misinterprets social clues
2. Learned helplessness
3. Memory deficits
4. Metacognitive deficits
5. Attention deficits
6. Poor social skills
7. Specific academic difficulties

Application Exercise 4b. Determining Eligibility Based on Severe Discrepancy

1. Jose: Reading
2. Chanpen: Written language
3. Julie: Reading, math, written language

Application Exercise 4c. Metacognitive Learning Strategies

Representations will vary according to each student's individual strategies employed.

ANSWER KEY: APPLICATION EXERCISES FOR CHAPTER 5

Application Exercise 5a. Identifying Emotional Characteristics

a. 3	d. 6	g. 5
b. 1	e. 1	h. 2
c. 4	f. 2	i. 7

Application Exercise 5b. Identifying Types of Observations

1. Latency
2. Frequency
3. Magnitude
4. Duration
5. Topography

Application Exercise 5c. A Collaborator's View of Emotional or Behavioral Disorders

Representations will vary according to the student applications.

ANSWER KEY: APPLICATION EXERCISES FOR CHAPTER 6

Application Exercise 6a. Identifying Types of AD/HD

1. Hyperactive-impulsive
2. Inattentive
3. Hyperactive-impulsive
4. Inattentive
5. Combined
6. Inattentive

Application Exercise 6b. Accommodations for Students with AD/HD

a. 7	c. 5	e. 3	g. 4
b. 6	d. 1	f. 2	

Application Exercise 6c. Coaching the Concepts

Examples will vary according to the student innovations.

ANSWER KEY: APPLICATION EXERCISES FOR CHAPTER 7

Application Exercise 7a. Identifying Multiple Intelligences

1. Bodily-kinesthetic
2. Interpersonal
3. Linguistic
4. Spatial
5. Spatial
6. Logical-mathematical
7. Naturalist
8. Musical
9. Intrapersonal

Application Exercise 7b. IQ Scores in the Classroom.

1. Total in class with similar IQ: Sam plus 26 others, total 27 kids.
2. Total in class with similar IQ: Mary plus 10 others, total 11 kids.
3. Total in class with similar IQ: Andrew plus possibly one other, total 1+.
4. Total in class with similar IQ: Julie is most unusual, and there are no others like her.

Application Exercise 7c. Mapping Giftedness in Action

Representations will vary according to the student applications.

ANSWER KEY: APPLICATION EXERCISES FOR CHAPTER 8

Application Exercise 8a. Identifying Limitations in Intellectual Functioning

1. Attention
2. Generalization
3. Motivation
4. Memory

Application Exercise 8b. Adaptive Behavior Limitations

1. Health and safety
2. Social skills
3. Functional academics
4. Communication
5. Self-care

Application Exercise 8c. Obstacles to Learning Challenge

Representations will vary according to each student's individual strategies employed.

ANSWER KEY: APPLICATION EXERCISES FOR CHAPTER 9

Application Exercise 9a. Determining the Likelihood of a Disability in a Newborn

Averages:

Miguel: 9, 10
Susannah: 3, 3
Vishnu: 9, 10
Felicia: 0, 3
Chin-Cheng: 8, 8

Ranking for at risk from greatest at risk to least:

Susannah: Below 4 and no change after five minutes
Felicia: Below 4, but some improvement after five minutes
Chin-Cheng: Well above 8, small risk
Miguel and Vishnu: Well above 8, almost no risk

Application Exercise 9b. Assessment Methods for Student Learning and Performance

1. a: Developmental Model
2. d: Making Action Plans
3. c: Behavior States
4. b: Ecological Model

Application Exercise 9c. Concept Application in Context

Summaries will vary according to each student's focus and applications.

ANSWER KEY: APPLICATION EXERCISES FOR CHAPTER 10

Application Exercise 10a. Identifying Characteristics of Autism

1. c
2. e
3. g
4. f
5. a
6. b
7. d

Application Exercise 10b. Functional Assessment: Matching Situation and Intervention

1. c
2. e
3. a
4. b
5. d

Application Exercise 10c. Social Stories to Convey Conceptual Understanding

Representations will vary according to each student's individual stories.

ANSWER KEY: APPLICATION EXERCISES FOR CHAPTER 11

Application Exercise 11a. Identifying Conditions and Symptoms of Health Impairments

1. g: Hypoglycemia
2. h: Childhood leukemia
3. a: Stage 2 of HIV
4. b: Prenatal substance exposure
5. e: Temporal lobe or psychomotor seizure
6. d: Asthma
7. c: Hypoglycemia
8. f: Stage 3 of HIV

Application Exercise 11b. Developmental Responses to Death

1. e: Teenagers
2. c: Ages six to nine
3. b: Ages three to six
4. d: Ages nine to twelve
5. a: Newborn to age three
6. b: Ages three to six
7. b: Ages three to six
8. d: Ages nine to twelve

Application Exercise 11c. Medical Vocabulary Applications

Representations will vary according to the student applications.

ANSWER KEY: APPLICATION EXERCISES FOR CHAPTER 12

Application Exercise 12a. Identifying Forms of Cerebral Palsy by Movement Difficulties

1. Ataxic
2. Athetoid
3. Mixed
4. Spastic

Application Exercise 12b. Identifying Characteristics of Spina Bifida

a. 2: Meningocele
b. 1: Spina bifida occulta
c. 3: Myelomeningocele
d. 3: Myelomeningocele
e. 1: Spina bifida occulta
f. 2: Meningocele
g. 3: Myelomeningocele
h. 3: Myelomeningocele

Application Exercise 12c. The Conceptual Impact of Inclusion and Collaboration on Physical Disabilities

Representations will vary according to each student's individual understandings and interpretations.

ANSWER KEY: APPLICATION EXERCISES FOR CHAPTER 13

Application Exercise 13a. Identifying Areas of Change

1. Physical
2. Social, Behavioral, and Personality
3. Cognitive
4. Physical
5. Linguistic
6. Social, Behavioral, and Personality

Application Exercise 13b. Curriculum Applications

1. b. Component training
2. c. Functional retraining
3. a. Compensatory strategy training
4. a. Compensatory strategy training
5. b. Component training

Application Exercise 13c. Improving Instruction and Retention of Content

Answers will vary according to the student applications.

ANSWER KEY: APPLICATION EXERCISES FOR CHAPTER 14

Application Exercise 14a. Identifying Characteristics of Typical Language Development

1.	Josi	Birth to 6 months
2.	Cedric	6 to 12 months
3.	Fidel	12 to 18 months
4.	Jana	18 to 24 months
5.	Yu-chen	24 to 36 months
6.	Thalalia	36 to 48 months
7.	Julienne	4 to 5 years
8.	Muhammad	5 to 6 years

Application Exercise 14b. Identifying Language Impairments by the Dimension of Language in Focus

a. Pragmatics
b. Syntax
c. Semantics
d. Pragmatics
e. Phonology
f. Morphology
g. Phonology

Application Exercise 14c. Expanding Your Understanding of Communication Disorders

Representations will vary according to the students' applications.

ANSWER KEY: APPLICATION EXERCISES FOR CHAPTER 15

Application Exercise 15a. Identifying Levels of Hearing Loss

In order of severity of hearing loss:

1. Sammie
2. Summea
3. Juliana
4. Pedro
5. Najee
6. Jaime

Application Exercise 15b. Differentiating Means of Communication

Read the different ways students communicate and identify the communciation mode being used.

1. Sully: Oral/aural or speech, speechreading, and auditory skills
2. NamPrik: Total communication or simultaneous communication
3. Griffin: American Sign Language
4. Sharon: Oral/aural or speech, speechreading, and auditory skills
5. Memo: American Sign Language
6. Kunti: Total communication or simultaneous communciation

Application Exercise 15c. Interpreting Key Components of Hearing Loss

Representations will vary according to each student's individual interpretations employed.

ANSWER KEY: APPLICATION EXERCISES FOR CHAPTER 16

Application Exercise 16a. Identifying Causes of Visual Impairment

a. 1
b. 4
c. 2
d. 1
e. 3
f. 2

Application Exercise 16b. Matching Educational Needs with Appropriate Teaching

a. 4 and 5
b. 7
c. 1
d. 3
e. 6
f. 1 and 2
g. 3

Application Exercise 16c. Seeing Beyond the Content

Representations will vary according to the student applications.

ANSWER KEY: SAMPLE QUIZZES—MULTIPLE CHOICE

CHAPTER 1		CHAPTER 2		CHAPTER 3		CHAPTER 4		CHAPTER 5	
1	C	1	C	1	D	1	A	1	A
2	A	2	A	2	D	2	B	2	D
3	B	3	A	3	D	3	C	3	B
4	C	4	A	4	C	4	D	4	D
5	D	5	D	5	C	5	A	5	B
6	D	6	B	6	A	6	D	6	D
7	C	7	B	7	D	7	C	7	A
8	B	8	C	8	B	8	A	8	A
9	C	9	D	9	C	9	C	9	C
10	A	10	D	10	A	10	C	10	B
11	B	11	D	11	A	11	B	11	A
12	C	12	B	12	D	12	A	12	B
13	A	13	D	13	A	13	A	13	C
14	B	14	B	14	A	14	C	14	D
15	D	15	A	15	D	15	A	15	A
16	D	16	A	16	D	16	C	16	D
17	B	17	B	17	A	17	D	17	D
18	C	18	C	18	B	18	C	18	B
19	D	19	A	19	C	19	A	19	D
20	C	20	B	20	C	20	B	20	C
CHAPTER 6		CHAPTER 7		CHAPTER 8		CHAPTER 9		CHAPTER 10	
1	C	1	B	1	D	1	A	1	A
2	A	2	C	2	D	2	D	2	D
3	D	3	D	3	A	3	B	3	C
4	A	4	B	4	A	4	A	4	C
5	D	5	A	5	C	5	C	5	A
6	A	6	B	6	D	6	A	6	C
7	B	7	B	7	A	7	D	7	B
8	B	8	A	8	B	8	B	8	A
9	D	9	B	9	A	9	B	9	A
10	C	10	C	10	C	10	D	10	A
11	A	11	C	11	D	11	C	11	A
12	C	12	A	12	D	12	B	12	B
13	D	13	D	13	B	13	B	13	B
14	D	14	C	14	A	14	B	14	D
15	C	15	A	15	D	15	B	15	A
16	A	16	C	16	C	16	C	16	B
17	D	17	B	17	A	17	C	17	C
18	B	18	A	18	D	18	B	18	D
19	D	19	D	19	C	19	A	19	D
20	D	20	C	20	A	20	C	20	A

CHAPTER 11		CHAPTER 12		CHAPTER 13		CHAPTER 14		CHAPTER 15	
1	D	1	B	1	C	1	D	1	A
2	C	2	B	2	A	2	C	2	B
3	B	3	A	3	D	3	D	3	B
4	B	4	B	4	D	4	B	4	D
5	D	5	A	5	C	5	B	5	B
6	D	6	B	6	D	6	C	6	A
7	D	7	A	7	A	7	C	7	D
8	C	8	C	8	C	8	D	8	C
9	A	9	D	9	A	9	D	9	A
10	B	10	B	10	C	10	D	10	B
11	D	11	C	11	A	11	B	11	A
12	C	12	C	12	D	12	B	12	C
13	A	13	B	13	B	13	A	13	C
14	C	14	B	14	C	14	A	14	B
15	B	15	D	15	B	15	D	15	C
16	C	16	A	16	A	16	A	16	D
17	B	17	A	17	C	17	C	17	D
18	A	18	C	18	B	18	B	18	D
19	D	19	A	19	A	19	D	19	D
20	A	20	B	20	C	20	C	20	A

CHAPTER 16	
1	C
2	D
3	B
4	C
5	A
6	A
7	C
8	D
9	B
10	B
11	B
12	A
13	D
14	A
15	C
16	A
17	B
18	A
19	C
20	C

ANSWER KEY: SAMPLE QUIZZES—SHORT ANSWER

CHAPTER 1

1-21 Specially designed instruction, including instruction in physical education, to meet the unique needs of a student with a disability

1-22 (1) The categorical element—The student must have a disability; (2) The functional element—The disability must cause the student to need specially designed instruction.

1-23 Specific learning disabilities and speech or language impairments

CHAPTER 2

2-21 Screening, prereferral, referral, and nondiscriminatory evaluation procedures and standards

2-22 Norm-referenced tests and criterion-referenced tests

2-23 Reliability refers to how well a test yields similar results across time and among raters. Validity refers to how well the test measures what it purports to measure.

CHAPTER 3

3-21 Ready to learn, school completion, student achievement and citizenship, mathematics and science, adult literacy and lifelong learning, safe, disciplined, and drug-free schools, teacher-education and professional development, parental participation.

3-22 Inclusion and collaboration

3-23 Supportive role, facilitative role, information-giving role, prescriptive role

CHAPTER 4

4-21 With learning disabilities, students generally manifest a statistically significant discrepancy between ability and achievement. Their IQs range from average to gifted. Students with mental retardation do not have this discrepancy, and their IQs are approximately 70 or lower. Also, students with mental retardation display significant difficulties with adaptive behavior, while those with learning disabilities generally do not.

4-22 *Inclusionary Criterion:* A demonstrated discrepancy between ability and achievement. *Exclusionary Criterion:* Not the result of other factors, such as sensory impairment, mental retardation, or cultural differences. *Need Criterion:* Student needs special education and/or related services.

4-23 Visual perception, memory, motor functions, language, abstract reasoning, metacognition

CHAPTER 5

5-21 (1) Anorexia nervosa, which occurs when the student cannot be persuaded to maintain normal weight because of a fear of gaining weight. (2) Bulimia nervosa, which causes the individual to eat huge amounts of food at one time and then purge it through vomiting, excess use of laxatives, or extreme exercise.

5-22 Child abuse and neglect include acts or failures to act that could result in an imminent risk of death, serious physical or emotional harm, sexual abuse, or exploitation by a parent or caretaker who is responsible for the child's welfare. If you suspect that a child is being abused or neglected, it is your responsibility to report it to your state's child protection agency.

5-23 Frequently off task, poor academic work-related skills, splinter skills in basic academics, underachievement, and poor language skills

CHAPTER 6

6-21 (1) Behavioral skill deficit, (2) problem-solving deficit, (3) cognitive distortion, (4) self-control deficit

6-22 Observe the student to determine effective, poor, and absent social behaviors. Focus on one or two behaviors for change. Directly coach, model, and role-play important behaviors. Praise and reward the student for appropriate behaviors.

6-23 Half-day schedule. Small class size. Low teacher-student ratio. Trained teachers who enjoy their work and who emphasize encouragement and "positively-toned discipline." Structured environment, which includes predictable routines; clear, consistently reinforced rules; limited down time; and exposure to some school-type activities that require sitting quietly and listening. Freedom for the child to choose from several activities that involve quiet and active play as well as freedom to use materials creatively. Emphasis on the development of socialization and appropriate behavioral skills.

CHAPTER 7

7-21 High general intellect, specific academic aptitude, creative productive thinking, leadership ability, and visual or performing arts ability

7-22 Integrated curriculum studies in areas of interest, modification of the pace of learning, and modification of the depth of content coverage in specific topics

7-23 Written reflective evaluations that monitor learning, evaluations of content areas, reflections on thinking procésses; lists of books, magazines, and other materials evaluated by student; lists of topics and authors in subject areas that interest the student; charts, and audio and video recordings of the student's learning; records of strategies used; interviews; regular evaluations of the portfolio of the student, and others

CHAPTER 8

8-21 Attention, memory, generalization, and motivation

8-22 <u>Intermittent</u>: Supports on an "as-needed basis"

<u>Limited:</u> Consistent support over time, time-limited but not of an intermittent nature

<u>Extensive:</u> Need for regular involvement and not time-limited

<u>Pervasive:</u> Need for constancy, high intensity with potential life-sustaining nature

8-23 Three years after graduation, only 41percent of students were competitively employed and 15 percent were living independently.

CHAPTER 9

9-21 The extent of the disability is beyond mild or moderate levels, and typically two or more disabilities occur simultaneously.

9-22 Developmental, ecological, behavioral states, and Making Action Plans

9-23 (1) They may not develop in the same sequence as children without disabilities. (2) This approach assumes that the students have to possess certain skills before they can acquire "higher-level" ones. (3) This approach emphasizes the form of the skill rather than its function.

CHAPTER 10

10-21 Delayed language and echolalia

10-22 A neuromotor impairment means that there is a breakdown in the brain's capacity to direct the body to engage in movement that produces speech, gestures, written formats, or other alternatives.

10-23 CARS is one of the most frequently used diagnostic scales. It requires behavioral observations in fifteen areas of a child's functioning to determine the presence of autism.

CHAPTER 11

11-21 (1) Limitations in strength, (2) limitations in vitality, and (3) limitations in alertness.

11-22 The dog is tied or leashed at all times. A specific toilet area is used by the dog. The dog has been thoroughly tested and screened for any aggressive tendency.

11-23 (1) Use precautions to help prevent the accidental contraction of HIV and (2) honestly inform your students about the disease.

CHAPTER 12

12-21 Orthopedic impairment

12-22 Spastic, athetoid, ataxic, mixed

12-23 Physical therapist and occupational therapist

CHAPTER 13

13-21 Anoxia and brain damage from disease

13-22 Accidents, sports and recreational injuries, and violence

13-23 (a) Component training provides intensive and systematic training of specific cognitive skills, (b) Compensatory strategy training helps the student clarify, organize, and express information, (c) Functional retraining makes use of a student's everyday curriculum and activities to teach cognitive skills.

CHAPTER 14

14-21 Phonology, morphology, syntax, semantics, and pragmatics

14-22 (1) Use interesting materials, (2) place some desirable materials out of reach, (3) provide small or inadequate portions of preferred materials, (4) present two or more options for activities or materials, (5) create situations in which children are likely to need assistance, (6) set up a "sabotage" by not providing all of the materials needed to encourage requests, (7) set up silly or absurd situations to create a need to communicate.

14-23 Collaboration with the pathologist can help you embed students' language objectives within the context of the naturally occurring routines in the classrooms.

CHAPTER 15

15-21 Parent-child interaction, peers and tutors, incidental learning, and language competence

15-22 Oral/aural, ASL, simultaneous communication; oral/aural, bilingual-bicultural, and total communication

15-23 Emphasize experiential learning, build on the students' current knowledge and skills, require them to interact with peers, capitalize on the visual medium, and reduce environmental distraction.

CHAPTER 16

16-21 An impairment in vision that, even with correction, adversely affects a person's educational performance.

16-22 (1) The transmission of light energy through the eye, (2) the conversion of light energy to electrical energy, and (3) the transmission and interpretation of electrical impulses by the brain.

16-23 Euphemisms are awkward and unnecessary since the word "blind" accurately and clearly describes the condition of being unable to see.

CHILDREN'S AND YOUNG ADULT LITERATURE

Chapter 1: Overview of Today's Special Education

Bode, J. (1989). *New Kids in Town: Oral Histories of Immigrant Teens*. New York: Scholastic Inc.

Byars, B. (1977). *The Pinballs*. New York: Harper & Row.

Byars, B. (1985). *Cracker Jackson*. Kestrel, NY: Viking.

Byars, B. (1982). *The Animal, The Vegetable and John D. Jones*. New York: Delacorte Press.

Freedman, R. (1980). *Immigrant Kids*. New York: E.P. Dutton.

Hunt, I. (1976). *The Lottery Rose*. New York: Berkley Books.

Levine, E. (1989). *I Hate English*. New York: Scholastic Inc.

Paterson, K. (1978). *The Great Gilly Hopkins*. New York: Crowell.

Uchido, Y. (1991). *The Invisible Thread*. Englewood Cliffs, NJ: J. Messner.

Walker, B. K. (1993). *Laughing Together: Giggles and Grins from Around the Globe*. Minneapolis, MN: Free Spirit Publishing Inc.

Westridge Young Writer's Workshop. (1994). *Kids Explore The Gifts of Children with Special Needs.* Santa Fe, NM: John Muir Publications.

Chapter 2: Implementing IDEA's Principles

Avi. (1991). *Nothing but the Truth: A Documentary Novel*. New York: Orchard Books.

Berger, L., & Lithwick, D. (1992). *I Will Sing Life: Voices from the Hole in the Wall Gang Camp*. Boston, MA: Little, Brown & Co.

Coman, C. (1997). *What Jamie Saw*. New York: Penguin Books.

Cronin, G. (1995). *Two Birthdays For Beth*. Indianapolis, IN: Perspectives Press.

Dewitt, H. (1996). *Sad Days, Glad Days: A Story About Depression*. Morton Grove, IL: Albert Whitman & Co.

Dineen, M. H. (1993). *If They Can Do It, We Can Too!* Minneapolis, MN: Free Spirit Publishing Inc.

Janover, C. (1993). *Josh: A Boy with Dyslexia*. Minneapolis, MN: Free Spirit Publishing Inc.

Kachenmeister, C. Photos by Tom Berthiaume. (1996). *On Monday When It Rained.* Boston, MA: Houghton Mifflin.

Karnes, F. A. (1993). *Girls and Young Women Leading the Way: 20 True Stories About Leadership*. Minneapolis, MN: Free Spirit Publishing Inc.

Mccully, E. (1994). *My Real Family.* San Diego, CA: Browndeer Press, Harcourt Brace & Jovanovich.

Schwartz, L. (1990) . *What Would You Do? A Kid's Guide to Tricky and Sticky Situations*. Santa Barbara, CA: Learning Works.

Shreve, S. (1984). *The Flunking of Joshua T. Bates*. New York: Knopf.

Chapter 3: Special Education Today: Inclusion and Collaboration

Blank, J. P. (1976). *19 Steps Up the Mountain: The Story of the Debolt Family*. Philadelphia, PA: Lippincott.

Cleary, B. (1983). *Dear Mr. Henshaw*. New York: Morrow.

Dejong, M. (1954). *The Wheel on the School*. New York: Harper.

Drimmer, F. (1988). *Born Different: Amazing Stories of Very Special People*. New York: A Bantam Skylark Book.

Lisle, J. T. (1990). *Afternoon Of The Elves*. New York: Orchard Books.

Voetberg. J. Photos by Taasha Owen. (1995). *I Am a Home Schooler*. Morton Grove, IL: Albert Whitman & Co.

White, P. (1978). *Janet at School*. New York: Crowell.

Children's and Young Adult Literature list copyright Marilyn Shank, Ph.D. and Dorothy Leal, Ph.D.
This list is not to be reproduced without prior written consent of the authors.

Chapter 4: Learning Disabilties

Dwyer, K. M. Photos by Barbara Beirine. (1991). *What Do You Mean I Have a Learning Disability*? New York: Walker & Co.

Dunn, K. B., & Dunn, A. B. (1993). *Trouble with School: A Family Story About Learning Disabilities*. Rockville, MD: Woodbine House.

Gehret, J. (1996). *The Don't-Give-Up Kid and Learning Differences*. Fairport, NY: Verbal Images Press.

Hall, L. (1985). *Just One Friend*. New York: Crowell.

Kennemore, T. (1983). *Wall of Words*. London: Faber & Faber.

Lasker, J. (1974). *He's My Brother*. Morton Grove, IL: Albert Whitman & Co.

Levinson, M. (1985). *And Don't Bring Jeremy*. New York: Holt, Rinehart, & Winston.

Most, B. (1990). *The Cow That Went Oink*. New York: Harcourt Brace & Co.

Philbrick, W. R. (1993). *Freak the Mighty*. New York: Scholastic.

Roby, C. (1996). *When Learning Is Tough: Kids Talk About Learning Disabilities*. Morton Grove, IL: Albert Whitman & Company.

Sachs, M. (1993). *Thirteen Going On Seven*. New York: Dutton Children's Books.

Schlieper, A. Illustrated by Mary Beth Schwark. (1995). *The Best Flight*. Morton Grove, IL: Albert Whitman & Co.

Stern, J., & Ben-Ami, U. (1996). *Many Ways to Learn: Young People's Guide to Learning Disabilities*. Washington, DC: Magination.

Wolff, V.E. (1988). *Probably Still Nick Swanson*. New York: H. Holt

Chapter 5: Emotional or Behavioral Disorders

Brooks, B. (1984). *The Moves Make the Man*. New York: Harper & Row.

Cain, B. S., & Patterason, A. (1990). *Double-Dip Feelings: Stories to Help Children Understand Emotions*. Washington, DC: Imagination.Gold, P. (1975). *Please Don't Say Hello*. New York: Human Sciences Press.

Garland, J. (1996). *Depression Is the Pits, But I'm Getting Better: A Guide for Adolescents*. Washington, DC: Magination.

Hamilton, D. Illustrated by Gail Owens. (1995). *Sad Days, Glad Days: A Story About Depression*. Morton Grove, IL: Albert Whitman & Co.

Hayden, T. L. (1980). *One Child*. New York: Avon Books.

Hayden, T. L. (1981). *Somebodys Else's Kids*. New York: Avon.

Holmes, M. M., & Pillo, C. (Illustrator). (2000). *A Terrible Thing Happened: A Story for Children Who Have Witnessed Violence or Trauma*. Washington, DC: Magination.

Hou, L. (1981). *Your Friend, Rebecca*. London: The Bodley Head.

Hyde, M. O. (1983). *Is This Kid Crazy?* Philadelphia, PA: Westminster Press.

Klein, N. Illustrations by Kay Choroa. (1979). *Visiting Pamela*. New York: Dial Press.

Konigsburg, E. L. (1970). *George*. New York: Atheneum.

Larsen, H. (1978). *Don't Forget Tom*. New York: Thomas Y. Cromwell.

Mildiner, L., & House, B. (1974). *The Gates*. London: Centreprise Publishing Project.

Chapter 6: Attention-Deficit/Hyperactivity Disorder

Carpenter, P.; Ford, M., & Horjus, P. (Illustrator). (2000). *Sparky's Excellent Misadventures : My A.D.D. Journal*. Washington, DC: Magination.

Colin, A. (1997). *Willie: Raising and Loving a Child with Attention Deficit Disorder*. New York: Viking

Cray, E. (1992). *I'm Frustrated*. Chicago, IL: Parenting Press.

Cray, E. (1992). *I'm Mad*. Chicago, IL: Parenting Press.

Cray, E. (1992). *I'm Proud*. Chicago, IL: Parenting Press.

Duncan, R. (1989). *When Emily Woke up Angry*. Hauppauge, NY: Educational Series Inc.

Children's and Young Adult Literature list copyright Marilyn Shank, Ph.D. and Dorothy Leal, Ph.D.
This list is not to be reproduced without prior written consent of the authors.

Dwyer, K. M. Photos by Gregg A. Flory. *What Do You Mean I Have Attention Deficit Disorder*. (1996). New York: Walker & Co.

Galvin, M.R., & Ferraro, S. (Illustrator). (1995). *Otto Learns About His Medicine : A Story About Medication for Children with Adhd.* Washington, DC: Magination.

Gehret, J. (1990). *The Don't-Give-Up Kid and Learning Differences*. Fairport, NY: Verbal Images Press.

Gehret, J. (1991). *Eagle Eyes: A Child's Guide to Paying Attention.* Fairport, NY: Verbal Images Press.

Gehret, J. (1992). *I'm Somebody Too.* Fairport, NY: Verbal Images Press.

Janover, C. Illustrated by Rick Powell. (1997). *Zipper, the Kid with Adhd.* Bethesda, MD: Woodbine House.

Korman, C., & Trevino, E. (1995). *Eukee the Jumpy Jumpy Elephant*. New York: Specialty Press.

Moss, D. M. Illustrated by Carol Schwartz. (1996). *Shelley the Hyperactive Turtle*. Bethesda, MD: Woodbine House.

Nadeau, K. G., Dizon, E. B., & Rose, J. R. (1997). *Learning to Slow Down and Pay Attention: A Book for Kids About Add,* (2nd ed.). Washington, DC: Magination.

Nemiroff, M. A., Annunziata, J., & Scott, M. (Illustrator). (1998). *Help Is on the Way: A Child's Book About Add.* Washington, DC: Magination.

Nolan, H. (1997). *Dancing on the Edge*. New York: Harcourt Brace & Company. (National Book Award)

Parker, R. (1993). *Slam Dunk: A Young Boy's Struggle with Add.* Plantation, FL: Impact Publications.

Parker, R. (1992). *Making the Grade: An Adolescent's Struggle with Adhd.* Plantation, FL: Impact Publications.

Quinn, P. O., & Stern, J. M. (Eds.) (2000). *The Best of "Brakes": An Activity Book for Kids with Add.*

Quinn, P. O. (1995). *Adolescents and Add: Gaining the Advantage.* Washington, DC: Magination

Richardson, J. (1988). *Bad Mood Bear*. New York: Barron's.

Sanford, D. (1986). *Don't Look at Me*. Portland, OR: Muttnomah Press.

Chapter 7: Giftedness

Fenner, C. (1996). *Yolanda's Genius.*

George, J. (1959). *My Side of the Mountain*. New York: Dutton.

George, J. (1973). *Who Really Killed Cock Robin?* New York: Dutton.

Hamilton, V. (1971). *The Planet of Jr. Brown*. New York: Macmillan.

Hayden, T. L. (1980). *One Child.* New York: Avon Books.

Hayden, T. L. (1995). *The Tiger's Child.* New York: Avon Books.,

Hayes, W. D. Illustrated by William D. Hayes. (1970). *Project: Genius*. Toronto, ONT: Scholarly Book Service.

Hermes, P. (1990). *I Hate Being Gifted.* New York: Putnam.

Keyes, D. (1983). Flowers for Algernon. In *A Book of Short Stories*. New York: Harcourt Brace Jovanovich Publishers.

Konigsburg, E. L. (1997). *A View from Saturday*. New York: Atheneum. (Newberry)

Konigsburg, E. L. (1976). *From the Mixed-Up Files of Mrs. Basil. E. Frankwiler*. New York: Atheneum.

L'engle, M. (1962). *A Wrinkle in Time.* New York: Farar, Strauss, & Giroux.

L'engle, M. (1973). *A Wind in the Door.* New York: Farar, Strauss, & Giroux.

L'engle, M. (1978). *A Swiftly Tilting Planet.* New York: Farar, Strauss, & Giroux.

Newman, R. Illustrated by Paul Sagsoorian. (1967). *Boy Who Could Fly*. New York: Atheneum.

O'Brien, R. (1971). *Mrs. Frisby and the Rats of Nimh*. New York: Atheneum.

Pfeffer, S. B. (1989). *Dear Dad, Love Laurie*. New York: Scholastic.

Children's and Young Adult Literature list copyright Marilyn Shank, Ph.D. and Dorothy Leal, Ph.D.
This list is not to be reproduced without prior written consent of the authors.

Chapter 8: Mental Retardation

Berkus, C. W. (1992). *Charlsie's Chuckle.* Rockville, MD: Woodbine House.

Byars, B. (1970). *The Summer of the Swans.* New York: Scholastic Inc.

Carrich, C. (1985). *Stay Away from Snow.* New York: Clarion Books.

Christopher, M. F. Illustrated by Foster Caddell. (1996). *Long Shot for Paul.* Boston, MA: Little Brown.

Clifton, L. (1980). *My Friend Jacob.* New York: Dutton.

Fassler, J. Illustrated by Jane M. Smyth. (1969). *One Little Girl.* New York: Behavioral Publications.

Fleming, V. Illustrated by Floyd Cooper. (1993). *Be Good to Eddie Lee.* New York: Philomel Books.

Friis-Baastad, B. (1967). *Don't Take Teddy.* New York: Scribner.

Hirsch, K. Illustrated by Nancy Indereiden. (1977). *My Sister.* Minneapolis, MN: Carolhoda Books.

Litchfield, A. B. (1984). *Making Room for Uncle Joe.* Morton Grove, IL. Albert Whitman & Co.

Little, J. (1968). *Take Wing.* Boston, MA: Little Brown.

Melton, D. (1976). *What About Me?* New York: Watts.

Rabe, B. (1988). *Where's Chimpy.* Morton Grove, IL: Albert Whitman & Co.

Rheingrover, J. S. Illustrated by Kay Life. (1996). *Veronica's First Year.* Morton Grove , IL: Albert Whitman & Co.

Rylant, C. (1985). *Every Living Thing.* New York: Bradbury Press.

Schwier, K. M. (1988). *Keith Edward's Different Day.* New York: The G. Allan Roeher Institute.

Shyer, M. (1988). *Welcome Home, Jellybean.* New York: Aladdin Books.

Smith, D. B. Illustrated by Alan Tiergreen. (1975). *Kelly's Creek.* New York: Thomas Y. Crowell.

Testa, M. (1996). *Thumbs Up, Rico!* Morton Grove, IL: Albert Whitman & Co.

Wright, B. R. Illustrated by Helen Cogancherry. (1992). *My Sister Is Different.* Austin, TX: Raintree Steck Vaugn.

Chapter 9: Severe and Multiple Disabilities

Berstein, J. E., & Fireside, B. (1996). *Special Parents, Special Children.* Morton Grove, IL: Albert Whitman & Co.

Blank, J. P. (1976). *19 Steps up the Mountain: The Story of the Debolt Family.* Philadelphia, PA: Lippincott.

Brown, F. G. (1977). *You're Somebody Special on a Horse.* Morton Grove, IL: Albert Whitman & Co.

Brown, T. Illustrated by Fran Ortiz. (1994). *Someone Special Just Like You.* New York: Henry Holt & Co.

Dwight, L. (1992). *We Can Do It!* New York: Checkerboard Press.

Emmert, M. (1996). *I'm The Big Sister Now.* Morton Grove, IL: Albert Whitman & Co

Fassler, J. (1975). *Howie Helps Himself.* Morton Grove, IL: Albert Whitman & Co.

Helfman, E. (1995). *On Being Sarah.* Morton Grove, IL: Albert Whitman & Co.

McMahon, P. Photos by Peter Simon. (1996). *Summer Tunes: A Martha Vineyard Vacation.* Mexico: Boyds Mills Press.

Metzger, L. (1997). *Ellen's Case.* New York: Puffin Books.Moran, G. (1994). *Imagine Me on a Sit-Ski!* Morton Grove, IL: Albert Whitman & Co.

Osofsky, A. Illustrated by Ted Rand. (1992). *My Buddy.* New York: Henry Holt & Co.

Powers, M. E. (1986). *Our Teacher's in a Wheelchair.*Morton Grove, IL. Albert Whitman & Co.

Prall, J. (1985). *My Sister's Special.* Chicago: Children's Press.

Rosenbert, M. B. (1983). *My Friend Leslie: The Story of a Handicapped Child.* New York: Lothrop, Lee & Shepard Books.

Sherkin-Langer, F. (1995). *When Mommy Is Sick.* Morton Grove, IL: Albert Whitman & Co.

Smith, D. B. (1975). *Kelly's Creek.* New York: Thomas Y. Crowell & Co.

Stein, S. B. Photos by Dick Frank. (1974). *About Handicaps.* New York: Walker & Co.

Vigna, J. (1993). *When Eric's Mom Fought Cancer.* Morton Grove, IL: Albert Whitman & Co.

Wolf, B. (1974). *Dont' Feel Sorry for Paul.* New York: J.B. Lippencott Co.

Children's and Young Adult Literature list copyright Marilyn Shank, Ph.D. and Dorothy Leal, Ph.D.
This list is not to be reproduced without prior written consent of the authors.

Chapter 10: Autism

Barrow, J., & Barrow, S. (1993). *There's a Boy in Here.* New York: Simon & Schuster.

Lane, H., & Pillard, R. (1978). *The Wild Boy of Burundi: A Study of an Outcast Child.* New York: Random House.

Rich, L.D. (1970). *Three Of A Kind.* New York: F. Watts.

Schulze, C. (1993). *When Snow Turns to Rain.* Rockville, MD: Woodbine House.

Stehli, A. (1991). *The Sound of a Miracle: A Child's Triumph over Autism.* New York: Doubleday.

Thompson, M. (1996). *Andy and His Yellow Frisbee.* Bethesda, MD: Woodbine House.

Williams, D. (1992). *Nobody Nowhere: The Extraordinary Autobiography of an Autistic.* New York: Times Books.

Williams, D. (1994). *Somebody, Somewhere: Breaking Free from the World of Autism.* New York: Times Books.

Yashima, T. (1965). *Crow Boy.* New York: Scholastic Inc.

Chapter 11: Other Health Impairments

Althea. (1993). *I Have Diabetes.* Hong Kong: Dinosaur Publications.

Althea. Illustrated by Angela Owen. (1991). *I Have Asthma.* Hong Kong: Dinosaur Publications.

Bach, A. (1982). *Waiting for Johnny Miracle.* New York: Bantam Books.

Bahr, M. Illustrated by David Cunningham. (1992). *The Memory Box.* Morton Grove, IL: Albert Whitman & Co.

Breebaart, J., & Breebaart, P. (1993). *When I Die Will I Get Better*? New York: Peter Bedrick Books.

Brown, L. K., & Brown, M. (1996). *When Dinosaurs Die: A Guide to Understanding Death.* New York: Little Brown & Co.

Carter, S. M., & Alden R. Photographs by Dan Young. (1996). *I'm Tougher Than Asthma.* Morton Grove, IL: Albert Whitman & Co.

Delton, J., & Tucker, D. (1996). *My Grandma's in a Nursing Home.* Morton Grove, IL: Albert Whitman & Co.

Getz, D. (1990). *Thin Air.* New York: Holt & Co.

Girard, L. W. (1993). *Alex, the Kid with Aids.* Morton Grove, IL: Albert Whitman & Co.

Gunther, J. (1949). *Death Be Not Proud: A Memoir.* New York: Harper Perennial.

Hanson, R. (1997). *The Face at the Window.* New York: Clarion Books.

Hermes, P. (1980). *What If They Knew?* New York: Harcourt Brace Jovanovich.

Jordan, M. (1993). *Losing Uncle Tim.* Morton Grove, IL: Albert Whitman & Co.

Krisher, T. (1993). *Kathy's Hats: A Story of Hope.* Morton Grove, IL: Albert Whitman & Co.

London, J. (1996). *The Lion Who Had Asthma.* Morton Grove, IL: Albert Whitman & Co.

Mcdaniel, L. (1991). *So Much to Live for.* New York: Bantam Books.

Miller, R. (1986). *Robyn's Book: A True Diary.* New York: Scholastic, Inc.

Mills, J.C., & Chesworth, M. (Illustrator) (1993). *Gentle Willow: A Story for Children About Dying.* Magination.

Ostrow, W., & Ostrow, V. Illustrated by Blanche Sims. (1989). *All About Asthma.* Morton Grove, IL: Albert Whitman & Co.

Paterson, K. (1977). *Bridge to Terabithia.* New York: Crowell.

Pirner, C. (1991). *Even Little Kids Get Diabetes.* Morton Grove, IL: Albert Whitman & Co.

Rubalcaba, J. (1997). *Saint Vitus' Dance.* New York: Clarion Books.

Rudner, B. Illustrated by Peggy Trabalka. (1992). *Will I Still Have to Make My Bed in the Morning?* Louisville, KY: Art Print & Publishing Co.

Rudner, B. Illustrated by Thomas Fahsbender. (1987). *The Littlest Tall Fellow.* Louisville, KY: Tiny Thought Press.

Schwartz, L. Illustrated by Beverly Armstrong. (1995). *Aids Questions for Kids.* Santa Barbara, CA: The Learning Works Inc.

Spyri, J. (1997). *Heidi.* Boston , MA: Puffin Books.

Thiele, C. J. (1988). *Jodie's Journey.* New York: Harper & Row.

Weaver, L. Illustrated by Aileen Arrington. (1993). *Close to Home, A Story of the Polio Epidemic.* New York: Viking.

Wilkinson, B. (1975). *Ludell.* New York: Harper & Row.

White, R., & Cunningham, A. M. (1983). *Ryan White: My Own Story.* New York: Penguin

Children's and Young Adult Literature list copyright Marilyn Shank, Ph.D. and Dorothy Leal, Ph.D.
This list is not to be reproduced without prior written consent of the authors.

Whitelaw, N. (1991). *A Beautiful Pearl*. Morton Grove, IL: Albert Whitman & Co.

Wild, M. (1993). *Remember Me*. Morton Grove, IL: Albert Whitman & Co.

White Pellegreno, M., & Kempf, C. (Illustrator). (1999). *I Don't Have an Uncle Phil Anymore*. Washington, DC: Magination.

Weiss, J. H., & Chesworth, M. (1994). *Breathe Easy: Young People's Guide to Asthma*. Washington, DC: Magination.

Chapter 12: Physical Disabilities

Calvert, P. (1992. *Picking Up the Pieces*. New York: Charles Scribner's Sons.

Carlson, N. (1992). *Arnie and the New Kid*. New York: Puffin Books.

Depaola, T. (1980). *Now One Foot, Now the Other*. New York: G.P. Putnam's Sons.

Delton, J. Illustrated by Alan Tiefreen. (1993). *Pee Wee Scouts, Fishy Wishes*. New York: A Dell Young Yearling

Fletcher, J. C. (1993). *Mama Zooms*. New York: Scholastic Inc.

Hesse, K. (1997). *Out of the Dust*. New York: Scholastic Press. (Newbery)

Imai, M. (1994). *Lilly's Secret*. Cambridge, MA: Candlewick Press.

Kehret, R. (1996). *Small Steps: The Year I Got Polio*. Morton Grove, IL: Albert Whitman & Co.

Killilea, M. (1952). *Karen*. New York: Dell Publishing.

Laskar, J. (1980). *Nick Joins In*. Morton Grove, IL: Albert Whitman & Co.

Little, J. (1962). *Mine for Keeps*. Boston, MA: Little Brown.

Mayer, G., & Mayer, M. (1992). *A Very Special Critter*. New York: Golden Books.

Powers, M.E. (1986). *Our Teacher's in a Wheelchair*. Morton Grove, IL: Albert Whitman & Co.

Rabe, B. Illustrated by Lillian Hoban. (1981). *The Balancing Girl*. New York: Puffin Books.

Roy, R. (1985). *Move Over, Wheelchairs Coming Through*. New York: Clarion Books.

Rudner, B. Illustrated by Peggy Trabalka. (1983). *The Handstand*. Louisville, KY: Tiny Thought Press.

Slepian, J. (1980) *The Alfred Summer*. New York: Macmillan.

Swells, R. (1990). *The Little Lame Prince*. New York: Dial Books for Young Readers.

White, P. (1978). *Janet at School*. New York: Crowell.

Useman, S., Useman, E., & Pillo, C. (Illustrator). (1999). *Tibby Tried It*. Washington, DC: Magination

Chapter 13: Traumatic Brain Injury

Burke, M. (1984). *Reflections of a Brother*. Washington, DC: National Head Injury Foundation.

Dickenson, M. (1987). *Thumbs Up: The Life and Courageous Comeback of White House Press Secretary Jim Brady*. Washington, DC: National Head Injury Foundation

Leaf, L. E. (1988). *Susan's Dad: A Child's Story of Head Injury*. Washington, DC: National Head Injury Foundation.

Mahanes, F. (1985). *A Child's Courage, A Doctor's Devotion: Triumph Over Head Trauma*. Washington, DC: National Head Injury Foundation

Warrington, J. (1981). *The Humpty Dumpty Syndrome*. Washington, DC: National Head Injury Foundation

Chapter 14: Communication Disorders

Black, I. S. Illustrations by Seymour Fleischman. (1995). *The Little Old Man Who Could Not Read*. Morton Grove, IL: Albert Whitman & Co.

Bourke, L. (1981). *Handmade ABC: A Manual Alphabet*. Reading, MA: Addison Wesley.

Bunting, E. Illustrated by Donald Carrick. (1989). *The Wednesday Surprise*. New York: Clarion Books

Kemp, G. (1981). *The Turbulent Term of Tyke Tiler*. Harmondsworth: Puffin.

Schneider, M. (1978). *If Only I Could Talk*. London: Heinemann.

Showers, P. (1966). *How You Talk*. New York: Harper Collins Publishers.

Small, D. (1992). *Ruby Mae Has Something to Say*. New York: Crown Publishers.

Stanek, M. Illustrated by Judith Friedman. (1989). *I Speak English for My Mom*. Morton Grove, IL: Albert Whitman & Co.

Children's and Young Adult Literature list copyright Marilyn Shank, Ph.D. and Dorothy Leal, Ph.D.

This list is not to be reproduced without prior written consent of the authors.

Thompson, M. (1992). *My Brother, Mathew*. Rockville, MD: Woodbine House.

Schaffer, C. E., & Friedman, J. (1993). *Cat's Got Your Tongue? A Story for Children Afraid to Speak*. Washington, DC: Magination.

Chapter 15: Hearing Loss

Abbot, D., & Kisor, H. (1996). *One TV Blasting and a Pig Outdoors*. Morton Grove, IL: Albert Whitman & Co.

Abramson, M. (1985). *Amy, The Story of a Deaf Child.* New York: Lodestar Books.

Aseltine, L., et al. (1996). *I'm Deaf and It's Okay*. Morton Grove, IL: Albert Whitman & Co.

Bergman, T. (1989). *Finding a Common Language.* Milwaukee, WI: Gareth Stevens Publications.

Booth, B. D. Illustrated by Lamarche, Jim. (1991). *Mandy*. New York: Lothrop, Lee, & Shepard Books.

Bornstein, H., & Saulnier, K. L. Illustrated by Patricia Peters. (1992). *Nursesry Rhymes from Mother Goose; Told in Signed English*. Washington DC: Kendall Green Publications.

Bourke, L., & Sullivan, M. B. (1980). *A Show of Hands Say It in Sign Language*. New York: Harper Trophy.

Bove, L. (1985). *Sign Language ABC; Featuring Jim Henson's Sesame Street Muppets*. US: Random House.

Butts, N. (1996). *Cheshire Moon*. Front Street Publications.

Fain, K. (1993). *Handsigns*. San Francisco, CA: Chronicle Books.

Flodin, M. (1995). *Signing Is Fun*. New York: A Perigree Book.

Gross, R. B. Illustrated by Susannah Ryan. (1991). *You Don't Need Words! A Book About Ways People Talk Without Words*. New York: Scholastic Inc

Hilbok. B. (1981). *Silent Dancer*. Englewood Cliffs, NJ: J. Messner.

Hirsch, K. (1981). *Becky*. Minneapolis, MN: Carolhoda Book.

Keller, H. (1954). *Story of My Life*. Garden City, NY: Doubleday.

Lakin, P. (1996). *Dad and Me in the Morning*. Morton Grove, IL: Albert Whitman & Co.

Lee, J. M. (1991). *Silent Lotus*. New York: Farrar, Straus, & Giroux.

Litchfield, A. B. Illustrated by Eleanor Mill. (1976). *A Button in Her Ear*. Morton Grove, IL: Albert Whitman & Co.

Litchfield, A. B. (1996). *Words in Our Hands*. Morton Grove, IL: Albert Whitman & Co.

Lowell, G. R. (2000). *Elana's Ears, or How I Became the Best Big Sister in the World.* Washington, DC: Magination

McMahon, P. Photos by John Godt. (1995). *Listen for the Bus; David's Story*. Mexico: Boyd's Mill Press.

Peterson, J. W. Illustrated by Deborah Kogan Ray. (1977). *I Have A Sister, My Sister Is Deaf.* New York: Harper Trophy.

Pollock, P. (1982). *Keeping It Secret*. New York: Putnam & Grosset Group.

Rankin, L. (1991). *The Handmade Alphabet*. New York: Scholastic.

Riskind, L. (1981). *Apple Is My Sign*. Boston, MA: Houghton Mifflin.

Rosen, L. (1981). *Just Like Everyone Else*. San Diego, CA: Harcourt Brace Jovanovich.

Chapter 16: Blindness And Low Vision

Brighton, C. (1984). *My Hands, My World.* New York: Macmillan.

Brown, M. (1979). *Arthur's Eyes*. New York: Little Brown & Company.

Butler, B. (1972). *Gift of Gold*. New York: Mead.

Curtis, P. Photos by Mary Bloom. (1982). *Greff: The Story of a Guide Dog*. New York: Lodestar Books.

Davidson, M. (1965). *Helen Keller's Teacher*. New York: Schoastic Inc.

Freedman, R. (1997). *Out of Darkness; The Story of Louis Braille*. New York: Clarion Books.

Haar, J. (1977). *The World of Ben Lighthart*. New York: Delacorte Press/ S. Lawrence.

Keller, H. (1954). *The Story of My Life*. Garden City, NY: Doubleday.

Kroll, V. L. Illustrated by Jill Kastner. (1995). *Naomi Knows It's Springtime*. Hong Kong: Boyds Mills Press.

Litchfield, A. B. (1996). *A Cane in Her Hand*. Morton Grove, IL: Albert Whitman & Co.

Markham, L. (1993). *Helen Keller*. Chicago, IL: Franklin Watts.

Raskin, E. (1968). *Spectacles*. New York: Aladdin Books.

Children's and Young Adult Literature list copyright Marilyn Shank, Ph.D. and Dorothy Leal, Ph.D.
This list is not to be reproduced without prior written consent of the authors.

Smith, L. (1991). *Glasses Who Needs 'Em*? New York: Viking.

Wild, M. (1993). *All The Better To See You With*! Morton Grove, IL: Albert Whitman & Co.

Wilder, L. I. (1953). *By The Shores Of Silver Lake*. New York: Harper & Row Publications Inc. (Newbery)

Yolen, J. Illustrated by Remy Charelip & Demetra Marasles. (1977). *The Seeing Stick*. New York: Thomas Y. Crowell Co.

Children's and Young Adult Literature list copyright Marilyn Shank, Ph.D. and Dorothy Leal, Ph.D.

This list is not to be reproduced without prior written consent of the authors.

VIDEOS ABOUT INDIVIDUALS WITH CULTURAL DIFFERENCES AND EXCEPTIONALITIES

Available at Local Retail, On-Line, and Rental Stores

Chapter 1—Overview of Today's Special Education

A Test of Love. (1984, PG, Australia, color, 93 minutes). A young teacher reaches out to a child with a disability.

Billy: Portrait of a Street Kid. (1977, NR, US, color, 96 minutes). A homeless teen tries to improve his life through education.

Blackboard Jungle. (1955, NR, US, B & W, 101 minutes). Glenn Ford plays a teacher of troubled young people in a low socioeconomic setting.

Conrack. (1974, PG, US, color, 107 minutes). Pat Conroy (Jon Voight) is a progressive teacher in a school on a rural southern island.

Criss Cross. (1992, R, US, color, 100 minutes). A single parent with low income has a rebellious 12-year-old son.

Dangerous Minds. (1995, R, US, color, 99 minutes). Marine turned teacher educates inner-city children.

God Bless the Child. (1988, NR, US, color, 93 minutes). A single mother is forced to live in the streets with her child.

Lovey, A Circle of Children, Part I. (1977, NR, US, color, 120 minutes). A teacher works in a classroom for students with emotional and behavioral disorders. (Part II, 1982).

Music of the Heart. (2000, PG, color, 123 minutes). A woman teaches music in a public school—against many odds.

The Outside Chance of Maximillian Glick. (1988, G, Canada, color, 96 minutes). A bright 12-year-old experiences conflict between his hopes for the future and his family's Jewish values.

Padre Padrone. (1977, NR, Italy, color, 114 minutes). Child overcomes poverty, abuse, and neglect to graduate college and master Latin and Greek.

The Prince of Central Park. (1977, NR, US, color, 76 minutes). Two orphaned children, living in a tree in central park, are befriended by an elderly woman.

Sarafina. (1992, PG-13, France-UK-US, color, 115 minutes). An African American teacher in South Africa encourages students to think for themselves.

Spare the Rod. (1961, Not rated, UK, b & w, 93 minutes). A teacher tries to help students in a tough London school.

Stolen Children. (1992, NR, France-Italy, color, 112 minutes). A policeman tries to help three children who have been abused and neglected to find some happiness after a children's shelter turns them away.

Sugar Cane Alley. (1984, PG, France, color, 107 minutes). An 11-year-old boy and his grandmother survive poverty and hope for the future during the 1930s.

To Kill a Mockingbird. (1962, Not rated, US, b & W, 129 minutes). Children learn about bigotry when their father defends a man who has been unjustly accused of rape.

To Sir, with Love. (1967, Not rated, UK, color, 105 minutes). Sidney Poitier teaches students in a London inner city school.

To Sleep with Anger. (1990, PG, US, color, 102 minutes). Portrays cultural differences between parents and children in an African American family.

Up the Down Staircase. (1967, NR, US, color, 124 minutes). Details struggles of a young English teacher in a New York City school.

Waterland. (1992, R, UK, color, 95 minutes). A high school history teacher relates to his students based on the emotional upheavals of his past.

Where the Day Takes You. (1992, R, US, color, 105 minutes). Portrays lives of homeless adolescents in Los Angeles.

Why Shoot the Teacher? (1977, Canada, NR, color, 101 minutes). A teacher's experience in a small, rural town during the Depression.

Video List copyright Marilyn Shank, Ph.D. This list is not to be reproduced without prior written consent of the author.

Chapter 2—Implementing IDEA's Principles

Crisis at Central High. (1981, NR, US, color, 125 minutes). Portrays events that occurred at Central High School in Little Rock, Arkansas, when integration was mandated after Brown v. Board of Education.

Inherit the Wind. (1960, NR, US, b & w, 127 minutes). Battle over whether evolution should be taught in public schools demonstrates that educational change sometimes occurs as a result of court cases.

Philadelphia. (1994, PG-13, US, color, 125 minutes). A young lawyer uses the Americans with Disabilities Act and Section 504 to build a case of discrimination after he was fired from his job for having AIDS.

Separate but Equal. (1991, NR, US, color, 200 minutes). Details *Brown v. Board of Education.*

When Billy Broke His Head and Other Tales of Wonder. (1995, NR, US, color, 60 minutes). Billy Golfus, who had difficulty finding work after a traumatic brain injury, discusses experiences of discrimination against those with disabilities.

Chapter 3—Special Education Today: Inclusion and Collaboration

Amy. (1981, US, G, color, 100 minutes). A teacher leaves her husband in the early 1900s to teach at a school for children with disabilities.

Bill. (1981, Not rated, US, color, 100 minutes). Mickey Rooney plays Bill Sackter, an adult with mental retardation who was released from a residential setting after 46 years.

Bill on His Own. (1983, NR, US, color, 100 minutes). The continued story of Bill Sackter.

The Caretakers. (1963, NR, b & w, 97 minutes). Portrays a hospital for people with emotional and behavioral disorders during the 1960s.

Educating Peter. (1992, US, color, 30 minutes). Oscar-winning documentary chronicles the third-grade year of Peter who has Down Syndrome and is fully included in a general classroom.

Larry. (1974, US, color, 80 minutes). A man with average intelligence, although he lived in a residential facility for people with mental retardation for 26 years, must adapt to life outside the facility.

Stand and Deliver. (1987, PG, US, color, 105 minutes). A talented teacher (Edward James Olmos) inspires East L.A. barrio students to pass an advanced placement calculus test.

Sylvia. (1985, PG, New Zealand, color, 98 minutes). Chronicles educator Sylvia Ashton-Warner's attempts to bring innovative educational methods to Maori children despite resistance by New Zealand's educational establishment.

Chapter 4—Learning Disabilities

The Loneliness of the Long Distance Runner. (1962, NR, UK, b & w, 103 minutes). A young man with learning difficulties robs a bakery and is sent to a reform school where he finds he has athletic ability.

The Mighty. (1998). A teen with learning disabilities who is physically strong forms a partnership with a teen who has a physical impairment and is gifted to become The Mighty.

Stanley and Iris. (1990, PG-13, US, color, 104 minutes). Stanley (Robert De Niro), who is illiterate and in his forties, is taught to read by Iris (Jane Fonda).

Chapter 5—Emotional or Behavioral Disorders

Alan and Naomi. (1992, PG, US, color, 96 minutes). A teenager (Lukas Haas), who is Jewish, befriends a girl who became catatonic after seeing her father murdered by Nazis.

An Angel at My Table. (1990, R, New Zealand, color, 158 minutes). Autobiography of Janet Frame (Kerry Fox), New Zealand's most famous novelist and poet, details her struggles with misdiagnosed schizophrenia as an adolescent and young adult.

Bless the Beasts and the Children. (1972, PG, US, color, 109 minutes). Six boys who don't fit in try to free a herd of buffalo scheduled for slaughter.

The Boy Who Cried Bitch. (1991, NR, US, color, 101 minutes). A 12-year-old who is violent and psychotic received inadequate psychiatric and parental care.

David and Lisa. (1963, NR, US, b & w, 94 minutes). Chronicles the life and treatment of two teenagers with emotional and behavioral disorders.

Dead Poet's Society. (1989, PG, US, color, 128 minutes). An outstanding student in a prep school struggles with depression and eventually commits suicide.

Video List copyright Marilyn Shank, Ph.D. This list is not to be reproduced without prior written consent of the author.

I Am the Cheese. (1983, PG, US, color, 95 minutes). A teenager receives psychiatric care after witnessing the death of his parents.

I Never Promised You a Rose Garden. (1977, R, US, color, 96 minutes). A teenager struggles with schizophrenia.

Lord of the Flies. (1963 and 1990, NR and R, US, b & w and color). Boys stranded on an island gradually become savage.

Lost Angels. (1989, R, US, color, 116 minutes). Adolescents in a residential setting receive treatment for emotional and behavioral disorders.

Lovey, A Circle of Children, Part I. (1977, NR, US, color, 120 minutes). A teacher works in a classroom for students with emotional and behavioral disorders. (Part II, 1982).

Marvin and Tige. (1983, PG, US, color, 104 minutes). An isolated man takes in an 11 year old who tried to kill himself.

Misunderstood. (1984, PG, US, color, 91 minutes). A teenager becomes increasingly withdrawn and desolate after the death of his mother.

My Little Girl. (1986, R, US, color, 113 minutes). A teenager from a wealthy family spends a summer working in a detention center for children.

No Big Deal. (1983, NR, US, color, 86 minutes). An adolescent with emotional and behavior disorders tries to fit in with his peers.

Nobody Waved Goodbye. (1965, NR, Canada, b & w, 80 minutes). Portrays a teenager who is alienated and frustrated.

One Flew Over the Cuckoo's Nest. (1975, R, US, color, 133 minutes). R.P. McMurphy (Jack Nicholson) is a convict who thinks he can get his sentence reduced by pretending to have emotional disorders. Tragedy occurs in the residential facility where he is placed.

Ordinary People. (1980, R, US, color, 123 minutes). Timothy Hutton plays an adolescent who becomes suicidal after the drowning of his brother and receives counseling from an excellent therapist (Judd Hirsch). Family and peer interactions are insightfully portrayed.

The Outsiders. (1983, PG, US, color, 91 minutes). The lives of three troubled teenagers as seen through the eyes of a gifted adolescent.

Over the Edge. (1979, PG, US, color, 95 minutes). Troubled suburban adolescents rebel against society.

Permanent Record. (1988, US, PG-13, color, 91 minutes). The suicide of a model student causes high school faculty and classmates to wonder who might be next.

Pixote. (1981, NR, Brazil, color, 127 minutes). An abandoned 10 year old pimps, sniffs glue, and commits murder.

Shine. (1995. PG-13, Australian, color, 105 minutes). A piano prodigy deals with mental illness and his father's abuse.

The Stone Boy. (1984, PG, US, color, 93 minutes). A boy withdraws after accidentally shooting his brother.

This Boy's Life. (1993, R, US, color, 115 minutes). A young boy must overcome severe physical and emotional abuse.

The Tin Drum. (1979, R, Germany, color, 142 minutes). A child copes with the rise of the Third Reich by developing unusual behaviors and willing himself not to grow.

The Wild Child. (1969, G, France, b & w, 85 minutes). A doctor tries to civilize a boy who was raised alone in the woods of France.

The Year My Voice Broke. (1987, PG-13, Australia, color, 103 minutes). A teenager becomes infatuated with a girl who has emotional and behavioral disorders.

Chapter 6—AD/HD

None noted

Chapter 7—Giftedness

Amadeus (1984, PG, color, 158 minutes). Life of gifted Wolfgang Amadeus Mozart (Tom Hulce) and his conflict with envious composer Salieri (F. Murray Abraham).

Dangerous Holiday. (1937, NR, b & w, 54 minutes). A gifted violinist, tired of practicing, runs away from home, leaving everyone believing he was kidnapped.

Video List copyright Marilyn Shank, Ph.D. This list is not to be reproduced without prior written consent of the author.

Fame. (1980, R, US, color, 134 minutes). Portrays gifted students at New York City's School for the Performing Arts who want to enter show business.

Finding Forrester. (2001, PG-13, US, color, 136 minutes). A gifted teen in an inner-city recruits an award-winning, reclusive writer as a mentor.

The Girl Who Spelled Freedom. (1986, NR, US, color, 90 minutes). A girl from Cambodia becomes a national spelling bee champion.

Good Will Hunting. (1997, R, US, color, 126 minutes). A young man takes a job as a custodian at MIT where his profound giftedness in mathematics is discovered.

A Hero Ain't Nothing but a Sandwich. (1978, PG, US, color, 105 minutes). A gifted adolescent in a ghetto begins to use drugs.

Little Man Tate. (1991, PG, US, color, 99 minutes). A single mother in a low socioeconomic environment struggles to give her child, who is profoundly gifted, the stimulation he needs.

The Manhattan Project. (1986, PG-13, US, color, 117 minutes). Fictional account of a teenager who is gifted and builds an atom bomb.

My Father's Glory. (1990, G, France, Color, 120 minutes). Childhood memories of a precocious boy and his family. Story continues in *My Mother's Castle*.

Real Genius. (1985, PG, US, color, 108 minutes). A comedy about gifted college students being used by their professor to create weapons he can sell to the government.

Say Anything. (1989, PG-13, US, color, 100 minutes). A teenage girl who is gifted lives with her father and dates a young man who wants to be a kickboxer.

Searching for Bobby Fischer. (1994, PG, US, 120 minutes). Portrays a child who is gifted at playing chess and the struggles of his family to balance his giftedness with his need to be a child.

Shine. (1995, PG-13, Australia, color, 105 minutes). A piano prodigy deals with mental illness and his father's abuse.

Space Camp. (1986, PG, US, color, 107 minutes). A group of gifted students at a NASA space camp accidently get launched into space.

To Be Young, Gifted, and Black. (1972, NR, US, color, 90 minutes). An autobiography of Lorraine Hansberry.

War Games. (1983, PG, US, color, 110 minutes). A computer whiz taps into the Pentagon computer with disastrous results.

Young Winston. (1972, PG, UK, color, 145 minutes). Chronicles Winston Churchill's early life.

Chapter 8—Mental Retardation

Andy. (1965, NR, US, b & w, 86 minutes). A middle-aged man with mental retardation copes with problems in New York City slum life.

Beautiful Dreamers. (1992, PG-13, Canada, Color, 107 minutes). American poet Walt Whitman (Rip Torn) befriends Dr. Maurice Bucke (Com Feore) who progressively treats persons with mental retardation.

Best Boy. (1980, NR, US, color, 111 minutes). Oscar-winning documentary about filmmaker Ira Wohl's fifty-two-year old cousin who has mental retardation.

Bill. (1981, NR, US, color, 100 minutes). Mickey Rooney plays Bill Sackter, an adult with mental retardation who was released from a residential setting after 46 years.

Bill on His Own. (1983, NR, US, color, 100 minutes). The continued story of Bill Sackter.

Board and Care. (1979, NR, US, color, 27 minutes). Two teens with mental retardation share their hopes and dreams.

Bravo Gloria. (1988, R, US, color, 30 minutes). A 32-year-old woman with mental retardation seeks a full life.

Charly. (1968, PG, US, color, 103 minutes). Fictional account of a man with mental retardation (Cliff Robertson) who becomes a genius after a science experiment.

A Child Is Waiting. (1963, NR, US, color, 105 minutes). Parents with a child who has mental retardation cope with his placement in a residential setting.

Digging to China. (1998, PG, US, color, 98 minutes). A ten-year-old girl befriends a thirty-year-old man with mental retardation, causing alarm when the two run away after some shocking news.

Eggs. (1995, Norway, color, 88 minutes). A man learns he has a son with mental retardation when the mother dies. The son, who is fascinated by birds, moves in with his father and his father's family.

Video List copyright Marilyn Shank, Ph.D. This list is not to be reproduced without prior written consent of the author.

Fany. (1996, Czech—English subtitles, color, 95 minutes). A woman has difficulty adjusting to having her sister with mild mental retardation live with her, especially because of her sister's love for stray animals.

Forrest Gump. (1994, PG-13, US, color, 120 minutes). Fictional account of a man with educable mental retardation who lives an extraordinary life.

The Kid from Nowhere. (1982, NR, US, color, 100 minutes). Based on a true story, a boy with Down syndrome becomes an an athlete in Special Olympics.

Le Huitième Jour (*The Eighth Day*). (1996, NR, French, color, 116 minutes). A self-absorbed businessman has his life changed by the friendship of a man with Down syndrome (played by an award-winning actor with Down syndrome).

L'Enfant d'Eau. (1995, Canadian, NR, color, 107 minutes). Two adolescents, one with mental retardation, are the only survivors of a plane crash and must live together on an isolated island.

Les Bois Transparents. (1994, NR, France, color, 87 minutes). A man with Down syndrome helps an artist overcome his creative block.

Like Normal People. (1979, NR, US, color, 96 minutes). A man and woman with mental retardation want to marry, but encounter obstacles.

Lucky Day. (1991, NR, US, color, 96 minutes). A young woman with mental retardation wins the lottery, changing the way her family treats her.

Nunzio. (1978, R, color, 87 minutes). A man with mental retardation who fantasizes about being Superman becomes a hero in real life.

Of Mice and Men. (1992, PG-13, US, color, 110 minutes). John Steinback's novel is adapted for film. Lennie, a quiet farm-worker, teams up with his cousin who has mental retardation.

The Other Sister. (1999, PG-13, US, color, 129 minutes). After spending years in a boarding school for students with mental retardation, a young woman's wealthy family confronts their guilt and overprotection as the woman strives for independence.

The Rain People. (1968, R, US, color, 102 minutes). A bored, pregnant housewife meets an ex-football player with mental retardation who changes her life on a road trip.

Sling Blade. (1996, R, US, color, 138 minutes). After being released from an institution for the criminally insane, a man with mental retardation befriends a boy from an abusive home.

Slipping into Darkness. (1988, R, US, color, 86 minutes). The college women are charged with the murder of a local boy with mental retardation.

Special People: Based on a True Story. (1984, NR, Canada, color, 100 minutes). The story of the woman who started the Famous People Players, a group of actors with mental retardation.

Square Dance. (1987, PG-13, US, color, 118 minutes). A teenager forced to leave her grandfather's farm for her promiscuous mother's home befriends a young man with mental retardation.

Tim. (1979, NR, Australia, color, 94 minutes). A middle age career woman hires a handyman with mental retardation. The bond that develops is difficult for the man's sister to accept.

Two of a Kind. (1989, NR, US, color, 102 minutes). An elderly man is rejuvenated by his grandson with retardation.

What's Eating Gilbert Grape? (1994, PG-13, US, color, 120 minutes). An adolescent provides support and encouragement for his younger brother with mental retardation.

Winnie. (1988, NR, US, color, 96 minutes). A woman with mental retardation tries to escape a residential facility and write a book about her thirty years of confinement.

The Yarn Princess. (1994, NR, US, color, 92 minutes). A woman with mental retardation must convince a judge that she can take care of her sons after her husband develops schizophrenia.

Chapter 9—Severe and Multiple Disabilities

Acorn People. (1982, MFTV, US, color, 97 minutes). An unemployed teacher learns to value children with disabilities at a summer camp.

A Child Is Waiting. (1963, NR, US, b & w, 102 minutes). Burt Lancaster and Judy Garland work with students who have mental retadation and multiple disabilities.

Dominick and Eugene. (1988, PG-13, US, color, 111 minutes). A young intern must make choices about his twin brother who depends on his care.

Video List copyright Marilyn Shank, Ph.D. This list is not to be reproduced without prior written consent of the author.

The Woman Who Willed a Miracle. (1983, NR, US, color, 92 minutes). A mother discovers that her son with severe and multiple disabilities has the ability to play the piano.

Chapter 10—Autism

House of Cards. (1993, PG-13, US, color, 109 minutes). Fictionalized account of a girl who develops autistic symptoms and her mother's and psychologist's confict over appropriate treatment.

Mercury Rising. (1998, R, US, color, 112 minutes). An FBI agent protects a boy with autism who accidentally cracks a government code.

Rainman. (1988, R, US, color, 140 minutes). Charlie Babbitt (Tom Cruise) kidnaps his brother, who is autistic, (Dustin Hoffman) from a residential setting after his father dies.

Silence. (1974, G, US, color, 88 minutes). A family movie about a young boy with autism who is lost in the wilderness.

The Wizard. (1989, PG, US, color, 99 minutes). A boy takes his brother with autism across the country to a video game contest.

Chapter 11—Other Health Impairments

Awakenings. (1990, PG-13, US, color, 121 minutes). During the 1960s, neurologist Dr. Malcolm Sayer (Robin Williams) temporarily "awakens" people who developed catatonia as a result of an encephalitis epidemic.

Common Threads: Stories from the Quilt. (1989, NR, US, color, 75 minutes). Documentary of five diverse individuals, including one child, who had AIDS.

Echoes of a Summer. (1976, PG, US, color, 99 minutes). A twelve-year-old (Jodie Foster) confronts death with courage.

The Elephant Man. (1980, PG, US, B & W, 125 minutes). John Merrick's (John Hurt) struggle with prejudice of others during the Victorian era because of having a condition that disfigures him.

Longtime Companion. (1990, R, US, color, 96 minutes). Traces the progress of HIV among the homosexual community.

Lorenzo's Oil. (1992, PG-13, US, color, 135 minutes). Parents of a son with a fatal, rare nerve disease seek to discover a cure.

The Man Without a Face. (1994, PG-13, US, color, 120 minutes). A teacher who was severely burned tutors a boy who wants to go to a military school.

Mask. (1985, PG-13, US, color, 120 minutes). Rocky Dennis (Eric Stoltz) is a teenager who copes with humor and courage with craniodiaphysial dyaplasia, which causes calcium deposits to form on his skull and leave him disfigured.

The Men. (1950, NR, US, b & w, 85 minutes). A man paralyzed during World War II sinks into depression until his girlfriend reaches out to him.

Promises in the Dark. (1979, PG, US, color, 115 minutes). A young girl who is dying of cancer finds support from a caring doctor.

Six Weeks. (1982, PG, US, color, 107 minutes). A girl dying from leukemia wants to dance in the Nutcracker Ballet.

Steel Magnolias. (1989, PG, US, color, 118 minutes). A young woman (Julia Roberts) with juvenile diabetes copes with humor and courage and the support of family and friends.

The Teacher and the Miracle. (1961, NR, b & w, 88 minutes). A man copes after the loss of his son.

Chapter 12—Physical Disabilities

Autumn Sonata. (1978, NR, US, color, 97 minutes). For the first time in years, a concert pianist is reunited with her two daughters, one of whom has been institutionalized because of a degenerative nerve disease.

Born on the Fourth of July. (1989, R, US, color, 145 minutes). Based on the life of Ron Kovic, the movie follows his life as a recruit in Vietnam, to an angry paralyzed veteran, to a vocal antiwar protestor.

Breaking the Waves. (1992, R, US, color, 143 minutes). A woman blames herself and struggles with her faith because of an accident that left her husband paralyzed.

Coming Home. (1978, R, US, color, 130 minutes). A veteran who was paralyzed in Vietnam seeks to make sense out of his life.

Video List copyright Marilyn Shank, Ph.D. This list is not to be reproduced without prior written consent of the author.

Crossbar. (1979, MFTV, US, color, 77 minutes). Based on the true story of Aaron, Komylo, who determined to achieve Olympic status in the high jump despite having only one leg.

El Cochecito (The Wheelchair). (1960, NR, Spanish, b & w, 90 minutes). A man who is nondisabled tries to gain acceptance into a group of friends united by their use of wheelchairs. English subtitles.

The Eleanor Roosevelt Story. (1965, NR, US, b & w, 91 minutes). Oscar-winning documentary of the First Lady's life.

Frankie Starlight. (1965, NR, US, color, 88 minutes). After World War II, a woman gives birth to a little person who becomes an astronomer and writer.

Frida. (1984, NR, Mexico, color, 108 minutes). Portrays renowned Mexican artist and radical who has polio and paralysis from an accident.

Gaby—A True Story. (1987, R, color, 110 minutes). Gaby Brimmer (Liv Ullman) is the daughter of European refugee parents in Mexico and has cerebral palsy and is almost completely paralyzed.

The Glass Menagerie. (1987, PG, US, Color,134 minutes). A woman with a physical disability lives the life of a recluse with only her glass animals for comfort.

Go Now. (1996, NR, US, color, 87 minutes). A construction worker discovers he has multiple schlerosis.

The Hunchback of Notre Dame. (1939, NR, US, b & w, 117 minutes). A Parisian bellringer with a physical disability provides sanctuary to a woman who is accused of being a witch.

I Don't Want to Talk About It. (1994, NR, Spanish with subtitles, color, 102 minutes). A woman strives to help her daughter, a little person, become as happy and accomplished as possible by denying her daughter's disability.

Inside Moves. (1980, PG, US, color, 113 minutes). A young man who has survived a suicide attempt becomes friends with a group of people with disabilities.

It's Good to Be Alive. (1974, MFTV, US, color, 100 minutes). Brooklyn Dodgers' catcher Roy Campanella faces life with quadriplegia.

Joni. (1980, G, US, color, 108 minutes). Artist Joni Eareckson (played by Eareckson) has a diving accident that leaves her with quadraplegia and finds strength in her religious beliefs.

Long Ago Tomorrow. (1970, PG, UK, color, 100 minutes). Two adults with paraplegia fall in love.

My Left Foot. (1989, R, Ireland, color, 103 minutes). Very human portrayal of Christy Brown (Daniel Day-Lewis) whose cerebral palsy leaves movement only in his left foot.

The Other Side of the Mountain. (1975, PG, US, color, 101 minutes). Skier Jill Kinmont is paralyzed in a sporting accident.

Passion Fish. (1992, R, US, color, 134 minutes). A TV soap actress learns to accept a disability after an accident with the help of a young nurse.

Simon Birch. (1998, PG, US, color, 110 minutes). A boy with a physical disability knows he is destined to be a hero.

The Sweet Hereafter. (1996, R, US, color, 110 minutes). A community deals with disability and death after a school bus accident.

Sunrise at Campobello. (1960, NR, color, 143 minutes). Biography of President Franklin D. Roosevelt, who had polio.

The Waterdance. (1992, R, US, color, 106 minutes). A young novelist becomes paraplegic after an accident and restructures his life in a rehabilitation center.

Chapter 13—Traumatic Brain Injury

All the Little Animals. (1998, R, US, color, 104 minutes). A young adult with a traumatic brain injury runs away from his stepfather and finds friendship with a recluse.

It Came from the Sky. (1998, R, US, color, 92 minutes). Strangers invade the lives of a bitter father, long-suffering mother, and their son with brain damage.

Knife in the Head. (1978, NR, German with subtitles, color, 106 minutes). A man loses his memory and physical coordination after being shot in the head. Along with adjusting to his injury, he is involved in a political dispute.

Light in the Piazza. (1962, NR, US, b & w, 101 minutes). A woman refuses to place her daughter who received a traumatic brain injury in a residential facility. The daughter falls in love in Italy, and her mother confronts doubts about her daughter's ability to be married.

Video List copyright Marilyn Shank, Ph.D. This list is not to be reproduced without prior written consent of the author.

Long Journey Back. (1978, MFTV, US, color, 100 minutes). A woman injured in a school bus accident receives rehabilitation.

The Rain People. (1969, R, US, color, 102 minutes). A pregnant woman hitchhikes and falls in love with a former football player with traumatic brain injury.

Regarding Henry. (1991, PG-13, US, color, 107 minutes). Henry (Harrison Ford) is a lawyer, who, after a head injury, becomes a more caring and sensitive person.

When Billy Broke His Head and Other Tales of Wonder. (1995, NR, US, color, 60 minutes). Billy Golfus, who had difficulty finding work after a traumatic brain injury, discusses experiences of discrimination against those with disabilities.

Chapter 14—Speech and Language Disorders

Amy. (1998, NR, US, color, 103 minutes). A girl develops elective mutism after her rock-star father dies.

Baxter. (1973, PG, US, color, 100 minutes). Speech therapist (Patricia Neal) tries to help an adolescent with emotional problems to overcome a lisp.

A Brief History of Time. (1992, NR, UK-US, color, 84 minutes). Documentary portrays cosmologist Stephen Hawking who has amyotrophic lateral sclerosis and communicates with a voice synthesizer.

Children of a Lesser God. (1986, R, US, color, 110 minutes). A teacher at a school for the deaf and a young woman working as a janitor at the school conflict over the importance of speech over sign language.

Johnny Got His Gun. (1971, PG, US, color, 111 minutes). A World War I soldier who was severely injured in battle finally develops a way to communicate his wishes with others.

The Piano. (1994, R, New Zealand, color, 120 minutes). A young woman who is mute communicates through music, sign language, and body language her frustration in an unhappy marriage.

Run Wild, Run Free. (1969, G, UK, color, 100 minutes). Portrays the bond between a child who doesn't speak and a white colt.

What the Deaf Man Heard. (1997, NR, US, color, 120 minutes). Before boarding a bus with his single mother, a boy is told not to say a word. When she disappears at a bus stop, the boy refuses to talk, and others assume he is deaf and mute.

Chapter 15—Blindness and Low Vision

Amy. (1981, G, US, color, 100 minutes). A teacher of students who are blind or deaf organizes a football game between them and neighborhood children.

At First Sight. (1999, PG-13, US, color, 128 minutes). An architect falls in love with a masseur who is blind. When she arranges a surgery that restores his sight, their relationship changes.

Breaking Free. (1995, PG, US, color, time unknown). A teen makes a life-changing decision to work at a camp for the blind to prevent being sent to a correctional facility.

Butterflies Are Free. (1972, PG, US, color, 109 minutes). A young man who is blind moves away from his overprotective mother and learns about life from his actress neighbor.

City of Conquest. (1940, NR, US, b & w, 101 minutes). After being blinded by acid on his opponent's gloves, a boxer works at a corner news stand, earning money to finance his brother's music education.

80 Steps to Jonah. (1969, G, US, color, 107 minutes). Fictional account of a loner charged with a crime, who changes his outlook on life after stumbling on a camp for children who are blind.

Eye on the Sparrow. (1987, PG, US, color, time unknown). A determined couple who are blind seek to adopt a child.

A Family Thing. (1996, PG-13, US, color, 109 minutes). An African American matriarch who is blind insists that the family welcome a new family member, a man who always thought he was European-American.

Good Luck. (1996, R, US, color, 95 minutes). A man left blind from a football injury sinks into despair until he meets a man who has paraplegia. The two form a partnership to enter a whitewater rafting race.

Ice Castles. (1979, PG, US, color, 109 minutes). Ice skating champion becomes blind after an accident.

If You Could See What I Hear. (1982, PG, Canada, color, 103 minutes). Writer, composer, athlete, and TV personality Tom Sullivan is blind.

Life on a String. (1991, PG, Chinese—English subtitles, color, 101 minutes). A musician who is blind is told by his master that when he breaks 1000 strings on his banjo, he will receive a script for his eyes.

Video List copyright Marilyn Shank, Ph.D. This list is not to be reproduced without prior written consent of the author.

Love at First Sight. (1977, PG, Canadian, color, 85 minutes). In this comedy a blind man falls in love with a young woman whose father objects to the relationship. Enter the grandmother to the rescue.

Love Leads the Way. (1986, NR, US, color, time unknown). One of the first Americans to use a seeing-eye dog fights barriers.

The Lovers on the Bridge. (1999, R, French, color, 120 minutes). A homeless young man falls in love with a homeless artist who has one eye and is losing her sight.

Mask. (1985, PG-13, US, color, 120 minutes). A teenager who is blind (Laura Dern) falls in love with a teenager who is disfigured with craniodiaphysial dyaplasia.

The Miracle Worker. (1962, NR, US, b & w, 107 minutes). Oscar-winning biography of Helen Keller (Patty Duke) who is deaf and blind and her teacher Annie Sullivan (Anne Bancroft).

A Patch of Blue. (1965, NR, US, b & w, 105 minutes). A young woman who is Caucasian and blind (Elizabeth Hartman) falls in love with a man who is African American (Sidney Poitier).

Places in the Heart. (1984, PG, US, color, 112 minutes). During the Great Depression, a widow takes in a blind border.

Proof. (1991, PG, Australia, color, 86 minutes). A blind man takes pictures to prove the world is as others say.

To Race the Wind. (1980, NR, US, color, 93 minutes). A blind Harvard student copes with university life.

Scent of a Woman. (1992, R, US, color, 137 minutes). The colonel, who has recently become blind and is alcoholic and self-pitying, teams with Charlie, a misfit student at a local prep school, for a weekend adventure.

Wait Until Dark. (1967, NR, US, color, 107 minutes). In this thriller, a woman who is blind must outwit three intruders.

Wild Hearts Can't Be Broken. (1991, G, US, color, 88 minutes). Sonora Webster (Gabrielle Anwar) is a 1930s "diving girl" who continues her career after losing her sight.

Chapter 16—Hearing Loss

Beethoven Lives Upstairs. (1992, NR, US, 52 minutes). A young boy is fascinated by Ludwig, his parent's boarder.

Beethoven's Nephew. (1985, NR, US, 103 minutes). Beethoven believes he is the only one who can help his nephew develop into a musical genius, much to his nephew's chagrin.

Beethoven: Triumph over Silence. (1983, NR, US, color, 37 minutes). Would Beethoven's music have changed if he were not deaf?

Beyond Silence (Jenseits der Stille). (1996, PG-13, Germany, color, 109 minutes). A young woman whose parents are deaf communicates with them by International Sign Language, which is shunned by the superstitious community.

Bridge to Silence. (1989, NR, US, 95 minutes). A deaf woman asks her mother to care for her child while the woman is grieving the death of her husband. After joining an acting troupe, she recovers from her depression, but when she asks her mother to return her daughter, she discovers her mother has applied for custody.

Children of a Lesser God. (1986, R, US, color, 110 minutes). William Hurt portrays a new teacher at a school for the deaf who develops a relationship with an intelligent deaf woman (Marlee Matlin) working as a janitor.

Choices. (1981, NR, US, color, 90 minutes). A young man is prevented from playing football because of a hearing loss.

Dummy. (1979, NR, US, color, 90 minutes). An attorney with a hearing impairment defends a man who is deaf-mute and accused of murder.

Edison the Man. (1940, NR, US, color, 108 minutes). The film depicts Thomas Edison's life, including his hearing impairment.

For the First Time. (1959, NR, US, color, 97 minutes). An opera singer's life is changed by a woman who is deaf.

Un Grand Amour de Beethoven. (1936, NR, US, b & w, 135 minutes). A chronicle of the life of Beethoven.

The Heart Is a Lonely Hunter. (1968, G, US, color, 125 minutes). A man who is deaf and mute (Alan Arkin) helps others.

Johnny Belinda. (1948, NR, US, color, 105 minutes). A doctor teaches a young deaf woman who lives in a rural area how to communicate using sign language. (More recent versions are also available.)

Video List copyright Marilyn Shank, Ph.D. This list is not to be reproduced without prior written consent of the author.

Love Is Never Silent. (1985, US, color, 105 minutes). A woman's parents who are deaf depend on her for communicating with the outside world, making her independence from them difficult.

The Magnificent Rebel. (1961, NR, US, b & w, 91 minutes). A Disney take on the life of Beethoven.

The Man of a Thousand Faces. (1957, NR, US, color, 122 minutes). The life of horror film actor Lon Cheney, whose parents were deaf, is depicted.

Mandy. (1952, NR, US, color, 93 minutes). A child who is deaf overcomes discrimination and isolation through special education.

The Miracle Worker. (1962, NR, US, b & w, 107 minutes). Oscar-winning biography of Helen Keller (Patty Duke) who is deaf and blind and her teacher Annie Sullivan (Anne Bancroft).

Mr. Holland's Opus. A well-loved music teacher must learn to accept his son's deafness.

When the Whales Come. (1989, G, UK, color, 100 minutes). Children befriend a hermit who is deaf and loves birds.

...And Your Name Is Jonah. (1979, NR, US, time unknown). Parents dispel the myth that their deaf son has mental retardation by teaching him to communicate.

Video List copyright Marilyn Shank, Ph.D. This list is not to be reproduced without prior written consent of the author.

COLLABORATING FOR SUCCESS

Collaboration Goal: ______________________________

Collaborators	*Roles and Preparation*	*Possible Barriers*	*Solutions to Barriers*	*Modifications to Implementation*	*Ongoing Evaluation*
Students with Disabilities					
Parents					
General Educator(s)					
Special Educator(s)					
Related Service Providers					
Administrative Personnel					
Students without Disabilities					
Others:					
ALL					